MW00803583

Erotic Love in Sociology, Philosophy and Literature

Also available from Bloomsbury

Enduring Time, Lisa Baraitser
Conflicting Humanities, ed. By Rosi Braidotti and Paul Gilroy

Erotic Love in Sociology, Philosophy and Literature

From Romanticism to Rationality

Finn Bowring

BLOOMSBURY ACADEMIC
LONDON • NEW YORK • OXFORD • NEW DELHI • SYDNEY

BLOOMSBURY ACADEMIC
Bloomsbury Publishing Plc
50 Bedford Square, London, WC1B 3DP, UK
1385 Broadway, New York, NY 10018, USA

BLOOMSBURY, BLOOMSBURY ACADEMIC and the Diana logo are trademarks of
Bloomsbury Publishing Plc

First published in Great Britain 2019

Copyright © Finn Bowring, 2019

Finn Bowring has asserted his right under the Copyright, Designs and Patents Act,
1988, to be identified as Author of this work.

Cover design by Anna Hidvegi
Cover image: *Two Hugging Women*, drawing by Egon Schiele, 1911

All rights reserved. No part of this publication may be reproduced or
transmitted in any form or by any means, electronic or mechanical,
including photocopying, recording, or any information storage or retrieval
system, without prior permission in writing from the publishers.

Bloomsbury Publishing Plc does not have any control over, or responsibility for, any
third-party websites referred to or in this book. All internet addresses given in this
book were correct at the time of going to press. The author and publisher regret any
inconvenience caused if addresses have changed or sites have ceased to exist, but can
accept no responsibility for any such changes.

A catalogue record for this book is available from the British Library.

A catalog record for this book is available from the Library of Congress.

ISBN: HB: 978-1-3500-9222-8
ePDF: 978-1-3500-9223-5
eBook: 978-1-3500-9224-2

Typeset by Newgen KnowledgeWorks Pvt. Ltd., Chennai, India
Printed and bound in Great Britain

To find out more about our authors and books visit www.bloomsbury.com
and sign up for our newsletters.

For Vicky, Tiz and Rhin

Have you ever loved the body of a woman?
Have you ever loved the body of a man?
Do you not see that these are exactly the same to all in all nations
       and times all over the earth?

*****

Among the men and women the multitude,
I perceive one picking me out by secret and divine signs,
Acknowledging none else, not parent, wife, husband, brother,
       child, any nearer than I am,
Some are baffled, but that one is not – that one knows me.
Ah lover and perfect equal,
I meant that you should discover me so by faint indirections,
And I when I meet you mean to discover you by the like in you.

*****

Sometimes with one I love I fill myself with rage for fear I effuse
       unreturn'd love,
But now I think there is no unreturn'd love, the pay is certain one
       way or another,
(I loved a certain person ardently and my love was not return'd,
Yet out of that I have written these songs.)

                    Walt Whitman, *Leaves of Grass*

Contents

Introduction: Love is love is love

After the Orlando nightclub attack in 2016 – at the time the deadliest mass shooting by a single aggressor in US history – a slogan became ubiquitous on social media and in popular visual culture. 'Love is love is love' was taken from the lines of a sonnet delivered by the playwright Lin-Manuel Miranda during an emotional Tony Awards acceptance speech in the evening after the terrorist attack. At one level it was a heartfelt plea for loving kindness and compassion – virtues that Christian thinkers have historically associated with the Greek term *agapē*. As the French sociologist Emile Durkheim observed in the closing decade of the nineteenth century, a community's values shine brightest when they have been violently assaulted, and the values that animate secular Western societies revolve around the preciousness of human life and the dignity of the person. Love is love is love, because love is the proliferation of a generosity too abundant to be destroyed by an act of hate.

Nineteenth-century humanism was a false universalism, however. Its concept of 'the person' was an abstraction modelled on the singular coherence of the intellect, rather than on the diversity of bodies, feelings, values and longings. The prestige of reason was itself founded on an irrational repudiation of the different and the strange, of cultures, practices and appearances that diverged from the narrow norms of a Western male monoculture whose internal uniformity was misconceived as a harmonious and inclusive objectivity. Love is love is love, because love is diverse as well as plentiful, and because only a plurality of love can measure up to the plurality of peoples.

Of course there is a third layer to the line from Miranda's poem, which explains its widespread adoption by the LGBT community. The venue was a gay nightclub and the attacker was a homophobe. 'Love is love' also means: when sex is loving, it is love – it is human connection, mutual generosity, attentiveness to the other as a sensuous and desiring being. Not 'sex is sex', nor even 'sex is love' – which is clearly not always true – but 'love is love', because the aspiration to find love through physical intimacy can be found in all sexualities and all forms of desire. Here we are in the domain not of *agapē* but of *eros*; not of selfless generosity, but that passionate cherishing of and yearning to bond with another person which we associate with sexual love.

Looking inwards, towards our desires, however, also reveals our unique capacity to frustrate ourselves, to deceive ourselves and to collude in social arrangements which, while passing under the name of love, may actually be destructive of our own and others' well-being. As the psychoanalyst Adam Phillips notes, because human beings are incapable of desiring without also imagining the satisfaction of desire, our desires are fulfilled in the realm of fantasy before we ever try to realise them in practice. Our keenest desires, moreover, are often for things we have had no, and indeed need no, actual experience of. Because of this, our yearning for the 'unlived life' can easily turn fantasies of satisfaction into defences against desire, into a flight from the more fearful risk of having our actual wants frustrated, rejected or scorned. 'Our fantasies of satisfaction,' Phillips (2012: 140) writes, 'are where we hide from the possibility of real satisfaction.'

Our fantasies of satisfaction are fed by the cultural practices, social relations, images, norms and meanings of our society. Two centuries of romantic literature, as well as ever more powerful industries of visual, musical, scientific and political storytelling, have given the romantic desire for intimate union with another person unprecedented nourishment in modern Western societies. That this desire has been shaped and imagined in self-destructive and exclusionary ways is now well known, for private paradises are a common disguise worn by political and economic interests that often have no respect for the autonomy of the person.

It is therefore hardly surprising that suspicion of romantic love also has an established pedigree in our intellectual culture. The bathroom and the bedroom, the intimacy of bodies and emotions, the seemingly unique, mysterious or idiosyncratic feelings and events that appear to define people's personal lives and experiences and mark their distinctiveness as individuals have long been the target of socially informed critique. For sociology in particular, love is as good a test as any of the discipline's claim to make familiar what is strange, and of its promise to show how social forces and interests penetrate the most private and irrational recesses of human existence. 'There is a broadly based popular mythology about the character of love as a violent, irresistible emotion that strikes where it will', Peter Berger wrote in his *Invitation to Sociology* (1963). 'The sociologist investigating our patterns of "courtship" and marriage,' however, 'soon discovers a complex web of motives related in many ways to the entire institutional structure within which an individual lives his life – class, career, economic, ambition, aspirations of power and prestige. The miracle of love now begins to look somewhat synthetic' (48).

Sociological investigation shows how the 'synthetic' idea of love as an inexplicable passion has historically served an ideological role, concealing the way economic inequality is strategically reproduced through the nuclear family, with the normative enforcement of endogamy in marriage ensuring that property and wealth are transmitted only to the carefully matched offspring of the dominant class. Their eyes may have met across a crowded room, but the crowd is likely to have been a culturally homogenous group, and what felt like a personal epiphany was really an over-rehearsed and endlessly repeated script. The moment of 'exchanged recognition', to borrow a term from D. H. Lawrence, is not the reciprocal confirmation of two people's mysterious and singular desires, but rather the mutual familiarity and understanding of common social backgrounds, and the effortless legibility of socially constructed looks, gestures and words.

As women have been constructed as the primary consumers of and enthusiasts for the idea of romantic love, feminist critics have also attacked the way sentimental depictions of intimate life have long disguised the power asymmetries in heterosexual relationships, pulling a veil over the cruelty, violence and self-abnegation suffered by many women in their private lives. The religion of love is an 'idolatrous love', Simone de Beauvoir argued in *Le Deuxième Sexe* (1949), deceiving women with the belief that they can remedy the effects of their social and economic dependency by making themselves essential to a superior power, to a demigod, a transcendent freedom – in other words, to a man. Here begins the female lover's characteristic self-abasement, which flirts with masochism, collusion and bad faith. Such is the woman's devotion to her partner's freedom, Beauvoir observes, that the man's inescapable mediocrity, his inevitably uncertainty, his irresistible inertia and facticity are as much a torment to her as his power to command and to possess: 'she wakes him up simply to keep him from sleeping', for her 'god must not sleep lest he become clay, flesh'. Meanwhile the deity to whom she sacrifices herself grows tired of his lover's selflessness, and the harder she tries to please him the more he loses interest: 'Giving herself blindly, woman has lost that dimension of freedom which at first made her fascinating. The lover seeks his reflection in her; but if he begins to find it altogether too faithful, he gets bored. It is, again, one of the loving woman's misfortunes to find that her very love disfigures her, destroys her; she is nothing more than this slave, this servant, this too ready mirror, this too faithful echo' (Beauvoir 1972: 667, 675).

In Shulamith Firestone's account, romantic idealisation is more typical of the man than the woman, since only by means of a 'false idealisation' of the woman can a man fall in love with someone whom a patriarchal society has degraded and condemned to a lower caste (Firestone 1979: 126–7). This idealistic projection is a narcissistic fantasy prone to swift disillusionment, however, and it is promptly followed either by flight or by feigned loyalty and sexual exploitation of the socially unequal but nonetheless desiring woman. 'The concept of romantic love affords a means of emotional manipulation which the male is free to exploit, since love is the only circumstance in which the female is (ideologically) pardoned for sexual activity', Kate Millett wrote in *Sexual Politics*. 'Romantic love also obscures the realities of female status and the burden of economic dependency' (Millett 1970: 37).

So long as men and woman are not equal, Firestone argued, any love between them will be 'corrupted by its power context' and therefore 'diseased'. The love we call 'romantic' is the most prevalent form of this corrupted, perverted love. 'Romanticism is a cultural tool of male power', Firestone writes, a tool that has grown more prominent as women's sexual autonomy has increased and the biological bases of patriarchy have crumbled: 'where formerly women had been held openly in contempt, now they are elevated to states of mock worship'. False flattery conceals a harsher truth, which is that women's affectionate devotion to men is used by the dominant sex to sustain the self-serving accomplishments of economic, political and cultural action. 'Culture was built on the love of women, and at their expense. Women provided the substance of those male masterpieces; and for millennia they have done the work, and suffered the costs, of one-way emotional relationships the benefits of which went to men' (Firestone 1979: 139, 122).

Our discourses of romantic love have also been dominated by norms of heterosexuality, by a Western cultural model of marital monogamy and by a white European imaginary that historically disparaged or mythologised black sexuality while recoiling at the thought of cultural, ethnic or religious intermarriage. Many of these taboos, it is true, have been relaxed over the last 50 years, but others remain surprisingly entrenched. Women's claim to be recognised as desiring beings, for example, has been a long and arduous struggle. Our heterosexual masculine culture can accommodate, if only voyeuristically, the idea of lesbian sexuality, much more easily than it can homosexuality. The contrasting receptions of the films *Blue Is the Warmest Colour* (2013) and *Nymphomaniac* (2013) also suggest that women's desire for women, particularly when it is emotionally inflected by love, is far more palatable to the hegemonic masculine consciousness than a heterosexual woman's pursuit of her own sexual pleasure. In both cases, male heterosexuality is threatened by the idea of being at the mercy of another's desire, as if the masculine conception of desire were too saturated with power to imagine facing an encounter with desire that does not demand submission.

The social changes of the last few decades have, nonetheless, led some social commentators to argue that the sphere of intimacy is undergoing an egalitarian transformation. In the less structurally predictable, more diverse and more individualised society theorised by many contemporary Western sociologists, space has opened up for what some believe is the emergence of a rational democratic model of love. Declining marriage rates, high rates of divorce, women's greater sexual and economic autonomy, the legalisation of same-sex marriage, the growth of single-person households, increasing numbers of interethnic relationships and a much more liberal culture of sexual expression and entitlement suggest the breakdown of the racially endogenous, heteronormative and patriarchal regulation of intimate life, and its replacement by a more equal, but also more fluid and uncertain, form of emotional reciprocity that has been called 'confluent love' (Giddens 1992).

The veracity of this more egalitarian picture of personal relationships has been contested from a number of perspectives. Today's more generous culture of tolerance and understanding exists alongside a worrying growth in right-wing extremism in many parts of the world. The explosion in the use of social media over the last decade has allowed the hardening of social prejudices as well as the questioning of them, and the confidence with which sexist, racist and homophobic people can now threaten others and publicise their views online has been a reckoning of sorts for many comfortable and generous-minded liberals. Misogyny in particular, as Mary Beard has observed first hand, appears louder and more aggressive today than in the recent past, even though the social practice of silencing women has a long and ignoble history, dating back at least as far as classical antiquity (Beard 2017). We'd like to believe that public utterances, especially when they are made in anonymity, are not always a reliable indicator of private behaviour. But a quarter of women in the United Kingdom are estimated to have experienced domestic abuse at some time since the age of 16 and, although there are also significant numbers of male victims, women are twice as likely to be victims of domestic abuse as men.

Small wonder, then, that the claim that a more rational, more reflexive type of love is emerging based on an egalitarian model of contractual exchange has been interpreted by some feminist scholars as an ideological smokescreen, a new form of commodity fetishism designed to conceal social relations that remain stubbornly unequal (Jamieson 1999; Langford 1999). Other social commentators have stressed the way the greater freedom enjoyed today to separate and divorce, and to select new sexual partners from an ever-expanding catalogue of choices, has ironically breathed new life into the toxic fiction of romantic love. Freed from the oppressive moral constraints of marital monogamy and class and ethnic endogamy, the ideology of erotic passion, it is argued, today makes humdrum relationships feel even more unhappy and intolerable than in the past (Kaufmann 2011; Bruckner 2013). The powerful cultural narratives and imagery of romantic love continue to feed our private fears and unconscious longings, abetting what Phillips (2012: 118) calls 'this strange form of authority – the authority of inexperience, the conviction we gain from not having done things'. Meanwhile infidelity, disengagement and desertion find ready-made legitimacy in the mysterious but transcendent pull of 'true' love, the apparently irresistible force of which, Mary Evans (2003) observes, disqualifies all attempts to raise rational moral complaints about lovers' behaviours.

Although differences remain between many of these theorists, there is a general consensus that personal life would be happier and more fulfilling if people resisted the utopia of romantic love and set their relationships on a more rational and realistic footing. This is a sincere and humane sentiment, but it is not without its limitations. On the one hand, the sober repudiation of fantasy and faith underestimates the extent to which personal life has already been rationalised, and overlooks the way the process of rationalisation has corroded emotional bonds and undermined the trust on which loyalty and commitment to another person is built. As Illouz argues in *Why Love Hurts* (2012), so dominant is the narrative of autonomous selfhood in today's Western societies that rational choice has usurped the ritual performances by which the emotional dimension of interpersonal attachments was previously constructed, validated and sustained. Romantic joy and suffering is no longer considered in a cultural and symbolic framework that might lend it moral sense and dignity, but is instead held up as evidence of the self-defeating delusion of love, and as proof that people – especially women – should invest their emotions more strategically. Such has become the importance to us of freedom of choice in our personal lives that promise-making is no longer associated with a deepening of social ties and an enrichment of their meaning, and faithfulness is instead experienced as an obstacle to our rational autonomy and self-realisation. Feminist psychoanalysis has exposed this fetishising of reason and transcendence as a masculine paradigm that ironically occludes the true vitality of women's desire. The latter 'can be found', Jessica Benjamin (2008: 201) argues, 'not through the current emphasis on *freedom from:* as autonomy or separation from a powerful other, guaranteed by identification with an opposing power. Rather, we are seeking a relationship to desire in the *freedom to:* freedom to be both with and distinct from the Other.'

On the other hand, the call for a more rational, reasonable, respectful love neglects the role that fantasy and imagination play in all sustainable relationships. It was Emile Durkheim who, over a century ago, observed the 'eternal truth' of religion, which is that for human beings to live with each other in solidarity they must have 'faith' in the *sui generis* force that is engendered by their association – they must believe in a unity of selves that is superior to the profane motives and meanings of its constituent members. Even our ideas about individual freedom and the principle of mutual respect derive, Durkheim stressed, from a secular cultural discourse – he called this 'moral individualism' – which must inspire our faith, for there is nothing in our existence as empirical beings which can justify or explain the dignity we accord, or should accord, to the human person (Durkheim 2001: 172). We live for an idea of love, just as we live for an idea of freedom, an idea of justice, an idea of beauty, an idea of truth. We live for ideas because ideas live longer than us, attaching us to something that religions have always thought of as divine. Even non-sexual love, affectionate friendship, the tender mercies of mutual acceptance and practical companionship require their own art and rituals, their forms of elegance and tact. Even the most tolerant love, the most intelligent realism, requires an aesthetic sublimation, an imaginative belief in the moral authority of an interpersonal bond, an idealisation of compassion and togetherness vivid enough to defy the matter-of-fact imperatives of functional demands and unromantic distractions, of arbitrary differences and incommunicable feelings. If nothing else, the desire that many same-sex couples have to solemnise their partnerships with civil ceremonies and weddings testifies to the moral symbolism of romantic love, the hunger for a love that lasts – a love that can last – because it is more than a private endeavour.

Love as value and as ideal is of course meaningless if it does not arouse, articulate and sustain love as feeling and desire. But by the same token, love as value and as ideal draws us out of ourselves, sharpens our attentiveness to others, sensitises us to the joy and suffering of another's existence. According to the French philosopher Luc Ferry, we have entered a new epoch characterised by a 'second humanism' whose spirit reverberates outwards from the emotional crucible of the modern family, extending the diversity and reach of human fellowship with copious acts of kindness. The 'revolution of love', Ferry argues, repudiating all moral and intellectual cynicism, is inescapably political. It has liberated marginalised and repressed sexualities, attacked cultural racism and the arrogance of an earlier metaphysical humanism, and aroused a feeling of care and sympathy for distant others, for nature, for future generations, which is without precedent. Love has become both a sacred value and an ethical act – the active consecration of the person. It does not enclose us in an inward-looking private world, but 'impels us to intervene in the public sphere' (Ferry 2013: 55). Love is love is love.

Love is an idea as well as a passion, a cultural story as well as a bodily feeling. To love is to hope and to imagine, but also to desire and to suffer. Adam Phillips, in his psychoanalytic discussion of desire, reminds us that we need to recognise how frustration is as much a part of 'real' desire as it is part of fantasy; desires are born of frustration – of denial, lack, dependency, powerlessness. Fantasies of satisfaction, Phillips points out, can easily become a hiding place from real frustration as well as real satisfaction – we escape the risk of disappointment using fantasies of enjoyment which conceal what we really want, thus deepening the malaise of the unlived life. But fantasies of satisfaction, to reiterate, are unavoidable, because to desire is always to imagine the satisfaction of desire; disappointment, equally, is unavoidable, because the imagination always precedes, and is thereby destined to fail, the test of reality. Since 'there can only be unrealistic wanting', Phillips observes, 'the quest for satisfaction begins and ends with a frustration'. To bear the inevitable frustrations of missing out, Phillips argues, we should at least avoid those self-deceiving desires whose satisfaction 'is too exactly imagined' (2012: 26, 32–3). To be free from neurotic misery and self-repression, we need to devote time, thought and imagination to getting to know better the real frustrations of having, pursuing and inadequately satisfying desires.

> Waiting too long poisons desire, but waiting too little pre-empts it; the imagining is in the waiting. In consciously contrived instant gratification neither desire nor the object of desire is sufficiently imagined. Wanting takes time; partly because it takes some time to get over the resistances to wanting, and partly because we are often unconscious of what it is that we do want. But the worst thing we can be frustrated of is frustration itself; to be deprived of frustration is to be deprived of the possibilities of satisfaction. If we are not, say, to use sex to get rid of sex, if we are not to abolish our pleasure by the too slick seeking of it, we will need to recover, or even to refine, our frustration. We will have to resist our wanting being stolen from us before we have realised it. (Phillips 2012: xx)

Crudely simplistic images, ideas and stories of love may, as the critics of romanticism suggest, steal our wants and leave us at the mercy of more hostile and unscrupulous powers. Their too-easily-imagined purity may also thwart the radical polymorphism of desire, channelling it into the well-worn grooves of a sexist, racist and homophobic culture. But finding time to read, listen, imagine and think about desire may also help us resist the manipulation and debasement of human feeling, and give us the confidence to be curious, hopeful and even uncertain in love. The worst thing we can be frustrated of, Phillips says, is 'frustration itself', and this frustration includes the disquiet of not knowing, of not understanding or being understood – of 'not getting it', as Phillips playfully puts it. To make inevitable frustration tolerable, Phillips suggests, we need the imagination to work out modes of thinking and communicating that allow us to keep 'not getting it', or to keep partially and incompletely getting it, in order to resist the more insidious allure of perfect happiness and flawless understanding. As feminist critics of science, such as Evelyn Fox Keller, have argued, an emotionally mature relation to the world 'implies a sense of reality that is neither cut off from, nor at the mercy of, fantasy; it requires a sufficiently secure sense of autonomy to allow for that vital element of ambiguity at the interface between subject and object' (Keller 1985a: 84).

I want to argue that in matters of sexual love this 'vital element of ambiguity' requires a language capable of recognising, and appreciating, the strangeness of desire, as well as the mystery and uncertainty of its object. I want to argue that the cultural history of sexual love, if studied carefully and with an eye to ambiguity, provides a language that, notwithstanding its well-documented prejudices and limitations, may dignify the passion, turbulence and uncertainty of intimate relationships in a way that sustains our faith in ourselves as lovers as well as our faith in others as worthy of love. What from the sceptical standpoint may be a conspirator in a self-thwarting fantasy is thus from another perspective a resource from which we can draw when we seek to bear the frustrations, as well as illuminate the exhilarations, of the human heart. As well as scrutinising, in a rational and realistic way, the deployment of power and deception in personal relationships, we need to explore the different possible ways of making sense, however obliquely, of what is most unfathomable, but also most transcendent, in our relations to one another. We need to know, as Raymond Carver put it, what we talk about – and indeed what we *can* talk about – when we talk about love.

In this book I look at how people have talked about sexual love from the ancient Greeks to modern-day sociologists. I am interested not only in the intellectual history of love but also in how discourses of love have intersected with social and economic trends, as well as with personal events and experiences. In the first chapter I look at the queering of *eros* in antiquity, and use historians' knowledge of classical Greece to explore the social construction of sexuality and the political and ethical translations of desire. The second chapter focuses on the Athenian intellectuals' understanding of *eros*, with Plato's *Symposium* taking centre stage. Often criticised for depersonalising desire and making love a purely cerebral endeavour, Plato's theory is not, I argue, a completely desexualised one. Although the 'ladder of love' points towards the sublime transcendence of mortal bodies, and there are major discordances, as well as some surprising continuities, between Plato's conception and modern understandings of interpersonal subjectivity and desire, this first philosophical version of *eros* is important for the way it allowed subsequent Christian thinkers to theorise love as both a divinising and a morally consecrating force. With the twelfth-century formation of courtly love, as I discuss in Chapter 3, both the agent and object of this love were finally understood to be a singular human being. Denis de Rougemont famously argued that courtly love was an aesthetic expression of the pagan beliefs of the Cathar heretics, that it provided a mythical framework for articulating an essentially narcissistic, death-loving desire to be free of the corruptions of the material world, and that when it subsequently shed its religious symbolism it became – in the guise of modern 'romantic love' – a crude excuse for sexual promiscuity and marital infidelity. Following Octavio Paz and Irving Singer, however, I argue against this interpretation, and emphasise the way courtly love, by idealising the beloved, made cherishing the body and soul of another person a sacred endeavour. The love songs of the Provençal troubadours and *trobairitz* mark the beginning of the tradition of Western romantic love – love which is passionately faithful and exclusive, which is illicit and threatening to social conventions, which must be tested and ennobled by obstacles, prohibitions, and by rejection and suffering, and which must be deepened and refined by aesthetic stylisation and narrative memory. Romantic love, and the literature that sanctified and reproduced it, may begin with twelfth-century *fin'amors*, but it is worth noting that *even in the beginning* the lovers in the Medieval romance were conceptualised as artists, commemorators and storytellers of an already existing history of love. Thus, in Gottfried von Strassburg's version of *Tristan* (written in the first decade of the thirteenth century), the lovers, before they enter the grotto and lie together on the crystal bed, are found doing their own romantic storytelling, as they recollect the tragic stories of ancient *eros*:

They debated and discussed, they bewept and bewailed how Phyllis of Thrace and poor Canacea had suffered such misfortune in Love's name; how Biblis had died broken-hearted for her brother's love, how love-torn Dido, queen of Tyre and Sidon, had met so tragic a fate because of unhappy love. To such tales did they apply themselves from time to time. (Cited in Wandhoff 2012: 53)

Chapter 4 jumps forward to consider the history of the European family, focusing on the changes to personal life and relationships that began in the late 1600s, and which appeared to result in critical transformations by the late eighteenth and early nineteenth centuries. The growth of affective individualism, the conviction that love rather than family interests should determine people's partnership choices, and the emergence of a marital ideal of moral and intellectual companionship have been documented by a range of historians. These changes were refracted by social class and gender, of course, and even in the middle-class Victorian family companionate marriage was more likely to be regarded as a serene spiritual union than as a passionate fusion of dreaming and desiring selves. The nineteenth-century novel, which is the subject of Chapter 5, was making romantic love a more persuasive cultural ideal, however. Although the ideological function of the novel, which venerated wedlock, concealed or legitimised the patriarchal repression of women, and often used racist tropes to represent the unruliness of natural desire, cannot be denied, I also use this chapter to discuss the more subversive themes of Victorian literature, and the way the reading of that literature unsettled as well as reproduced the dominant norms and expectations of heterosexual monogamy.

Focusing more on his essays and correspondence than on his novels, Chapter 6 explores D. H. Lawrence's philosophy of love. Condemned as pornographic in his lifetime, Lawrence's work is even today commonly regarded as a standard bearer for sexual liberation. I argue, however, that there is a strong romantic theme in Lawrence's thinking, and I look at the way his understanding of sexual love was both fostered and contradicted by the more uninhibited philosophy and attitude of his wife. Chapters 7 and 8 then look at the way love was theorised by the classical sociologists of the nineteenth and early twentieth centuries. Alongside shorter discussions of Marx and Simmel, I give Durkheim's work more sympathetic attention than many critics would say he deserves, dwelling on his analysis of the tensions and ambiguities of sexual love, and emphasising his insight that relationships between people, if they are to be sustained, require an imaginative faith in the existence of a union greater than the sum of its parts. The second half of the chapter introduces Max Weber's theory of rationalisation.

I do this in some detail in order to set up the discussion, in Chapter 8, of his theory of eroticism, exploring in the process Weber's personal experiences and the indirect mutual influence, on both Weber and D. H. Lawrence, of the Austrian sexual revolutionary Otto Gross. While Weber is commonly thought of as a pessimistic thinker who saw Western modernity as an unstoppable march towards the mechanisation of feeling and the petrification of the soul, his analysis of the independent sphere of the erotic suggests a more dynamic understanding of the modernisation process. It also allows us to position love as a component of that cultural lifeworld which, Habermas later argued, remains at risk from being colonised by cognitive–instrumental reason.

Chapter 9 brings the analysis up to date by discussing the way love has been tackled in social theory and contemporary sociology over the last 50 years. Rising divorce rates, greater political and economic individualism, and more liberal attitudes towards sexual pleasure are some of the factors that have led to the idea that a new normative model of personal life has come to replace the antiquated fictions and prejudices of romanticism. This model retains the egalitarian ideals of the companionate relationship, but combines it with a more instrumental attitude towards sexual gratification and a more communicative model of intimacy, in which the monitoring, analysing and verbalising of feelings is the therapeutic 'work' deemed necessary to sustain a gratifying relationship. Although this model – often associated with Giddens' theory of the 'pure relationship' – has been criticised for glossing over the continued inequities and repressions in heterosexual relationships, this demystified version of love is certainly evident in the discourse of contemporary popular culture (Hochschild 2003; Shumway 2003), and versions of it appear in the post-romantic attitudes and understandings of sociological research participants (Illouz 1999; Swidler 2001). Drawing at length on Eva Illouz's work, I explore the tensions, inequalities and conflicts which ensue from this apparent rationalisation of love and argue in defence of the older tradition of romantic love as an imaginative resource better capable of mobilising interpersonal passions and feelings.

As an intellectual history of love, this book is both idiosyncratic and interdisciplinary, combining chapters on philosophy with others on social and cultural history, literary studies, and classical and contemporary social theory. Trying to cover such a wide field, and to do so in a way that doesn't overstretch my own knowledge and expertise, there are inevitably gaps and omissions. I am also aware that in my desire to do justice to some of the marvellous books I have read while researching this topic, the exegeses of other people's ideas – including some ideas that, on balance, I probably disagree with – at times occlude my own voice. I should therefore clarify at the outset that what I am advocating in this study is a greater appreciation of the role of the imagination in personal life, and a recognition that relations between autonomous people that are both just and meaningful require belief as well as knowledge (they require something akin to that secular religion which Durkheim called 'moral individualism', or what Fevre (2016) refers to as 'sentimental', as opposed to 'cognitive', individualism). In an era when social scientists are understandably keen to distinguish verifiable knowledge claims from the ideological world of 'alternative facts', I realise that this appeal to belief may strike some readers as unduly reckless. For some time now, however, it has been argued that strong ideological convictions are not what sustain most people's complicity with an unjust world, and that we need to focus instead on the pragmatic acquiescence of the downtrodden (Lodziak 1988), on the over-knowing disenchantment of those who cynically carry on (Sloterdijk 1988) and on the unconditional authority that accrues to an irrational world from the inexplicable trauma of our colluding with it (Žižek 2008: 24ff). If transformative acts, by contrast, acquire their urgency from feelings, and feelings, as Fevre (2000: 72ff) argues, are energised by beliefs, then it may well be time, both ethically and politically, to reconsider romantic love as one species of belief that deserves more diligent stewardship. David Shumway intimates something similar in a comment on the theme of love in *The Great Gatsby* (1925). Fitzgerald depicts the young millionaire's dogged infatuation with Daisy Buchanan as a colossal idealisation of a shallow socialite, and yet, for all its association with modern consumerist make-believe, Gatsby's romantic extravagance is still respected rather than condemned by the novel's narrator.[1] Fitzgerald's point, Shumway (2003: 61–2) suggests, is 'that romantic love is not merely a metonymy but a synecdoche. If we cannot believe in love, then belief is impossible.'

---

[1] Most of the classical texts and literary works referred to in this book are listed in the bibliography, though when my references to them are cursory and lacking in detail the bibliographical entry is omitted. As many of the canonical literary texts I cite, particularly in Chapter 5, have been republished multiple times with different layouts and paginations, when quoting from them I have added to the in-text citations the chapter number (and, before that, if relevant the 'book' or 'part' number) in roman numerals, followed by the page number of the copy I have read. The original year of publication is always displayed when I first mention a literary work; the year that my own copy was published is included in the corresponding bibliographical entry.

1

Eros in ancient Athens

The *History of the Peloponnesian War* tells the story of the protracted conflict between the expanding Athenian empire and the forces of Sparta and its allies, a conflict which, when Athens finally surrendered in 404 BC, brought to a close the golden age of classical Greece. In an important passage on the expedition to invade Sicily in 415 BC, its author, Thucydides, who served as an Athenian general during the early years of the war, draws a connection between the public mistrust of Alcibiades, who commanded the military venture, and the traumatic birth of Greek democracy a century earlier. The fear and suspicion of Alcibiades' daring leadership, which saw him ordered to return to Athens to answer charges that he was plotting against the state, were an echo, in Thucydides' view, of Athenians' confused narrative memory of the dictatorship of Pisistratus and his sons, the toppling of which, a hundred years before, had led to the founding of the democratic polis. In 514 BC, with Pisistratus dead and his sons, Hipparchus and Hippias, in power, Hipparchus was attacked and killed. Though Hippias ruled vengefully for another four years, his ultimate defeat and exile was forever linked, in the popular Athenian consciousness, to the apparent thirst for freedom that originally inspired the murder of Hipparchus.

Thucydides (6.54–57) reminds us, however, that the fearless act of resistance by the two assassins, Aristogeiton and Harmodius, 'was in fact the chance result of a love affair'. Aristogeiton was a middle-class citizen of Athens, Harmodius 'a famous beauty now in the full bloom of youth'. The tyrant Hipparchus had courted Harmodius and, when his advances were spurned, shamed him by humiliating his sister in public. While Harmodius was angered, Aristogeiton suffered 'a fit of lover's jealousy' fuelled by the 'fear that Hipparchus might use his power to take Harmodius by force'. The lovers hatched a plan to murder the tyrant brothers during a public festival and, in doing so, liberate the city. Seeing a fellow conspirator talking with Hippias, however, they feared that they had been betrayed and were about to be arrested. Acting peremptorily – 'as men possessed, in one case by the passion of love and in the other by wounded pride' – they seized a window of opportunity and struck down Hipparchus. Harmodius was killed by guards, while Aristogeiton was arrested and put to death.

Such was the association made between the actions of the two insurgents and the subsequent founding of the democratic state that Aristogeiton and Harmodius became, after the reforms of Cleisthenes, civic heroes to the people of Athens, honoured with the official title of 'Liberators' (*eleutherioi*) and 'Tyrannicides' (*tyrannophonoi*). The men's daring exploits were remembered with a publicly commissioned statue (the city's first commemorative statue of a mortal), songs were written comparing them to Achilles and Diomedes, and special privileges were granted to their descendants (McGlew 1993: 152–3). Ever the dispassionate historian, Thucydides complains, however, that the cult of the tyrannicides was founded on collective amnesia. According to Thucydides, Pisistratus and his sons administered a benign dictatorship, and 'compared with other tyrants they set the highest standards of behaviour and good sense' (6.54.5). Moreover, it was really Hippias, as the eldest son, who held the reins of power, not Hipparchus, and the family's rule became oppressive only *after* the assassination of Hipparchus. The eventual deposing of Hippias was also accomplished only thanks to the help of the Spartans. And finally, Thucydides emphasises, the 'reckless audacity' of the assassins originated not in a patriotic passion for liberty, but in 'the pangs of love' (6.59.1).

The popular image of Harmodius and Aristogeiton as liberators of Athens almost certainly derived from a deliberate rejection, or at least revision, of history (McGlew 1993: 152). And yet this wilful retelling of history is interesting because of what it says about the conception of love in fifth-century Greece. It reminds us, of course, about the veneration of male beauty in classical Greek culture, our knowledge of which can only denaturalise heterosexuality and highlight the plasticity of human desire as well as the social and historical construction of sexual 'normality'. It also shows how the normative regulation – today we might say 'sublimation' – of sexual desire may be saturated with ethical and political interests. The Greeks in particular seemed to believe that love for a specific individual could be the hearth on which is ignited the flame of a higher, more sublime, more glorious love – love of the *polis*, and of the liberty, strength and wisdom of its citizens.

And yet, we should not be too hasty here either. Until a revival of research on Greek antiquity in the 1970s, it was not unusual to assume that the Greeks' attitude to love and sexuality was polarised between the pagan sexual licentiousness of the common people and the austere, high-minded ideals of the philosophising aristocracy for whom sexual love was a mere conduit for the sublime pursuit of freedom and truth. Dover writes of the former:

> At first glance many aspects of Athenian life might appear to justify the belief, favoured by some popular writers in our own day, that the Greeks lived in a rosy haze of uninhibited sexuality, untroubled by the fear, guilt and shame which later cultures were to invent. The Greeks did, after all, treat sexual enjoyment as the province of a goddess, Aphrodite … . In the Dionysiac festivals at Athens giant models of the erect penis were taken in procession, to the accompaniment of suitably happy songs; a minor but affectionately regarded deity, Phales, seems to have been the personification of the erect penis … . The poets represented the gods themselves as enjoying adultery, fornication and sodomy, and the vase-painters of the late archaic and early classical periods often depicted sexual intercourse, masturbation and fellatio. Xenophon's Socrates, although hostile to the body on such issues as appeared to involve a clear body/mind antithesis, lists among the blessings conferred on mankind by beneficent providence … the fact that we, unlike so many animals, can be sexually active at all seasons. (Dover 1974: 205–6)

In partial contrast to this is the philosophical conception of love we have come to call 'Platonic', which is defined in my dictionary as a 'purely spiritual love' and which, in the form originally offered by Plato, has been disparaged for advocating a 'spiritualised egocentrism' denuded of physical passion and incapable of cherishing people as ends in themselves. Both the popular-sexual and the aristocratic-spiritual versions of Attic love have, in fact, attracted the refrain that they are devoid of the close intimacy and emotional reciprocity that we would normally associate with amorous relationships. In Alvin Gouldner's assessment of the philosophical ideal of love, 'Plato strives to strip love of its Dionysian qualities and to make it a thing of the mind, rather than something of the deepest emotions or of the whole, embodied man' (1967: 244). The sublime love apparently recommended in Plato's dialogues seems a long way from our own modern ideal, which instead aspires 'to enrich the lives of persons who are themselves worthy of love for their own sake' (Vlastos 1981: 31).

Eros, erastes, eromenos

I shall return to look in more detail at Plato's philosophy of love in the next chapter. Here I want to examine what we know about the way the Greeks understood erotic relationships in the classical era of Athens, for more recent work on this topic has suggested that the extremes of popular-Dionysian and aristocratic-intellectual love may be an inaccurate and artificial division of Greek attitudes to love and sexuality. In particular, our understanding of homosexuality in fifth-century Athens has been significantly deepened thanks to Foucault's study of the delicate ethical regulation of Greek sexual relations – what he called a 'stylistics' or 'aesthetics' of existence.

We should be aware that when the Greeks spoke of love, the term they most commonly used was '*eros*', a word with a range of meanings including what in English we would think of as 'desire' and 'lust'. The earliest evidence of the word is in the writings of Herodotus and Hesiod from the eighth century BC. Both Eros and Aphrodite were Greek deities, and although in Hesiod's *Theogony* Eros seems to be predated by the birth of Aphrodite, in another passage in the same text, Ludwig (2002: 9) points out, Eros is 'a primary, cosmogonic hunger, which precedes Aphrodite and most of the other gods'. All intense yearnings and desires would, from this latter account, be traced back to Eros. In vase paintings, sculptures and jewellery, Eros was commonly depicted as a young winged male whose arrows, as Greek poetry frequently attested, could wound mortals with pangs of helpless desire (Dover 1989: 43, 67n11). The description of Eros as a 'sickness' or 'madness' was also a staple of the poets, playwrights and philosophers of classical Athens (Dover 1974: 210–11). The poetry of Ibycus, from the sixth century BC, includes references to the irresistible force of both Eros and Aphrodite: 'Eros, again looking at me meltingly with his eyes under dark eyelids, flips me with manifold charms into the inescapable nets of Aphrodite.' Anacreon, another lyric poet of the same period, wrote: 'The dice of Eros are madnesses and uproars' (Stigers 1981: 48–9). Eros was not only a dangerous force of compulsion to the lover but could also assault the object of love with fatal effect. In Euripides' *Hippolytus*, for example, when Semele is 'put to bed' by Zeus, she is burnt to death by the 'flaming thunderbolt' of his *eros* (Nussbaum 2002: 60).

'*Eros*' was a term that was also used, at least in earlier antiquity, to refer to both non-sexual and non-amorous passions. Thus, Ludwig (2002: 124–6) reports that in Homeric Greek the word had a generic meaning that denoted desire for a wide range of objects, from the banal to the glorious, including food, dancing, war and weeping. In later writings, the tendency for *aphrodisiac* to be used by the Greeks in specific reference to purely sexual appetites and pleasures began to allow '*eros*' to assume a more restricted meaning that was in some respects closer to the passion we today associate with romantic love, and which also enabled the Greeks to speak, as we do, about sex without love.[1] *Eros* for the Greeks rarely had connotations of altruistic care, however, which was a later conception of love that probably originates in Christian theology, St Paul's interpretation of the Greek term *agapē* and Augustine's notion of *caritas*, concepts which refer to the humility and selflessness necessary to achieve communion with the Divine.

In the prose and spoken Greek of the classical period, a more specific sense of *eros* prevailed. In his famous speech at the public burial of the soldiers killed during the first year of the Peloponnesian War, Pericles urged the patriotic citizens of Athens 'to gaze, day after day, upon the power of the city and become her lovers [*erastai*]' (Thucydides 2.43.1).[2] When Pericles and later Greek statesmen used the term *erastes* in political discourse, they were almost certainly exploiting the erotic associations of a word which was ordinarily used to distinguish the dominant figure in a sexual encounter – normally an adult male 'lover' (*erastes*) whose adolescent male partner assumed the passive status of 'beloved' (*eromenos*). The call to citizens to be 'lovers of the polis' was, in other words, a reminder of the citizen's duty to be an active and virile participant in public affairs and a contributor to the renown of the city. As Ludwig puts it: 'Pericles does not only ask his fellow citizens to feel passionately about the city; rather, he asks them on the basis of their passion to play, in relation to the city, the social role that lovers play toward a beloved. They are to serve her chivalrously, sacrifice for her, compete for her favours, rival one another to show who is most worthy' (2002: 148).

Among the key features of *eros* as it appears to have been understood in fifth-century Athens, both in public culture and, as we shall see in the next chapter, in philosophy, three elements stand out according to Ludwig (2002: 12–14). The first is that *eros* is a response to something perceived as beautiful, the appetite for beautiful things being taken as natural to human beings. This could be a person, but it might also be a truthful insight, a moral ideal or, as in Pericles's claim that the passions of Athenians should be aroused by the allure of their 'powerful' city, a political community. The second is that *eros* is desire that has been intensified by the remoteness of the goal or by the presence of obstacles to its fulfilment. Not only are readily available goods therefore not likely to arouse *eros*, but such

---

[1] The best example of this is Lysias' speech in the *Phaedrus*, which explores the justification for a boy having a sexual relationship with a man who desires him but is 'not in love' with him.

[2] Translation from Hornblower (1991: 311). In the Penguin Classics edition of Thucydides, 'become her lovers' is rendered 'fall in love with her', a translation that misses the specific sexual connotations of '*erastai*'. The same distinction prevails in modern English: we can 'love' all sorts of mundane things – football, chocolate, sunshine – but it would be awkward to describe oneself as these things' 'lover' (Ludwig 2002: 147).

goods may be willingly risked because of the powerful force of *eros*, this strong and obsessive desire being distinguishable from the more ordinary affection or dearness (*philia*) felt for a spouse, child, parent or friend (Dover 1974: 212).[3] The third is that *eros* seeks something beyond itself; it is a fierce and sometimes fatal drive towards transcendence that may skirt perilously close to madness.

All things in moderation

Ludwig's view is that *eros* in its narrow, amatory sense has always been a driving force for human beings, but the degree to which this force has been channelled, stylised and sublimated into non-sexual forms – courtship and romance, art and philosophy, patriotism, politics and war – has varied from one society to another. For the Greeks – or more accurately, for Greek masculinity in classical Athens – a free and virile citizen was someone in command of his pleasure as well as his city. Resistance to tyranny, in other words, required resistance to tyrannical desire, *eros* being a force of necessity that could endanger a citizen's autonomy and reason. The ethical importance of resisting tyrannical impulses is apparent in the way Pericles praised the war dead for standing their ground and suffering death instead of surrendering to fear and the desire to flee (Thucydides 2.42.4). It is also implicit in Thucydides' description of the feverish lust which Athenians initially felt for the Sicilian expedition. 'Eros afflicted them all alike to sail forth', he reports, but this was an 'excessive passion' that blinded them to the rashness of the ultimately doomed enterprise (6.24.2–4).[4]

In keeping with this cautionary attitude towards the domineering force of *eros*, the 'lover of the body' is described by Socrates in Xenophon's *Symposium* as 'more servile' than the 'lover of the mind' (8.23–24). Socrates' first speech in the *Phaedrus*, which he subsequently retracts for being reductive and undialectical, caricatures the 'madness' of *eros* and the degradations which its incontinent passions inflict on lover and beloved alike. In passages that evoke an ugly Proustian picture of self-centred love, Socrates sees the *eromenos* fatefully 'surrendering himself to a man who is untrustworthy, bad-tempered, jealous,

---

[3] The difference between *eros* and *philia* should not be overstated, and might better be understood by analogy with our own distinction between being 'in love' and 'loving'. *Philia* did not imply the absence of passion or emotion, and English translators often seem to find the word 'love' to be the best way of rendering its meaning. *Philosophia*, for example, is 'love of wisdom' (not 'friendship of wisdom').

[4] The wording used here is explained in Jeremy Mynott's translation of Thucydides (2013: 402) and in Connor (1984: 167–8).

unpleasant, and harmful not just to his property and his physical condition, but even more to his mental development' (241c). Similarly, Pausanias, in Plato's *Symposium*, describes the 'obsequious servility' of the actions of the intoxicated lover, who thinks it is acceptable 'to beg and beseech for his prayers to be fulfilled, to make promises under oath, to sleep in the other's doorway, to take on the kinds of degrading tasks even slaves wouldn't perform' (183a). Freedom from, or self-mastery of, such shameful passions was also associated (by Sophocles, among others) with the virtue of truthfulness: 'The freeman tells the truth because falsehood implies fear or need, and he should not be motivated by either' (Dover 1974: 115). A more generous understanding of the relationship between *eros* and dishonesty is offered by Pausanias in the *Symposium*: 'the only occasion when the gods pardon perjury is when a lover is the one making the promise. "A promise inspired by passion [*Aphrodite*]", as the proverb says, "is no promise at all"' (183b-c).

Alcibiades himself was the personification of *epithumia* ('intense desire'), driven by the pursuit of personal fame and glory, which in his political oratory he skilfully associated with the public good of the democratic polis and the Athenian valorisation of the active citizen: 'a city which is accustomed to activity would be very quickly destroyed by a change to inactivity' is how Thucydides reports Alcibiades' speech to the Assembly, where he successfully canvassed support for the invasion of Sicily. 'A city that is inactive wears itself out from within' (6.18.6–7). Although the city found itself passionately in favour of the daring naval expedition, it was also scandalised by Alcibiades' lavish personal lifestyle and unscrupulous political associations, believing, for all his achievements in the realm of public administration and military strategy, that he was ultimately out for his own advancement (6.15.3–4). The subsequent attempt to recall Alcibiades to Athens to face charges implicating him in the vandalising of *hermai*[5] and his sentencing in absentia to death were linked by Thucydides to the earlier actions of Harmodius and Aristogeiton, because in both cases, it seems, uncontrolled *eros* resulted in self-destructive hubris. Just as the erotic boldness of the tyrannicides provoked a more repressive regime, so too the Athenians' lust for war rebounded as a growing atmosphere of fear and suspicion in the polis, forcing Alcibiades himself to defect to the Lacedaemonians. The qualities of openness and tolerance which Pericles lauded his democratic city for

---

[5] These were stone columns topped with the bust of a head – normally of the God Hermes – and engraved below with male genitalia. They were often placed at boundaries, crossroads and outside buildings, and were believed to ward off evil and bring good luck.

(2.37) thus seemed to be endangered by *eros* when it was allowed to rule without moderation. Connor summarises this oblique morality tale in Thucydides' narrative: 'The efforts to avoid a tyranny have resulted in a loss of some of the most essential features of the free civic order Athens prized so highly. In seeking to protect itself from a tyranny Athens begins to become a tyrant whose effects are felt not so much by its subjects as by its own citizens' (1984: 180).

If incontinent desire is a risk to democracy, it is perhaps no surprise that in the *Republic* Plato has Socrates define the 'democratic man' as one who 'enjoys every pleasure in perfect moderation', while the 'tyrant' is one who has 'purged out temperance, and filled himself with alien frenzy'. This is why 'love [*eros*] has of old been called a tyrant' (572d-573d). The ethical requirement for the rational control of *eros* is also apparent in an important sentence in Pericles' funeral oration. 'We love fine things but are not extravagant', he says in praise of the cultured Athenian temperament, 'and we love learning but are not effete' (2.40.1).[6] While the idea that to rule over one's pleasures is to bring them under the authority of the *logos* is unremarkable, Pericles pushes this argument further in suggesting that wisdom may itself be a seductive source of self-degradation, and that indulgent ideas must also be held in check by prudent action and dialogue. Desire must be sublimated by reason, but reason too must be restrained to avoid excess. In both cases, lack of self-restraint implies passivity and acceptance of bondage, qualities which to the Greek mind were essentially feminine and typical of barbarians and slaves. What defined a free male citizen, by contrast, was the sublimation and controlled stylisation of desire. Foucault elaborates:

> To be immoderate was to be in a state of non-resistance with regard to the force of pleasures, and in a position of weakness and submission; it meant being incapable of that virile stance with respect to oneself that enabled one to be stronger than oneself ... . The dividing line between a virile man and an effeminate man did not coincide with our opposition between hetero- and homosexuality; nor was it confined to the opposition between active and passive homosexuality. It marked the difference in people's attitudes toward the pleasures; and the traditional signs of effeminacy ... were not necessarily associated with the individual who in the nineteenth century would be called an 'invert', but with the one who yielded to the pleasures that enticed him: he was under the power of his own appetites and those of others ... . In the eyes of the

---

[6] Hannah Arendt (1977: 213–14) renders this sentence: 'We love beauty within the limits of political judgement, and we philosophise without the barbarian vice of effeminacy.' It should be noted that all translations of this passage use 'love' or 'lovers' to denote what in the original Greek are compounds of *philia* rather than *eros*.

Greeks, what constituted ethical negativity par excellence ... consisted in being passive with regard to the pleasures. (Foucault 1992: 84–5)

Greek pederasty and the problematisation of pleasure

For the Greeks, Foucault argues, the difference between self-possession and loose morals in sexual behaviour was more significant than the kinds of pleasures pursued, or the sex of the person who was desired. The Greeks did not classify themselves according to the sex of their partner, and *eros* felt for the same sex was considered no different to *eros* felt for the opposite sex; both were assumed to be natural responses to the presence of beauty. Foucault suggests that the specific moral problematisation of sexual desire, as something separate from other forms of desire, is something we have inherited from Christianity rather than the ancients. However, while the Greek ethic of moderation extended to all types of pleasure and all types of desire, sex, being an interpersonal exchange, clearly has, and for them had, a distinctive moral significance. Gluttony and greed do not impugn the honour of food or heap indignity on the glass of wine, but an unrestrained sexual appetite can bring shame to the beloved as well as the lover. 'What is at stake in sex', Nussbaum points out, 'is not only one's own self-mastery, but also the well-being, happiness, and ethical goodness of another' (2002: 58).

Why is it, then, that most moral reflections from classical Greece on the nature of love focus on relations between men, and more specifically on the relation between an adolescent boy (*pais*), who is not yet old enough to claim the status of citizen, and an adult male lover (*paiderastes*)? The fact that every surviving word of ancient Greek was written by a man is one obvious reason why women's experience of sexual love is invisible in these accounts. That women were deemed capable of sexual enjoyment is undeniable, but the ability to experience physical pleasure was regarded by the Greeks as an animal faculty, and it was the man's capacity to actively moderate and control his desires which testified to the superiority of the free citizen.

The consensus among modern historians seems to be that love between husband and wife was probably a rare occurrence among the elite in Greek antiquity, and when it existed, as Engels put it, it was 'not so much subjective inclination as objective duty, not the cause of marriage, but its corollary' (Engels 1942: 68). Engels' reference to 'duty' notwithstanding, marital morality did not seem to *require* a close erotic bond for it to constitute a normative practice and relationship (Foucault 1992: 202). Socrates, in Xenophon's *Symposium*, says he has been told that Nikeratos feels *eros* for his wife, and that this is reciprocated (8.3), but this seems worthy of comment as an exception rather than the rule. Probably women's exclusion from participation in public affairs impaired the intimacy of heterosexual relations among the elite, making wives less interesting and attractive companions to their husbands than other men (Gouldner 1967: 62–3; Dover 1989: 88). Male citizens also had more respect for the educated company of the independent *hetairai* than they had for their own dependent wives. 'We have courtesans [*hetairai*] for pleasure,' the Athenian politician Apollodorus famously declared in his prosecution speech against the *hetaira* Neaira, 'concubines for the daily tending of the body, and wives in order to beget legitimate children and have a trustworthy guardian of what is at home' (Demosthenes 59.122).

Among the ranks of the Athenian aristocracy, from where arose the poets, statesmen, dramatists and philosophers whose accounts we must rely on, it therefore seems that marriage was primarily an economic arrangement for the transmission of property and the production of legitimate heirs, and the size of a woman's dowry, the social status of a potential bride's father, and a young woman's estimated competence at managing a household of children and slaves were the most important determinants of a man's marital choice. As Bakewell writes of Creon's description, in Sophocles' *Antigone*, of women as fertile soil to be 'ploughed' for children: 'within the context of male civic ideology, legitimate wives are like land: they are essentially identical parcels, with one tilled acre resembling another. Their primary purpose is to bring forth new life. And, like tracks of earth itself, they can be measured in standard units that simultaneously function as reservoirs of wealth' (2013: 83).

Of course, a married man in the Greek polis might also have had illicit sexual designs on other men's wives. But boys and girls were segregated from childhood in Athens, and once a girl was married this practice continued, with wives kept in separate quarters to limit their contact with men. The strict sexual segregation of women from men was likely to have been harder among the poorer citizens of the city, however, for there the responsibility for chores would have fallen on women rather than slaves; as well as this necessitating encounters with tradesmen and trips to the agora, some female citizens also had to accept the necessity of paid work, perhaps as wet nurses, or as harvest hands, vegetable sellers or weavers. Norms of sexual behaviour may well have varied between the classes, therefore, and below the strata of the wealthy elite heterosexual love affairs may have been easier and more common than historical records indicate (Dover 1974: 98, 211).

Evidence of lesbian relationships is even scarcer, however, and although the spatial separation of the sexes must have led to physical and emotional intimacy between women, the phallocentricity of Greek culture would have made love between women virtually inconceivable to the male mind. Given the association of active *eros* with the dominant role monopolised by the male citizen, women's desire *for men* was probably an even greater taboo. This may be why the only surviving self-representation of a woman as an erotic subject in Greek antiquity is the passionate love poems of Sappho (Stigers 1981: 47). Though there is no clear agreement as to the precise sexual significance of these poems, there is no doubt that they convey female desire, an appreciation of women as objects of female desire and, breaking free of the hierarchical *erastes-eromenos* dichotomy, the anguished desire to be loved and desired in return (Downing 1994).

Perhaps more critical to explaining the centrality of pederasty in Greek moral reflections on *eros*, however, is the way in which the Greeks valorised activity and denigrated passivity in sexual, as in other, relations. Sexual relations for the Greeks were, as Foucault puts it, 'isomorphic' with wider social relations. 'Pleasure practices were conceptualised using the same categories as those in the field of social rivalries and hierarchies', which meant that they were 'of the same type as the relationship between a superior and subordinate, an individual who dominates and one who complies, one who vanquishes and one who is vanquished' (1992: 215). Passiveness and compliance were signs of effeminacy; they were, in other words, 'natural' to women, and thus it was assumed that women naturally gained pleasure from sexual penetration. This was, in fact, one reason why wives were segregated, as the absence of contraception made women who were tempted by adultery a risk to the family's function as a mechanism for the inheritance of property. The perceived natural division between the dominant and passive partner in marriage was also why heterosexual relations attracted less ethical discourse and scrutiny.

The same rigid clarity of roles and expectations could not be established in relations between men and boys, however. While marital relations were regulated by gender segregation and the husband's legal right to govern the wife, there was a spatial and legal 'openness' in the relationships between men and boys, which were often conducted in the street, marketplace or gymnasium, and in which the man possessed no statutory authority over the boys he pursued. This openness meant that homosexual relationships were clear opportunities for the practising – or malpractising – of public virtues.

For the Greeks, on the one hand, the sexual attractiveness and availability of boys was virtually irresistible and beyond dispute. It was shameful for a free adult man to accept sexual servitude and domination by another man, and it was hubristic – and legally actionable – for the latter to demand that shameful acceptance. But free adolescent boys had not yet attained the critical status of a citizen, and the moral significance of the boy's consent was therefore weaker. This, combined with the Greek's aestheticisation of the young male body – which was valorised for its gracefulness, but only when there was also sufficient strength, dexterity and endurance to prevent its degeneration into effeminacy[7] – made adolescent boys an ethically admissible object of homoerotic desire.

On the other hand, the boy's junior status in this relationship was a transient and ambiguous one. Not only was his youthful bloom destined to disappear with the onset of adulthood and the first facial hair, but he was also a citizen-in-waiting, and could not therefore be treated in the same way as a submissive prostitute, slave or wife. The precarious – because transitory – nature of the pederastic relationship, the public visibility and agonal nature of its performance, and the ambiguous status of the beloved as both a legitimate erotic object and a pre-citizen who would soon become his own lover of boys therefore made relations between men and boys a delicate matter of moral problematisation and aesthetic choreography. Promoting homoerotism while attaching a certain stigma to the act of consummation, it is little wonder that the sublimated courtship practices of homosexual love were the most prevalent manifestation of *eros* in classical Athens (Ludwig 2002: 221). Relations between men and boys became, in Foucault's words, 'the object of a sort of ritualization, which by imposing certain rules on them gave them form, value, and interest. Even before they were taken up by the philosophical reflection, these relations were already the pretext for a whole social game' (1992: 196).

This was a game of honour and repute, and its rules were different for the two partners. The older lover, the *erastes*, was the suitor who was expected both to display and to restrain his ardour. This restraint was a demonstration of self-mastery, as Foucault stresses; but in its ideal form it was also, as Nussbaum (2002) points out, an expression of respect, if not indeed reverence, for the *eromenos*. The man would initially court the youngster with gifts which, if historical iconography provides an accurate representation of cultural practices,

---

[7] In Xenophon's *Symposium*, Socrates expresses admiration for Callias' love of the young athlete Autolycus: 'I see that the person you love is not pampered by luxury or enervated by effeminacy, but displays to the eyes of all his strength, endurance, courage and self-discipline. To be attracted by these qualities is evidence of the lover's own character' (8.8–9). The self-disciplining of the body was also regarded as a test of mental strength, and the intellect was regarded as an exclusively masculine virtue (Simmel 1971: 240).

were typically cockerels and hunted game (Dover 1989: 92). As the relationship developed, they would have also included educational instruction, musical tuition, athletic training, and political mentorship and preferment. Money would never have changed hands, however, for a free man who was proven, either as an adult or as a boy, to have prostituted himself for money would be demeaning his status as citizen, the punishment for which was permanent debarment from holding office, voting, and speaking in the assembly. The task of the *erastai* was therefore to compete among themselves to be the most attractive role model, showcasing to the courted boy the exemplary man he might become – athlete, warrior, musician, philosopher, statesman – if he were to accept a lover's affections and follow his lead.

For the *eromenos*, having older male admirers was a legitimate source of pride, but it was shameful to consent too quickly, and without having tested the lover's character and worth. A boy who yielded too easily would be regarded as a '*hetaira*', a kind of 'mistress' whose effeminacy signified an inability to defend himself and therefore an impaired future capacity to defend his city as a warrior-citizen. To excel in the sphere of love, as in the sphere of politics and war, the boy had to show firmness and self-mastery, refusing to be manipulated or to oblige his lover out of temerity, lust or unscrupulous self-interest.

The conventional understanding and moral norm was that the boy would, and should, get no physical pleasure from the sexual relationship, since that would be to identify with a passive, essentially feminine, role, and be poor training for the requirements of future citizenship. 'A boy does not even share the man's enjoyment of sexual intercourse as a woman does', Socrates observes in Xenophon's *Symposium*; 'he is a sober person watching one drunk with sexual excitement' (8.21). Depictions of homosexual relations in the sixth- and fifth-century vase-paintings studied by Dover (1989: 91–9) often show the *erastes* imploring or expostulating with an adolescent boy, rarely show sexual arousal in the youth, even when his affection is clearly apparent, and almost always represent copulation between man and boy as intercrural (between the thighs) and face-to-face (implying not reciprocity, but at least the absence of that relationship of domination and subservience apparent in depictions of heterosexual intercourse, as well as of homosexual intercourse with slaves, in which penetration always occurs from the rear). The boy demonstrates self-mastery and secures the respect of the man by refusing both his own sexual arousal and his lover's desire for penetration; he yields only partially and without losing control, and not for the sake of his own physical pleasure but in order to advance his education and social standing.

Philia, friendship and reciprocity

Described in these terms, pederastic relations in classical Athens sound some way removed from our modern conception of love, showing more of a resemblance to the inferior forms of friendship which Aristotle identified as being grounded in transient pleasure and utility. In Book 8 of the *Nicomachean Ethics*, Aristotle suggested that there are three types of friendship: perfect and enduring friendships based on wishing the well-being of the other for his own sake; friendships premised on the pursuit of pleasure, including sexual pleasure, which tend to be short-lived because appetites and tastes are subject to change; and equally accidental and transient friendships based on utility, which come to an end 'as soon as the advantage ceases, because they were attracted not by each other but by the prospect of gain' (1157a10-34). Though pederastic relationships seem like a hybrid of the second and third type – the boy is looking for utility, the man seeks pleasure – Aristotle actually cites the relation between *erastes* and *eromenos* as an example of a utility friendship, in which people with unequal resources exchange different goods: 'One might introduce here the relation between lover and beloved, or between a handsome person and an ugly one. This is the reason why lovers sometimes make themselves look ridiculous by demanding to be loved as much as they love' (1159a32-b22). That the *eromenos* is not expected to reciprocate the older man's love is consistent with Pausanias' speech, in Plato's *Symposium*, which refers to 'Aristogeiton's love [*eros*] and Harmodius's friendship [*philia*]' (182c).[8]

The cultural legitimacy of such relationships to the Greeks may be easier to grasp if we follow Dover's analogy between this normative construction of the homosexual *eromenos* and the conjugal narrative of 'respectable' women in nineteenth-century literature:

> The good woman, in this literature, does not desire or seek sexual intercourse. She does not even desire marriage; but if a man of good character and ability asks her to marry him, obtains her father's consent, displays patience, tact and modesty in all his dealings with her, and participates with her in a prolonged and complicated ritual of which the essential element is the utterance of formulae and responses in a church, thereafter she has sexual intercourse with him whenever he wishes. He has not at any time alluded directly to this aspect of marriage. She

---

[8] This is the W. R. M. Lamb translation. *Plato. Vol. III: Lysis, Symposium, Gorgias.* London: William Heinemann, 1925. Robin Waterfield's translation in the 1994 OUP edition is: 'Aristogiton's love and the constancy of Harmodius' loyalty'.

does not enjoy it or take the initiative in it; she accepts it because she loves him and because it is her duty. (Dover 1989: 90)

Helpful as it is, the analogy breaks down, of course, because the boy will not be a boy for very long. One might agree with Monoson (1994: 265) that there was 'erotic reciprocity' in pederastic relationships, in so far as these relationships revolved around the partners' shared commitment to sustaining an affair which had an honourable, graceful and aesthetically gratifying form. But sexual desire for a youthful body could not survive the maturing of that body, nor could it remain honourable when the boy became a citizen. In all pederastic relations, therefore, the *eros* of the lover stood in imminent danger of being exposed as little more than inconstancy and opportunism. As Pausanias explains in his speech in Plato's *Symposium*:

> A lover is bad if he is of the common type, who loves the body rather than the mind. This makes him inconstant, because there's no constancy in the object of his desires; as soon as the physical bloom that attracted him fades, he 'flies away and is gone', exposing the shabbiness of all his fine words and promises. On the other hand, a lover [*erastes*] who loves goodness of character is constant for life, because of the constancy of the object he's been united with. (183d-e)[9]

Although Pausanias uses *eros* and its compounds in this passage, for Aristotle constancy is a quality of the perfect *friendship*. It is evident in friendships between persons of 'good character', Aristotle says, because it is good to value goodness, and the goodness of another's character is precisely what a good person holds dear (*Ethics*, 1156b1-23). However, in the normal relationship between *erastes* and *eromenos*, the partners, Aristotle says,

> do not take pleasure in the same things: the one finds it in looking at his beloved, and the other in the attentions of his lover. And as beauty wanes, sometimes the friendship wanes too, because the one loses pleasure in the sight, and the other no longer receives the attentions; yet on the other hand many do remain friends if through their intimacy they have come to appreciate each other's characters as being like their own. (1156b23-1157a34)

---

[9] The same sentiment is expressed by Socrates in Xenophon's *Symposium*: 'the bloom of youth, as we know, quickly passes its prime, and when this fails, the affection must fade along with it; but so long as the mind is progressing towards greater wisdom, the more lovable it becomes' (8.14–15). 'Affection for the mind', Socrates also says, 'is less liable to satiety', whereas physical desire has a limit, 'so that one is bound to lose interest in a favourite in just the same way as repletion makes one lose interest in food' (8.15). A critic might argue that Socrates is talking here about sex, not eroticism (which always has an imaginative component). This is a distinction I will return to at the end of the next chapter.

Aristotle's allusion to a transient love evolving into a sustainable friendship was a common theme in Socratic literature, and suggests part of the provenance of our modern vernacular understanding of 'Platonic love'. The Aristotelian distinction between an essentially utilitarian *eros* and what Socrates, in Xenophon's *Symposium*, describes as a 'friendship [*philia*] of the mind' based on mutual admiration and respect (8.28–32) is the difference, Socrates suggests, between valuing someone as a means and valuing them as an end:

> It seems to me that a person who concentrates on outward appearance is like one who has rented a plot of land: his object is not to increase the value of the land, but to secure for himself as many crops as he can. But the man who desires friendship is more like the owner of his own holding; at any rate, he gathers together from every quarter whatever he can get to increase the worth of the one he loves. Besides, a favourite who knows that enough outward beauty will enable him to dominate his lover is likely to take little trouble over any other quality; but if he knows that, unless he is truly good, he will not retain the friendship, then it is natural that he should care more about virtue. (8.25-7)

Are we to understand, then, that it is 'spiritual friendship' which for the Greeks offered the only redemptive alternative to an otherwise self-defeating *eros*? It is certainly worth reiterating how a society more comfortable with homoeroticism than our own still subjected sexual desire to elaborate ethical sublimation and restraint. It is also worth reminding ourselves that in the sexually liberalised, if heterosexist, societies of the West today, libidinal longings play an increasingly central role in a culture of consumer capitalism that leaves many forms of misery and destruction in its wake. Since Foucault, we know, however, that the regulation of desire may mobilise what it regulates, and that the rule of reason often draws energy from the very passion it oversees. Socrates' repeated references to a 'heavenly Aphrodite' in Xenophon's *Symposium* should warn us, perhaps, against interpreting the love that is attracted to virtue as something purely intellectual in character. We must bear this in mind when we turn now to Plato's own famous *Symposium*, which has *eros* as its central topic.

2

Platonic love

It is to the Neo-Platonists of the Italian Renaissance that we owe the term 'Platonic love'. According to Kevin Sharpe (1987: 23–4), the concept was coined by Marsilio Ficino in a treatise on Plato's *Symposium* written in 1469. The idea that a chaste romance could yield sublime intellectual insight then spread to France, thanks partly to the literary writings and scholarship of Pietro Bembo and Baldassare Castiglione. There it became the inspiration for Honoré d'Urfé's pastoral romance, *Astreé*, which, once the novel had been translated into English in 1620, helped the French queen consort, Henrietta Maria, promote her own fashionable cult of Platonic love in the court of her husband, Charles I. Sharpe (1987: 24) cites a royal news bulletin from 1634, sceptically announcing its arrival:

> The Court affords little News at present, but that there is a love call'd Platonick Love, which much sways there of late; it is a love abstracted from all corporeal gross impressions and sensual Appetite, but consists in Contemplations and Ideas of the Mind, not in any carnal fruition. This love sets the Wits of the Town on work; and they say there be a Mask shortly of it, whereof her Majesty and her Maids of Honour will be part.[1]

Sharpe notes that the ethics of Platonic love were often ridiculed, not just from outside the court but also from within, with plays performed lampooning the Platonic lover as a charlatan and hypocrite. Far from sexual asceticism, in fact, the cult of Platonic love appeared to promote, in the words of one Stanford historian, 'libertine standards of marriage and love'. 'Platonics defended adultery and incest', Sensabaugh (1940: 459) writes: 'women, shrines of beauty and virtue, because of their beauty and virtue could not commit sin; and men, in worshipping beauty, could not err in placing Venus before Hymen,

---

[1] A mask, or *masque*, was a theatrical literary performance, normally accompanied by music, staged for the royal court.

should desire lead them from the straight road of custom'. Enraged by what they saw as the idolatrous worship of women's physical form, the Puritans made Platonic love their sworn enemy. Confusing courtly promiscuity with Catholic permissiveness, they demanded the departure of the Queen and her papist retinue, stoking in turn the religious antagonisms that would lead to the English Civil War.

If seventeenth-century England was confused about the meaning of Platonic love, perhaps this is a legitimate clue to the complexity of Plato's writings, a complexity which has been lost in our own vernacular association of Platonic love with sexless friendships purged of erotic desire. The *Symposium* is perhaps the most humorous of Plato's dialogues, but its intellectual significance cannot be overestimated. For along with Plato's *Phaedrus*, it offers the most systematic treatment in Greek philosophy on the concept of love, and opens a revealing window onto the different understandings of love popular at the time among the Athenian elite. For this reason I am going to present a detailed synopsis of it here.

The *Symposium*: Phaedrus and Pausanias

A symposium was literally a 'drinks party' (normally preceded by a meal), which upper-class Athenian men would attend for entertainment, singing, storytelling and conversation. Written around 385 BC, Plato sets his *Symposium* 30 years earlier, in 416 BC, a year before the disastrous Sicilian expedition led by Alcibiades. The host of the symposium is the poet and dramatist Agathon, who had just won a prestigious prize for the performance of his first play (this is what has enabled historians to date the setting of the event). The story really begins when the guests agree to dismiss the hired entertainers, and to amuse themselves instead by delivering speeches (*encomia*) in praise of the god Eros.

The first short speech (178a-180b) is given by Phaedrus, a prominent Athenian intellectual and former student of Socrates who appears in a number of Plato's dialogues. A year after this gathering, Phaedrus would be forced to flee Athens having been caught up in the paranoia of war and indicted for the profanation of the religious rites known as the Eleusinian Mysteries. Phaedrus begins by telling his companions that Eros is a 'primordial god' with no parents. The divine virtue of *eros*, Phaedrus claims, echoing the use of the term in Pericles' funeral oration, is that it rouses those in love to excel in bravery, loyalty and honour, 'for the last person a lover wants to be seen by, in the act of deserting or throwing away his weapons, is his boyfriend'. The gods honoured Achilles, Phaedrus says, because although he was the *eromenos* of Patroclus,[2] the courage he displayed in killing Hector to avenge Patroclus was more like the divine possession of an *erastes*. Phaedrus thus proposes a generative connection between the wilful passion of *eros* and the performance of noble deeds. He also signals the potential generosity of *eros*, which inspires the lover to excel before his beloved and even, as Achilles demonstrated, to lay down a youthful life in his honour.

The next speech to be reported in the text is given by Pausanias. In Plato's *Protagoras* (315de), Pausanias is described as the *erastes* of Agathon when the latter was young, and the relationship, as indicated in Xenophon's *Symposium* (8.32) and as implied by Aristophanes in his speech later in this current symposium (193b-c), seems to have been sustained since then. Perhaps not surprisingly, then, Pausanias speaks in praise of adult homosexual love, and claims to advance beyond Phaedrus by identifying a heavenly love superior to the crude lust of common *eros*.

Pausanias starts with an insight which would become central to Aristotelian ethics: an action cannot be judged right or wrong in itself, but only in terms of how well it is done. 'If it is done well and properly, it is right; if it is done badly, it is wrong. The same goes for loving and for Love [*Eros*]: only the Love who incites us to love properly is good and deserves our praise' (181a). Pausanias, who may feel he is on shaky moral ground for having retained an adult male lover in Agathon, is therefore keen to distinguish proper from improper love. The latter, he says, is indiscriminately attracted to bodies rather than minds, and to people who don't offer proper satisfactions (such as women). Virtuous love, on the other hand, is strong and enduring, and is therefore only drawn to boys once their physical and intellectual maturity has started to become apparent: 'It seems to me that not having affairs until then is a sign that one is ready to enter into a lifelong relationship and partnership, as opposed to intending to dupe the boy by getting on friendly terms with him while he's still young and foolish, and then scornfully abandoning him and running off to someone else' (181d). This emphasis on faithfulness, constancy, reciprocity and companionship is much

---

[2] This erotic reading of the *Iliad* probably derives from a trilogy by the tragedian Aeschylus, whose plays were popular at the time. Phaedrus agrees that Achilles and Patroclus were lovers, but disputes Aeschylus' casting of Achilles as the *erastes*, claiming that his youth and beauty must have made him the *eromenos* (180a). Socrates, in Xenophon's *Symposium*, rejects the erotic interpretation of the relationship altogether: 'Homer has made Achilles exact his famous vengeance for Patroclus not because Patroclus was his lover, but because he was a friend and was killed' (8.31).

closer to our own modern ideals of love than is the Greek model of pederasty, and indeed Pausanias' attempt to distinguish good and bad *forms* of love, and to associate the higher form of love with goodness and virtue, is also in tune with our intuition that lust and love are not entirely different, mutually antagonistic species.

Pausanias also rejects the sentiment that it is 'disgusting [for an *eromenos*] to gratify a lover', reminding us that this practice is perfectly acceptable so long as it is 'moderate and within the guidelines of convention'. States which condemn homosexual exchanges, he declares, are tyrannical regimes which fear the thirst for liberty and fraternity that is aroused by love between men, as was the case with Harmodius and Aristogeiton: 'it's not in the rulers' interests to have their subjects cultivate ambition[3] or the kind of firm loyalty and friendship which Love is particularly good at engendering' (182a-c). Pausanias also defends the game of chase and flight, arguing that it allows lovers to test each other's character and to construct from *eros* a relationship with elegant moral form: 'prompt submission is considered shameful: convention allows an interlude to occur, which invariably proves to be a good test'. The *eromenos* should not be seduced by money or the promise of political power, since neither of these things are 'reliable or constant', and both 'are incapable of forming a foundation for true friendship' (184a-b). It is acceptable for the *eromenos* to gratify his lover, Pausanias asserts, seemingly returning, somewhat contradictorily, to the legitimacy of the pederastic relationship, so long as by doing so his own self-improvement occurs. On the one side is 'the lover capable of increasing wisdom and other aspects of goodness', on the other 'the boy eager to learn and generally to increase his knowledge'. And though a boy who yields in the expectation of acquiring goodness may be unfortunate to discover that the *erastes* is a scoundrel with 'no goodness to his name', he should not feel dishonoured by this mistake, for while it is shameful to be motivated by the acquisition of external goods, it is not discreditable to 'do anything and everything for the sake of moral improvement'. Love of this higher, 'celestial' type, Pausanias concludes, is a blessing to the city. It should be 'highly prized by communities as well as individuals', since it 'impels a lover to pay a great deal of serious attention to the question of his own virtue, and does the same for the boy who is the object of a lover's affection' (184d-185c).

---

[3] The term used by Pausanias which Robin Waterfield translates as 'ambition' is '*phronemata megala*'. Ludwig (2002: 59) suggests 'proud thoughts' as a better translation. As we shall see in a moment, the same term is used by Aristophanes to describe the hubris of the original 'circle-men'.

Aristophanes

After a doting and unsophisticated testimonial by Eryximachus, who was a physician and friend of Phaedrus, the fourth encomium on Eros, which is arguably the most memorable of the speeches, is given by Aristophanes. The comic poet begins by saying that the importance of Eros to human beings has been greatly underestimated. Eros, Aristophanes claims, 'supports us and heals precisely those ills whose alleviation constitutes the deepest human happiness' (189d). This idea that love is a salve and a solace for wounded souls is part of a story that resonates particularly strongly with modern understandings of love.

Aristophanes offers his listeners a mythical account of the origin of the species. Humans, he says, were not originally formed as ambulant columns with a front and a back, but rather as 'circles', with four hands and four feet, who moved around like acrobats doing cartwheels. They had two sets of genitals, and two identical faces on either side of a single head. They also fell into three gender categories. Some were men, some were women, and some were androgynous, with both male and female organs. They were strong willed and displayed 'proud thoughts' (*phronemata megala*), and in their overweening ambition they tried to ascend to heaven to attack the gods. To clip the wings of the hubristic circle-people, and to enforce the virtues of moderation, Zeus split them all in half, then asked Apollo to twist the faces around so they were aligned with the severed side of them, their torn bodies being healed with skin which was smoothed out and then tied in a final knot (the navel). The weakened halves of the former circle-people were now forced to walk in an upright fashion; and as their number was now doubled, there could be more sacrificial offerings for the gods.

The split human beings now yearned to be made whole again by being grafted together with their missing half. Nothing else mattered to them, and in their apathy and failure to attend to the necessities of life, they began to starve. Zeus took pity on them, Aristophanes says, and moved their genitals around to the front of their bodies so they were on the same side as their faces. Before this, Aristophanes explains, sexual reproduction occurred through intercourse with the ground rather than each other. Thanks to Zeus' surgical adjustments, when couples embraced face-to-face they could now also have sex. People who prefer sex with their sexually opposite half were obviously cut from the hermaphrodites, whereas people who are most attracted to their own sex are the divided halves of either male or female circle-people (here we see a rare, if cursory, reference to the possibility of Sapphic eroticism). Aristophanes states that the purpose of sexual intercourse is to provide a respite from the painful longing for reunification, and to encourage people, once their passions have been discharged, to attend to the more humble matter of their own survival. In male-female unions, sex yields offspring who can populate and sustain the household; in relationships between men, the temporary gratification of *eros* enables the partners to 'relax, get on with their work and take care of other aspects of life' (191c).

Preceding the natural sexual preference that derives from the gender of each person's original progenitor, Aristophanes' fable describes a more primordial desire, which is the passionate pursuit of one's actual missing half. 'Love [*Eros*] draws our original nature back together; he tries to reintegrate us and heal the split in our nature. Turbot-like, each of us has been cut in half, and so we are human tallies, constantly searching for our counterparts' (191d). The melancholic longing to find completeness in a soulmate seems to be well understood here: 'We human beings will never attain happiness unless we find perfect love, unless we each come across the love of our lives and thereby recover our original nature' (193c). Aristophanes also conveys love's timeless joy: 'Anyone who has brought Love round to his side will find, as if by chance, the love of his life, which is a rare event at the moment' (193b). When this rare event happens, when someone 'actually meets his other half, it's an overwhelming experience. It's impossible to describe the affection [*philia*], warmth, and love [*eros*] they feel for each other; it's hardly an exaggeration to say that they don't want to spend even a moment apart' (192b-c). Although these lucky people 'form lifelong relationships together', the assumption that it is sex which draws them together is incorrect, because the yearning for completion existed before Zeus shifted the sexual organs to enable sexual intercourse. The evanescent goal that illuminates lovers' enjoyment of each other is in fact their physical reunification – something which remains, even for those lucky enough to find their missing half, impossible, for even in love we must accept that our beloved is a separate being, the interpenetration of bodies never quite delivering the merging of two into one that we desire. ' "Love" is just the name we give to the desire for and pursuit of wholeness' (192c-e).

Aristophanes' speech may be read as a straightforward vindication of the modern ideal of romantic love, moderated by realism and an awareness of love's inescapable solitude and frustration. The myth of the circle-people certainly appealed to the twentieth-century psychoanalytic imagination, although both Freud and Erich Fromm were guilty of a heterosexist reading of the fable, treating it as an explanation, in Fromm's words, of 'the desire for union between the masculine and feminine poles', in the light of which, Freud wrote, homosexuality 'comes as a great surprise' (Fromm 1956: 33; Freud 1991: 46).

Freud later corrected this misinterpretation, presenting Aristophanes' story as a phylogenetic metaphor for the ontogenetic formation of sexual desire which perceptively 'traces the origin of an instinct to *a need to restore an earlier state of things*' (Freud 1955: 57, his emphasis). The primacy of the sex instinct in Freud's theory of psychological development nonetheless departs from Aristophanes' claim that the yearning to be completed by one's other half preceded the desire and the capacity to have sexual intercourse with them. Freud also wrongly implied that this story reflected Plato's own view, overlooking the comic aspect of Aristophanes' speech as well as the fact that it is superseded in the *Symposium* by Socrates' theory of love.

That Plato does not accept Aristophanes' version of love will be evident from what follows, but there are also some discordant notes in the story of the circle-people that first deserve comment. Finding one's 'other half' is a rare event, Aristophanes says, so 'it necessarily follows that in our present circumstances the best thing is to get as close to the ideal as possible' (193c). Put this way, love sounds like a doubly egocentric disposition: we are searching for the missing half, the mirror image, of ourselves, and since we are unlikely to find it, the next best thing is to love another person not *as* another person, but as an approximation to what we are missing of ourselves. There is a strong undercurrent of narcissism lurking in this vision, which clashes with the modern, humanist idea that love is the cherishing of another person as a unique and independent being. Undoubtedly this was what attracted the interest of Freud, who also believed that the preferred object of adult sexual desire is a person who can replicate the love we received when, as infants, we were incapable of loving anyone except ourselves (Freud 1957). But in the words of Ortega y Gasset, this is 'desire', not love; it misses both the shock – the unforeseen 'falling' – of love, and the passionate and generous attentiveness to another person which is the activity of loving when in love.

> Desire for any object is ultimately a desire to possess it … . Hence the desire dies of its own accord when it is fulfilled … . Love, on the other hand, is an eternal dissatisfaction. Desire has a passive character, and in this sense, when I desire something, I want it to come to me. I am the centre of gravity and expect things to fall in my direction. Love, on the other hand … is all activity. The lover goes out of himself to the object and lives in it. Love is perhaps the highest attempt nature makes to lift the individual out of himself and to lead him to another … . In its first stage love resembles desire because it is aroused by some person or thing outside one's self. The soul feels disturbed and gently wounded by a sting inflicted by the object … . From the wound that the provocative sting of

the object opened up, love flows and turns itself actively toward the object ... .
This incessant process of moving over to another is called love. (Ortega y Gasset
1933: 527–9)

The confusing of an active, striving love with passive and satiable desire
is also apparent in the way Aristophanes treats sexual relations as a means of
dampening human longings and bringing them into line with the practical
necessities of life. It is notable in this respect that his encomium warns against
the values of manliness and bravery which Phaedrus and Pausanias said were
the excellences inspired in men by Eros. Instead Aristophanes implicitly
recommends a more lowly, homely *eros*, one which turns adjacently in search
of a sexual mate rather than reaching upwards for fame and glory, and which
finds contentment in domesticated coupling and the marital conventions of
heterosexuality. The warm exclusivity of this 'lateral' love may still strike an
emotional chord with us, but this comes at the cost of severing *eros* from its
distinctive Greek association with higher public virtues and the grandeur of
political action.

This may not be immediately apparent from a single reading of Aristophanes'
speech. In a curious and much-debated passage, Aristophanes refers to the boy
'offcuts' of the original male gender who, as a consequence, 'enjoy sex with men'.
'I know they sometimes get called immoral', Aristophanes says, referring to the
feminisation of young men who are willing to play the passive role of *eromenos*,
'but that's wrong: their actions are prompted not by immorality, but by courage,
manliness, and masculinity'. The proof of this, he asserts, is that 'as adults, they're
the only men who end up in government' (191e-192a).[4]

Aristophanes was a satirist who regularly poked fun at homosexuality,
using his plays to laud rural life and heterosexual *eros* in the household, while
denigrating the cult of homoerotic masculinity and militarism that pervaded the
polis (Ludwig 2002: 61–5). The clue to the possible irony in the above passage
appears in a subsequent remark, where Aristophanes warns that 'if we fail to
behave towards the gods with moderation, we'll be further divided', this time
sawn in two down the front of our faces. 'That's why it is everyone's duty to
encourage others to behave at all times with due reverence towards the gods,
since this makes it possible for good rather than bad to come our way, with
Love as our leader and commander' (193a-b). Aristophanes began his mythical
story with an account of how the original circle-people were punished for their

---

[4] Ludwig (2002: 28) translates this last line as '... they alone end up in politics as real men'. *Aner* can be
translated as 'big man', 'leader', 'real man', 'he-man'.

hubris, and the term he used – *phronemata megala* ('proud thoughts') – is the same term used by Pausanias to praise the courage and ambition engendered by homosexual *eros*. Aristophanes agrees with Pausanias that pederasty breeds the masculine ambition of 'real men', but his assessment of this wolfish ambition is more critical. For Aristophanes, it appears that the 'manliness' of the *eromenos* is really a description of the latter's shameless contempt for sacred moral conventions. The passive boy consents to the indignity of being 'feminised' by the active *erastes* because the reward will be political preferment and future opportunities for power and advancement. The boy's manly courage is really just an unscrupulous utilitarianism that cares nothing for piety, humility and honour. Such is his lust for power, he is willing to sleep his way to the top, and when he gets there who knows what else he may do to endanger the city and anger the gods. His self-aggrandisement, Aristophanes implies, is really just a civilised version of humans' original bestial desire to attack the gods and ascend to the heavens (Ludwig 2002: 101). Only heterosexual domesticity can dampen this vainglorious *eros*.

Socrates and Diotima

Aristophanes is followed by the poet Agathon, whose success the symposium is celebrating. He delivers a rousing, if intellectually unsophisticated, encomium on love, praising Eros for being young, sensitive, just, courageous, self-disciplined and wise. Agathon then cedes to Socrates, who begins with a signature admission of ignorance: 'what a fool I was to have agreed to join in and deliver a eulogy of Love when it came to my turn, and to have claimed expertise in the ways of love, when in fact I didn't have the slightest clue about the matter' (198c-d). Socrates then suggests that Agathon and the others have delivered attractive speeches without actually interrogating the nature of love. Obsessed with Love's divine beauty, they have overlooked the phenomenological experience of loving. To get closer to the truth, Socrates reverts to his dialogic method, pressing Agathon to recognise, first, that love is always a love *of* something; second, that what love desires is necessarily something that is lacked; and third, that when we desire something that we already possess this is because what we really desire, which we lack, is the continued possession of that thing into the future, for we are mortal beings who lack the permanence of the good (199c-200d). Then he gets Agathon to agree that, if love desires things that are attractive, not repulsive, and if love for an attractive thing is lack of that attractive thing, then love cannot itself be attractive, and we should stop being so complacent and so unself-critical about love.[5]

After this brief prelude, Socrates begins his speech proper. This is a speech with a difference, however, for what he offers is in fact the report of what he claims was an educative dialogue he once had with a woman who 'taught me the ways of love'. This 'expert in love', named Diotima, appears to be a kind of itinerant sage or mystic, though whether she was a real person or a fictional invention of Plato used to illustrate Socrates' alter-ego is unclear. Socrates discloses that it was Diotima who disabused him of Agathon's view, which he had previously shared, regarding the attractiveness of Eros. When he retorted that it was inconceivable that divine Eros, lacking the beauty that it desired, could be 'repulsive', Diotima advised him to stop thinking in terms of absolutes: desire for knowledge is not the same thing as ignorance; desire for beauty does not necessitate ugliness. There is an 'intermediate area' that falls 'between these extremes' (201d-202b). As 'good fortune and beauty' must already belong to all gods, Diotima surmises that Eros cannot be a god but must be a 'spirit' (a *daemon*) which occupies 'the middle ground between humans and gods', mediating between the two (202c-e). This intermediate position also stands between ignorance and knowledge. The gods are wise, and therefore cannot love knowledge because they already have knowledge to perfection. Ignorant people also cannot love knowledge, however, because they are ignorant of what they are missing. 'If a person isn't aware of a lack, he can't desire the thing which he isn't aware of lacking' (204a). Plato is of course moving us towards Socrates' basic epistemological stance: the foundation of wisdom is knowledge of one's own ignorance.

Knowledge is a matter of concern for Eros because 'knowledge is one of the most attractive things there is, and attractive things are Love's province. Love is bound, therefore, to love knowledge, and anyone who loves knowledge is bound to fall between knowledge and ignorance' (204b). But why does a lover love beautiful things, and what does the lover hope to achieve by their acquisition? Diotima answers this question by substituting 'beautiful' (*kalon* – that which

---

[5] Socrates' reasoning here is of course flawed, since lack of a beautiful thing that is desired does not mean that the person who desires lacks all beauty. The aim of Socrates' argument, however, seems to be to expose Agathon's self-satisfied eulogising of Eros, which treated love as an attractive, beautiful entity, worthy of poetic praise, without enquiring into what it means to love. As Diotima says, correcting Socrates' rehearsal of Agathon's position: 'you saw Love as an object of love, rather than as a lover; that would explain why you imagined that Love was so attractive' (204c). Diotima explains that love is a pauper, a vagrant with no money and 'no shoes on his feet' (203cd). This is clearly an allegorical reference to Socrates himself, the barefoot lover of wisdom whose only certainty is his lack of certainty.

looks or sounds good) with 'good' (*agathon* – that which is good for us), and then pointing out the self-evident fact that good things are the source of happiness or *eudaimonia* (which is not simply an elevated mood, as we are today inclined to understand 'happiness', but a state of moral and intellectual well-being).

Love of beauty is love of goodness, therefore, because beauty is how things that are good for us attract our attention. Plato's doctrine of Forms lurks behind the dialogue here: Plato believed that the three-dimensional objects of sensory experience present faint and imperfect glimpses, or shadows, of the pure Forms or Ideas, the latter being visible only in rare moments of supreme philosophical illumination. Earthly things, which are partial, particular and transient in our encounters with them, acquire meaning and value to mortals only insofar as they evoke an outline of their permanent and absolute nature. Like the metaphysical Forms that lie behind actual empirical objects, the soul of the individual, according to Plato, is invisible to the physical senses; also like the Forms, the soul is eternal, being reincarnated in a new body after death. The imperishable soul originally belonged to that metaphysical realm of absolute Forms, and its ability to see the dim reflection of Being in imperfect and perishable things derives from its pre-earthly acquaintance with those heavenly images. A person's beauty thus provokes love, Plato argues, because it awakens in the soul of the beholder an unconscious memory of the eternal Forms, of Beauty as a general Idea. In Simmel's words: 'the beautiful person evokes love … not because he is beautiful, but because a ray of that substantial beauty which has been seen in its purity and substantiality has fallen on him and stayed there' (1971: 238). This memory is both the precondition for knowledge and the cause of an eternal yearning which love catalyses and brings to fruition. 'It is the providential role of love to remind the lover, via beauties and Beauty itself, of the lost world of Forms' (Price 1997: 86).

The ladder of love

Love of goodness, Diotima claims, trumps Aristophanes' account of the search for one's missing half, because our other half would only be attractive to us if it were good. This goodness, however, cannot be guaranteed just because it is, or once was, part of us: 'we're even prepared to amputate our arms and legs if we think they're in a bad state' (205e). Love is vertical, not horizontal, as Aristophanes described it. Human beings want what is good; they want what they don't have and what is better than what they are. They reach upwards towards what is good for them, and seek to acquire this goodness permanently (206a). For human goodness to last, Diotima says, it must be perpetuated or reproduced. *Eudaimonia* is not the consumption of pleasing goods, therefore, so much as their procreation. Every person is 'physically and mentally pregnant' (206c), and bringing the pregnancy to term is how we create something good that will last. In the *Laws* Plato had described the longing for immortality as an attribute of human nature, identifying both 'fame' and 'children' as a means of achieving this (721b-c). In the *Symposium*, beauty is the stimulus for this endeavour, the goal of love, inspired by the presence of beauty, being 'birth and procreation in a beautiful medium' (206e). 'Why procreation?' asks Diotima. 'Because procreation is as close as a mortal can get to being immortal and undying. Given our agreement that the aim of love is the *permanent* possession of goodness for oneself, it necessarily follows that we desire immortality along with goodness, and consequently the aim of love has to be immortality as well' (206e-207a).

The desire for immortality – 'which is love' – is shared by animals, Diotima says, and that is why they will go to extraordinary lengths to nurture and protect their offspring (207b-d, 208b). In the human world, acts of courage, heroism and sacrifice in the face of adversity are done for 'the prospect of undying virtue and fame' by people who are 'in love with immortality' (208d-e). Men who are 'physically pregnant', Diotima explains, echoing Plato's belief that fully formed humans already exist in miniature form in the semen of the man, seek this immortality and renown by having children who will remember their fathers and emulate them. Men who are 'mentally pregnant' (or 'pregnant in soul'), on the other hand, need a 'beautiful medium' and intellectual partner to 'share in raising their offspring'. 'This is a person he immediately finds he can talk fluently to about virtue and about what qualities and practices it takes for a man to be good. In short, he takes on this person's education' (209a-c). The link with homosexual pederasty is obvious here: sex between men is physically sterile – the man's germ-cell homunculus must still be incubated in the womb of a woman – and, combined with the moral constraints on the sexual feminisation of the *eromenos*, the movement from physical to mental procreation is almost inevitable. The nurturing of virtue and wisdom is then linked by Diotima to creations which are potentially less perishable than biological children – the poetry of Homer and Hesiod, the social and political institutions created by the legendary Lycurgus of Sparta, the legal reforms of the Athenian statesman Solon. 'All over the world, in fact, in Greece and abroad, various men in various places have on a number of occasions engendered virtue in some form or other by creating works of beauty for public display. Quite a few of these men have even been awarded cults before now because of the immortality of their children, whereas no human child has ever yet earned his father a cult' (209d-e).

Although heroism, poetry and legislation illustrate the value of immortality, their relationship to *eros* and 'generation in beauty' is unclear. Diotima is more consistent, however, when she describes how the relationship of educative pederasty leads to the creation of mental offspring – to the propagation and veneration of wisdom and goodness which, in turn, will be passed on, one assumes, as the *eromenos* matures and becomes himself a lover. But here the argument is also challenging to our modern sensibility, implying at times a certain depersonalisation and asceticism of love.

Diotima describes love as an ascent, in which 'the things of this world' are used 'as rungs in a ladder' (211c). The lover first begins by loving 'just one person's body', and in doing so is able 'to give birth in that medium to beautiful reasoning' (210a). He then realises that beauty is an attribute shared by many bodies, and so the attachment to a particular body 'grows less intense and strikes him as ridiculous and petty'. After this, he realises that mental beauty (or the 'beauty of souls') is more attractive than physical beauty, and 'that even if someone is almost entirely lacking the bloom of youth, but still has an attractive mind, that's enough to kindle his love and affection, and that's all he needs to give birth to and enquire after the kinds of reasoning which help young men's moral progress' (210b-c). This then prompts the realisation that there is beauty in 'activities and institutions', and that physical beauty is 'unimportant' (210c). Attractive activities are then superseded by attractive ideas, which then bring the lover to the threshold of a higher truth: 'No longer a paltry and small-minded slave, he faces instead a vast sea of beauty.' This is the medium in which the lover 'gives birth to plenty of beautiful, expansive reasoning and thinking', until a 'constant and eternal' beauty – 'not beauty tainted by human flesh and colouring and all that mortal rubbish, but absolute beauty, divine and constant' – is revealed. The lover is thus finally able to contemplate the Form of Beauty: 'he'll see that every other beautiful object somehow partakes of it, but in such a way that their coming to be and ceasing to be don't increase or diminish it at all, and it remains entirely unaffected' (210c-211e). And not just beauty, for there is now a visionary beholding of 'truth' and 'goodness' as well (212a).

What about me?

Is the highest form of love therefore imagined by Plato to be a kind of spiritual or intellectual substitute for sexual desire, which leaves behind eroticism and physical love of a mortal person in order to contemplate the universal and eternal world of Forms? This is certainly a legitimate and well-worn interpretation. It is the one that gained traction during the Italian Renaissance and which has since shaped our vernacular understanding of 'Platonic love' as dispassionate friendship. If this were Plato's definition of true love, however, we would be hard-pressed to defend it today, and not just because of cultural and institutional changes to family life and the realm of intimacy over the last two centuries. We should not overlook that it was this cerebral, 'Ideocentric' conception of love which, once its homoerotic origins had been repudiated, arguably bequeathed to Western civilisation the fateful belief in an 'objective' form of knowing, in which what was seen to be the servile and essentially 'female' qualities of material nature, bodies and feelings were excluded from the rational pursuit of truth (Keller 1985b).

We know that the Greeks lived in what they believed was an immutable, unified, self-contained cosmos whose rational perfection and intelligibility meant it was difficult, notwithstanding their intellectual virility, for them to attribute to the individual the independence and uniqueness that is so precious to our modern conception of selfhood. Plato understood something of the creative fervour of love, its elevating power and its searching, divinising exuberance, and these associations are still evoked in the more familiar tradition of romanticism in which love is tested and ennobled through extravagant adventure, heroic determination and purifying self-sacrifice. 'The way in which love makes us creators, makes us outdo our strength, renders it a symbol for every quest', Andreas-Salomé (2014: 69) wrote, 'not only for the object of our erotic desire, but for every higher value to which it makes us aspire.'

But love for Plato was not an unpredictable, spontaneous, free and distinctive act of the soul, so much as a kind of logical necessity imposed by the appearance of beauty. This means that the converse idea, that we find beautiful what we love, and that beauty is therefore in the eyes of the beholder, would have been ridiculous to Greek understanding.[6] Even with Aristotle's doctrine of

---

[6] In the (typically inconclusive) discussion of the nature of piety in *Euthyphro*, Socrates distinguishes between a thing whose nature is defined by how it is treated, and a thing whose nature defines how it should be treated. It is noteworthy that, when it comes to the gods, 'the god-loved ... is so [i.e. is lovable] because it is being loved by the gods, by the very fact of being loved', but when it comes to a human virtue – in this case piety, though we could also substitute beauty – and humans' appreciation

perfect friendship – which is essentially the 'mean' between the two extremes of sexual desire and utilitarian self-interest – the possibility that love may be an autonomous, creative feeling that bestows value on a mortal and imperfect individual is discounted. For although Aristotle had a keener interest in love of people rather than love of Forms, he agreed with Plato that nothing can be worthy of love unless it is good; love (*philia*) doesn't *create* goodness, but simply appreciates the perfection of character that is displayed by good people.

In an essay on the *Symposium* first published in 1923, the German sociologist Georg Simmel noted how, from the vantage point of modernity, Plato's conception of love is a curiously depersonalised one, with both lover and beloved treated as vessels of an intellectual idea. For just 'as the beloved is here loved not as an individual but as the messenger of a supraindividual beauty, so is the lover himself also deindividualised, because his love ... comes not from the creative personality but from his former beholding of the Idea of the beautiful' (1971: 246). Simmel argues that it is only with the differentiated structures and practices of modernity that social actors become so autonomous and individualised as to render the self a unique entity that is both ethically and emotionally valued while at the same being ultimately opaque to rational scrutiny and total understanding. Our love for another individual therefore cannot be fully rationalised as it was for the Greeks, since for us the act of loving aims not at the possession of a universal truth, but at the articulation of a singular feeling, and the hope and possibility of that feeling being felt in return:

> modern love is the first to recognise that there is something unattainable in the other: that the absoluteness of the individual self erects a wall between two human beings which even the most passionate willing of both cannot remove and that renders illusory any actual 'possession' that would be anything more than the fact and consciousness of being loved back. This is the consequence of that ultimate deepening and individualisation of the self-feeling. What this leads to is a becoming rooted in oneself and an isolation within oneself which turns the wish to 'possess' into a contradiction and grasping into the void. (Simmel 1971: 246)

Depicting Plato's confidence in the totalising reach of reason as an 'intoxication unparalleled in the history of philosophy', Simmel thus emphasises

---

of it, 'the pious is being loved for this reason, that it is pious, but it is not pious because it is being loved' (10a–e). If a virtue lies in the eyes of the beholder, in other words, these can only be the eyes of the gods.

the separation of logic and meaning that is, in the memorable words of his friend Max Weber, 'the fate of an epoch that has eaten of the tree of knowledge'[7]:

> what mankind grown old, differentiated, and sophisticated can no longer support is this: to transform the world in its reality, its love, its meaning, and its spiritual values into a logical structure of abstract concepts and analogous metaphysical essences and to perceive this as the deepest happiness of the spirit; to derive from logical thought those tremors and awesome relations to the ground of things which later times can attain precisely only by a rejection of pure thought, through a cleavage between logical structure and that living feeling existence whose immediacy is caught neither in the Platonic concepts nor in ours, but can only be experienced in its own depths. (Simmel 1971: 248)

Our greater appreciation today of the depth and uniqueness of the personality is of course a specific cause of conflict and discomfort in the domain of intimate life, with modern ideals of romantic love sometimes adding to these troubles. For it matters to us, in a way that almost certainly never concerned the Greeks, that not only should we be loved but that we should *feel* loved. Or to put it another way, it is important not simply that I am *loved*, but also that it is *I* that am loved, and not some figment of the lover's romantic imagination, some independently existing definition of beauty or desirability, or some non-essential, non-unique or non-permanent element of my existence that I do not myself value or see as definitive of the individual whom I am. Because of the autonomous sense of self-identity that seems to be so precious to our modern way of understanding ourselves, we can, therefore, suffer not only from the absence of love but also from the presence of a love that feels misplaced, which loves something that doesn't properly tally with our own self-perception and self-appreciation. Putting it slightly differently, Simon May argues that love is therefore what we feel for people when they inspire in us a sense of 'ontological rootedness': 'We experience their mere presence as grounding – or as a promise of grounding – because it seems to be receptive to, to recognise, to echo, to provide a powerful birth to, what we regard as most essential about us' (May 2011: 240). Although this formulation better captures the personal prejudices, idiosyncrasies and inherent conditionality of love that is missing from the Platonic love of timeless universals, it reduces the essence of love from an active doing to a passive

---

[7] 'The fate of an epoch which has eaten of the tree of knowledge is that it must know that we cannot learn the *meaning* of the world from the results of its analysis, be it ever so perfect; it must rather be in a position to create this meaning itself' (Weber 1949: 57). I shall be considering Weber's work in more detail in Chapters 7 and 8.

feeling: 'love is the intense desire for someone whom – or something which – we experience as grounding and affirming our own existence' (May 2011: 13). As this quote indicates, May's more self-centred conception of love also results in the rather crude claim that love for a person is essentially no different to love for a thing – an idea, a political cause, a landscape, a work of art – that inspires the same feeling of groundedness.

Notwithstanding our better sociological understanding of power asymmetries and their abuse, the greater sensitivity we feel today towards the importance of the self in matters of love also sheds additional light on one of the things we find unsettling about the kind of love between a mature man and a youth that the Greeks were so accepting of. For although the process of individualisation has weakened many of the structural barriers – of class, ethnicity, heteronormativity – that have historically impeded love's capacity to embrace difference and find fulfilment in diversity, the deepened understanding of selfhood that we possess today has also created new categories of subjectivity, including that of childhood. Medieval society effectively ignored childhood, regarding it as a brief transitional period of no importance. But from the fourteenth century onwards, as Philippe Ariès (1962) documented, childhood began to be thought of in Western culture as a distinct stage of human development whose fragility and innocence justly arouses in adults both sentimental amusement and a morally solicitous concern to quarantine children from coarse influences and ensure their properly paced emotional and psychological maturation.

Growing life expectancy, the extension of educational opportunities for young people, the delaying of marriage and parenthood – the average age at which people first get married, and first have children, has over the last 50 years increased by four to eight years in most Western countries – plus the harsher structural conditions faced by young people in their pursuit of economic independence, have further shifted the point of balance between youth and adulthood in late modernity. In the Middle Ages, when five decades of life would have been an unusually lengthy sojourn, children shared in the work and play of the adult community as soon as they were deemed capable of doing without maternal care – which Ariès (1962: 411) estimates was around the age of 7. Today the period of pre-adulthood lasts at least until the late teens, with some medical commentators arguing that adolescence should now be understood as continuing into the mid-20s (Sawyer et al. 2018).

Greater life expectancy, however, may also have brought with it a sharper, lonelier and less culturally elaborate consciousness of mortality. For the ancient Greeks, who lived in sufficient proximity to their gods to feel rivalry as well as reverence towards them, the pursuit of immortality through excellence and renown was an abiding concern. The existential fact of the modern Western individual, by contrast, is the pitiless certainty of death, the prematurity of which, in a culture of relentless futurity, feels so senseless, as Max Weber (1970c: 356) observed, that it seems 'to put the decisive stamp upon the senselessness of life itself'. Today we are therefore more inclined, existentially at least, to view the threshold of 'maturity' as the point at which we experience and acknowledge the deeply personal truth of our own mortality, a truth which inevitably asserts itself through physical ageing and the loss of favoured attributes. Definitive of youth, by contrast, is an existential repudiation of mortality. Death, when we are young adults, is a known fact of life, but rarely a meaningful fact of *our* life, and the personal contemplation of death which we know will come always appears, from the viewpoint of youth, to be another category of existence entirely, as if being old were a separate state of being rather than something that happens, slowly and inexorably, to *us*.[8] To love a young person from the vantage point of maturity, then, is to love both something that is lacking in value (we call this necessary, if transitory, state of ignorance 'immaturity') and something incapable of knowing itself (to be young is to be ignorant of one's ignorance). When we are young, we think we are mature – and thus perfectly capable of having a relationship of reciprocity with an older person – because youth only reveals its immaturity to us once we have transcended it.

All this, of course, is implicit in the natural ethos of parents and teachers whose loving care for children and young people stops short of the physical intimacy accepted, with qualifications, by the Greeks, partly because childhood and adulthood have for us become too differentiated in experience and responsibility to permit the kind of deep, if always uncertain, emotional reciprocity we associate with sexual love. We may still recognise the Socratic-Platonic ideal of nurturing the blossoming faculties of a young person, and of promoting those well-practised virtues that Aristotle saw as the embodiment of moral character. Oscar Wilde famously invoked Plato at his first trial in 1895,

---

[8] Tolstoy's short story, 'The Death of Ivan Ilyich', shows what is required for the mature recognition of one's own mortality, but depicts this insight as a rare achievement rather than a customary mark of adulthood. Ilyich is terminally ill, but still, like most people, in denial: 'The example of the syllogism that he had learned in Kiseveter's logic – Caius is a man, men are mortal, therefore Caius is mortal – had seemed to him all his life correct only as regards Caius, but not at all as regards himself. In that case it was a question of Caius, a man, an abstract man, and it was perfectly true, but he was not Caius, and was not an abstract man; he had always been a creature quite, quite different from all others … . Caius certainly was mortal, and it was right for him to die; but for me, little Vanya, Ivan Ilyich, with all my feelings and ideas – for me it's a different matter. And it cannot be that I ought to die' (VI, 110).

defending a love which 'repeatedly exists between an elder and a younger man, when the elder man has intellect, and the younger man has all the joy, hope and glamour of life' (cited in Singer 1984: 82). But as the differentiation of childhood and adult has become a more conscious concern for us, we are more likely to be persuaded by Aristotle's observation, in the *Nicomachean Ethics*, that love (the ideal of which for Aristotle is *philia* not *eros*) cannot exist between partners who are too unequal, this being as impossible as reciprocity between a mortal and a god (1159a1-1159a9).

Love in Plato's *Phaedrus*

I mentioned before that, until fairly recently, most readings of Plato had treated the ladder of love as a progressive de-sexualisation of desire and a progressive depersonalisation of the object of love. A revival of interest in classical Greek philosophy has challenged that interpretation, however, and argued for a greater continuity between Plato's ideas and modern understandings of sexual love. A. W. Price (1997: 38) has argued against the conventional reading, for example, stressing the intensity of desire that Plato indicated was aroused by the beloved, and how this desire appears to reach an even greater pitch when the ascent of the ladder is complete. Sexual desire certainly seems to be controlled and sublimated, but it is not completely repudiated or replaced by something entirely different. As Gregory Vlastos, who is hardly uncritical of Plato's conception, puts it: 'that form of passionate experience invented by Plato, which should count as the original, and always primary, sense of "Platonic love", is a peculiar mix of sensuality, sentiment, and intellect – a companionship bonded by erotic attraction no less than by intellectual give-and-take' (1981: 39).

Price also rejects the idea that the lover, as he ascends the ladder, discards those people and things that had previously been the object of his passions. The ravishing appeal of beauty and goodness in the *Symposium* would be inconceivable, he emphasises, 'if bodies were entirely supplanted as objects of interests by souls' (1997: 45). Nussbaum's formulation points in the same direction: the intellectual aspiration towards the truth, she notes, 'has an internal structure closely akin to that of the lover's sexual yearnings and fulfilments' (2001: 217). If lovers sublimate their physical desire, it is not because desire has been subdued by the intellect, but because integral to the passion of true *eros* is a *reverence* for the beloved which would be violated and demeaned by crude sexual lust.

Moreover, appreciation of beautiful bodies and minds 'in general' need not imply the abandonment of a particular body and mind, just as love of the eternal Forms does not exclude loving an individual, who is a reflection of those Forms, as an end. As White (1990) points out, because the Forms of Beauty, Wisdom, Justice and the like do not have 'interests', they cannot be loved 'for their own sake' in the way that a human being can be so loved. Instead of loving someone, whose appearance is an image of Beauty, as simply a means of communing with the Forms, the resemblance between the beloved and the Form of Beauty could equally be understood to be the stimulus for the lover 'to act with zeal to further what he judges to be the genuine interests of that beloved' (White 1990: 402). Or to put it more boldly: a person is not loved as a means of grasping the ideal Forms, but rather the ideal Forms are what enable us to love a person with imaginative fervour.

Socrates' palinode in *Phaedrus* supports this reading of a more generous, more human-centred *eros*. The first speech in the dialogue, reported by Phaedrus but purported to belong to Lysias, recommends that a boy should choose a 'non-lover' as his partner, the latter offering educational instruction and character development in exchange for sexual favours. A non-lover is more preferable to a lover, Lysias had apparently argued, because the former would spare the boy the jealousy, inconstancy and possessiveness of an *erastes* in mindless thrall to the youngster's physical beauty. The speech is interesting as it conveys the idea, more familiar to our own 'desublimated' culture, of sex without *eros*, suggesting something close to the kind of utilitarian friendship described in the previous chapter in reference to Aristotle, and perhaps also invoking the normative Greek understanding of loveless sexual relations in marriage (Nussbaum 2002: 68). In the second speech, Socrates appears to endorse Lysias's recommendation, elaborating on the morally demeaning nature of unchecked desire. In the subsequent retraction of this assessment, however, Socrates offers a more generous eulogy of passionate love, the madness of which is now described as a divinely inspired blessing, an irrational inspiration which arouses the beloved as well as the lover, and prepares them both for mutual understanding and shared access to a higher truth.

Lysias, to reiterate, had distinguished the non-lover's interest in the boy's soul from the true lover's fascination with his body (the non-lover receives sex as a kind of payment, but this is a carefully weighted transaction rather than the gratification of a burning desire). Socrates, by contrast, emphasises how the sight of the beloved's beauty stirs awe and reverence that goes beyond the mere appearance of the beloved, marvelling at the plenitude of his existence 'as if he were a god' (251a). The exclusivity of *eros*, the obsessiveness that makes Eros 'oblivious to mothers, brothers, and all its friends', which torments the lover with painful longing whenever the beloved is absent, and cures him of suffering whenever he returns, is now described without ridicule by Socrates (251d-252b), for this love lacks the 'malice or mean-spirited ill-will' which he had previously associated with the jealous and spiteful lover (253b). Out of this benevolent passion, Nussbaum (2002: 72) suggests in her own reading of *Phaedrus*, reverence and gratitude for the beloved is born. These are strong *ethical* sentiments, Nussbaum points out, which the tame friendship of Lysias's non-lover could never have engendered, and which serve to harness *eros* in a way that protects the well-being of the beloved from instrumental violation.

Socrates then envisages a beloved who eventually comes to see and appreciate the benevolence of the *erastes*: 'the lover's good will astonishes the beloved and he realises that the friendship of all his other friends and relatives put together does not amount to even a fraction of the friendship offered by a lover who is inspired by a god' (255b). And then the unexpected happens: sensual desire, flowing from the *erastes* into the eyes of the *eromenos*, enters the soul of the latter, 'excites him', 'irrigates his wings', 'makes his plumage start to grow, and fills the soul of the beloved in turn with love'. This is a subversion of the traditional *erastes/eromenos* dichotomy, in which the beloved must be innocent of desire in order to accentuate the dominance and potency of the lover, as well as the suprapersonal nature of Eros as an irresistible allure: 'Oh child, virgin-glancing, I seek you,' one of Anacreon's poems goes, 'but you do not hear, not knowing that you are the charioteer of my soul' (cited in Stigers 1981: 51).

Greek convention may thus require that the *eromenos* offers friendship rather than love, but Socrates now observes that desire, like wisdom and goodness, is infectious, and that convention therefore doesn't tell the whole truth. The beloved 'has contracted counter-love [*anteros*] as a reflection of his lover's love, but he calls it and thinks of it as friendship rather than love', Socrates says. 'His desires are more or less the same as his lover's, though weaker – to see, touch, kiss, lie down together.' On the basis of this physical intimacy, the most honourable lovers will rise higher to 'a life of self-control and restraint', steering their love 'towards orderly conduct and philosophy'. But even those couples who come to 'live a more ordinary life', who physically 'consummate their relationship' because they 'choose the course which is considered the most wonderful of all by the common run of mankind', will be blessed by the gods in the afterlife: they will 'live a life of brightness and happily travel in each other's company', Socrates says, 'and sooner or later, thanks to their love, gain their wings together' (255c-256e).

Even when Socrates insists of speaking of love in its higher, more intellectual form, we are also reminded that this is a reciprocal rather than egocentric affair. That the love of truth, as much as the truth of love, remains an interpersonal exchange between partners rather than a solitary act of philosophical contemplation is illustrated by Socrates' reflections in *Phaedrus* on how dialogue nourishes the lifespan of ideas, offering a path to immortality that is superior to the sterile longevity of written artefacts. Pericles' comments on the 'effeminacy' of untested reason are faintly echoed here. Written words, Socrates says, 'just go on and on for ever giving the same single piece of information', whereas through conversation and teaching the lover of wisdom is able to germinate 'offspring and brothers' which are 'duly grown in others' souls'. This mental procreation, Socrates states,

> is what happens when an expert dialectician takes hold of a suitable soul and uses his knowledge to plant and sow the kinds of words which are capable of defending both themselves and the one who planted them. So far from being barren, these words bear a seed from which other words grow in other environments. This makes them capable of giving everlasting life to the original seed, and of making the man who has them as happy as it is possible for a mortal man to be. (*Phaedrus* 276e-277a)

Enter Alcibiades

There is perhaps a final indication that Plato did not see the *eromenos* as simply a useful, and disposable, stepping stone on the way to the solitary consummation of the lover's divine knowledge. As Socrates finishes his speech in the *Symposium*, Aristophanes' attempt at a reply is interrupted by the entrance of the handsome and charismatic Alcibiades, heavily drunk and decorated with ribbons, his appearance evoking the very image of Dionysus. At the beginning of Plato's *Protagoras*, Alcibiades is described as the most attractive young man in Athens (309c). His political ambitions are also legendry, and his hubris will soon be exposed by the disastrous Sicilian expedition. He represents, in Ludwig's interpretation, the danger which Aristophanes, had he not been interrupted, was about to allude to in his reply to Socrates' encomium on the ladder of love. 'Polemically put, Socrates has scarcely finished his benign picture of the "vertical" eros when a circle man walks in' (Ludwig 2002: 23).

But the presence of this 'circle man' ironically allows Plato to deliver a richer and more rounded portrait of Socratic love than might otherwise have been possible. As Alcibiades enters, Socrates refers modestly to his 'love for this man', and then playfully asks Agathon to protect him from what he says is Alcibiades' sexual possessiveness and jealousy. On seeing Socrates in the party, Alcibiades draws the guests' attention to the barefoot philosopher's extraordinary self-composure. No matter how much alcohol he consumes, Alcibiades says, Socrates never gets drunk. And the reach of his sobriety does not stop there.

This becomes the starting point for Alcibiades' own speech, which is a eulogy not of Eros but of Socrates himself. His initial description is not promising: he likens Socrates to an ugly Satyr, adding that like Satyrs he treats people 'brutally'. The irony here is that while Satyrs would rape their victims, Socrates' brutality is his refusal to yield to the sexual invitations of others. Socrates overwhelms people not with his looks, Alcibiades says, but with his words. 'I've heard some great speakers, including Pericles, and while I thought they did a good job, they never had that kind of effect on me, and they never disturbed my mental composure or made me dissatisfied with the slavishness of my life' (215e). Alcibiades admits that his passion for Athenian politics and his desire for the 'adulation of the masses' feel shameful in the face of Socrates' lessons in self-understanding. To avoid the conclusion that 'the life I lead isn't worth living', he therefore tries to keep away from him (216a-c).

Socrates is attracted to youthful boys, Alcibiades points out, and is 'constantly hanging around them in a stupor'. But appearances are deceptive, because inside he is 'chock-full of self-control' (216d). Although Alcibiades himself thought that he could successfully seduce him, Socrates resisted his increasingly brazen advances. Alcibiades, priding himself on his looks, managed to persuade Socrates to spend the night with him. But the philosopher 'spurned and disdained and scorned my charms', leaving Alcibiades 'full of admiration for his character, self-control, and courage' (219c-d). Further examples of Socrates' honourable qualities are then given by Alcibiades, including his indifference to the cold and endurance of hardship during the military siege of Potidaea, his protection of a wounded Alcibiades during combat and his calmness on the battlefield when the retreating Athenian army was routed by the Boeotians (219e-221c).

What Alcibiades' confessional praise reveals is that Socrates' sublime love of wisdom has effected a reversal of roles. His intellectual self-mastery has become the passionate object of young men's love. 'He takes people in by pretending to be their lover,' Alcibiades explains, 'and then he swaps roles and becomes their beloved' (222b). And in this reversal, the rules of the game have been transformed. Instead of a conventional utilitarian exchange between *erastes* and *eromenos*, Alcibiades reports that Socrates refused to 'trade our respective beauties' – beauty of the mind in exchange for beauty of the body – because in his view this would leave him short-changed ('gold for bronze', as Socrates put it). Socrates will give his wisdom, in other words, but not in exchange for physical pleasure or the contemplation of a boy's physical beauty. What he wants in return is the same golden coin: the flourishing of the boy's goodness. When virtue takes precedence over beauty, the distinction between active *erastes* and passive *eromenos* is superseded by a relationship of erotic reciprocity (Halperin 1986). In Waterfield's formulation: 'The attraction of his followers towards Socrates is attraction towards realised goodness, and the attraction of Socrates towards his followers is attraction towards potential goodness' (1990: 223). On this latter score, Aristophanes says that Socrates told him he'd 'got a long way to go yet' (218e-219a). But Aristophanes, for all his vanity, acknowledges that he has been irrevocably 'struck and bitten' by 'the madness and ecstasy of philosophy' (218a-b). We know that his political ambitions will eventually win out; but we also know that this is a flight from the truth of *eros* and from his burning desire to share with Socrates the erotic pursuit of goodness and truth.

The double flame

Sex, eroticism and love are, according to Octavio Paz, like the successive stages of growth in a blossoming plant: 'sex is the root, eroticism the stem, and love the flower' (1995: 38). Eroticism is to sex, Paz suggests, what poetry is to language: 'Poetry places communication in brackets in the same way that eroticism brackets reproduction.' It is the human imagination that 'turns sex into ceremony and rite', and the same imagination that turns 'language into rhythm and metaphor' (1995: 5, 3). In sex, the function of pleasure is to serve biological reproduction; in eroticism, the pleasure of sex is sublimated, transfigured and crystallised into an infinite variety of cultural forms.

> In the heart of nature, humans have created for themselves a world apart, composed of this entirety of practices, institutions, rites, ideas, and artefacts that we call culture. By origin, eroticism is sex, nature; by its being a human creation and by its functions in society, it is culture. One of the aims of eroticism is to take sex and make a place for it in society. Without sex there can be no society, since there can be no procreation; but sex also threatens society. Like the god Pan, it

is creation and destruction. It is instinct: tremors, panic, the explosion of life. It is a volcano and any one of its eruptions can bury society under a violent flow of blood and semen. Sex is subversive: it ignores classes and hierarchies, arts and sciences, day and night – it sleeps and awakens, only to fornicate and go back to sleep again … . Hence we have had to invent rules that channel the sexual instinct and protect society from its overflow … . The human race, subjected to the perpetual electrical discharge of sex, has invented a lightning rod: eroticism. (1995: 10–11)

Paz rightly defends the eroticism of Plato's philosophy of love, but he also expresses dissatisfaction with what he sees as the lack of human relatedness in Plato's conception, which in his view reduces love to a journey that is always essentially solitary and in which 'there is no true dialogue' (1995: 20). This, we have seen, is not altogether fair on Plato. Nonetheless, even if we settle on the idea that love is a sublime journey of mutual conversation and passionate engagement, it is hard not to feel that something important is still missing from this conception, or at least that some critical element of erotic love is not yet fully delineated. The best Platonic lovers are intellectual companions on a shared journey; they are travelling in the same direction, but they are not looking into each other's eyes. For C. S. Lewis, this was the hallmark of friendship rather than *eros*: 'Lovers are normally face to face, absorbed in each other; Friends, side by side, absorbed in some common interest.' For friends, 'as Emerson said, *Do you love me?* means *Do you see the same truth?*' (Lewis 2012: 73, 79). This mutual attentiveness to the world, whether it is the realm of ideas or the realm of virtues, is also very close to what Hannah Arendt called 'wordliness' – essential to the vitality of civic life, she argued, but the very antithesis of love which, by contrast, looks beyond the moral accomplishments of the individual towards the essence of a singular and indefinable being:

For love, although it is one of the rarest occurrences in human lives, indeed possesses an equalled power of self-revelation and an unequalled clarity of vision for the disclosure of *who*, precisely because it is unconcerned to the point of total unworldliness with *what* the loved person may be, with his qualities and shortcomings no less than with his achievements, failings, and transgressions. Love, by reason of its passion, destroys the in-between which relates us to and separates us from others … . Love, by its nature, is unworldly. (Arendt 1958: 242)

Erotic love of the 'who' is neither the same as friendship nor is it the same as simple physical desire. This is not a straightforward moral distinction – erotic love has broken countless hearts, betrayed many solemn promises and is more than capable of abandoning children, destroying families and abusing the loyalty of friends. But loveless physical desire misses the lover's preoccupation with the totality of another's being, a preoccupation that is loftier and more consuming than the mere pursuit of sexual pleasure. To the heterosexual man in love, C. S. Lewis points out, 'The fact that she is a woman is far less important than the fact that she is herself.' Lewis contrasts this with the words of Winston Smith to his sexual partner Julia in Orwell's *1984*: 'You like doing this? I don't simply mean me: I mean the thing in itself?' This is sex not as the bonding of persons, but as the exchange of universal bodily pleasures, which is precisely how Orwell imagined sexual life would be in the depersonalised dystopia of bureaucratic reason. 'Sexual desire, without Eros, wants *it*, the *thing in itself*, Lewis emphasises. 'Eros', by contrast, 'wants the Beloved' (Lewis 2012: 113–14).

Paz's preferred literary model of loveless desire is Molly Bloom's verbal torrent of erotic affirmation at the close of Joyce's *Ulysses* (1922), which a harsh reading of Plato might find prefigured in the ascent from the beauty of a body to the attraction of all bodies – 'he kissed me under the Moorish wall and I thought well as well him as another'. To this Paz responds:

> No, it is not the same with this one or that one. And this is the borderline that separates love and eroticism. Love is attraction toward a unique person: a body and a soul. Love is choice; eroticism is acceptance. Without eroticism – without a visible form that enters by way of the senses – there is no love, but love goes beyond the desired body and seeks the soul in the body and the body in the soul. The whole person. (1995: 32–3)

This whole person is a person in the world, and thus for Paz it is wrong to associate love with worldlessness, as Arendt does. 'Human love – that is to say, true love – denies neither the body nor the world … . Love is love not *of* this world but *from* this world, bound to the earth by the body's gravitation, which is pleasure and death' (1995: 257). It would be foolish, of course, to think that the passionate and mysterious feeling of attraction towards a unique person is a phenomenon invented by the moderns. We know from what the Socratics said regarding the madness of love that this *sentiment* has always existed. What is more recent, however, and what seems more foreign to the culture of the Greeks is the elaboration of this amatory feeling into an art, a discourse and an ideal. When 'reflection on love becomes the ideology of a society', Paz emphasises, 'then we find ourselves in the presence of a way of life, an art of living and dying, an ethic, and aesthetic, and an etiquette' (1995: 34).

The anthropology of love

What are the origins of the aesthetic ideal of love that Paz alludes to? Anthropological findings suggest that the romantic idealisation of a uniquely meaningful personal bond has been part of the culture of numerous different societies with diverse social formations, the attempt to escape structural contradictions or ecological pressures 'through the transcendental love of another person' being one common denominator, at least according to Charles Lindholm (1999: 258). Cultural historian William R. Reddy (2012) acknowledges that a 'longing for association', comprising diverse drives and sentiments, is probably universal, but he argues that the dualism between sexual appetites on the one hand and, on the other, a love which sublimates and civilises biological desire by converting it into reciprocal and exclusive appreciation of another person is a socially constructed experience that emerged in twelfth-century Europe and is therefore specific to the West. Other anthropologists have disputed the social construction of erotic love and have instead drawn both on cross-cultural empirical research and on neurobiological studies of emotional bonding to argue that passionate love is a panhuman evolutionary universal, and that we should therefore expect it to 'be present, albeit not necessarily valued, in every culture' (Jankowiak and Fischer 1992; Chisholm 1995; Fisher 1995; Jankowiak and Paladino 2008: 9). The 'official' culture of many societies may proscribe public displays of intimacy, outlaw the right to choose a mate or lover, and regard falling in love as a pathological intoxication or evil enchantment, but anthropologists now stress the need 'to look past official culture to the actual behaviour and motivation of individuals' (Collins and Gregor 1995: 88). In precisely this vein, research in various countries, including Sri Lanka (De Munck 1996) and Southwest China (Du 2008), has debunked the long-standing assumption of Western historians and social scientists that arranged marriages are incompatible with romantic intimacy, and that passionate marital bonds can be formed only in economically independent nuclear units which have broken free of extended kinship structures demanding more defuse emotional attachments. Research in Africa has also challenged the Western moral conception of love as selfless humility abstracted from instrumental attachments and interests. This rarefied conception is rejected because it disqualifies the love felt – most frequently by women – for people on whom they are economically dependent, and because it overlooks the way material transactions communicate feelings as well as interests, love and money being, as Jennifer Cole puts it, 'mutually constitutive' rather than intrinsically 'hostile worlds' (Zelizer 2005; Rebhun 2007; Cole 2009: 113).

Passionate feelings of erotic attachment may therefore be a cultural universal, but studies of intimate relationships in different societies today also show that the desirability of 'marriage for love' has grown in many communities in recent decades partly under the influence of Western cultural ideals, and partly because, as Lindholm (1995) argues, erotic love offers people a means of transcending the self-conscious feelings of contingency and loneliness that are more characteristic of complex urban lives. The wilful appreciation of the individual that is so central to the modern Western conception of romantic love has also made that conception particularly attractive to young people in different cultures who are searching for a more globally communicable and more forward-looking identity (Wardlow and Hirsch 2006). While we can confidently refute the claim that erotic love is an exclusive product of Euro-American culture, Western ideals of romantic love have clearly influenced the personal understandings and aspirations of diverse peoples around the world today. The history of these ideals is also more readily available to research thanks to Western literary and documentary traditions. For these reasons reviewing this history, as I shall be doing in the following chapters, is neither an arbitrary choice nor a narrowly ethnocentric project.

In Europe during the Middle Ages, Plato's ladder of love was converted by Christianity into an ordered ascent towards divine salvation. Although in one sense this perpetuated the spiritual depersonalisation of the object of love that haunted the Greek conception of *eros*, the influence of the Judaeo-Christian concept of *agapē*, as well as St. Augustine's notion of *caritas*, pushed Christian thinking in a different direction. With the belief in God's merciful, lavish, indiscriminate love of all human and non-human existence, and the invitation to the most saintly followers that they emulate Christ and dedicate their amorous imaginations to the task of bestowing value on the world, there appeared for the first time the doctrinal idea that love is the *creation* of goodness, rather than the pursuit of a perfection that already – objectively, permanently – exists. Moreover, by giving the spirit of love an anthropomorphic form, and imagining an Aristotelian friendship, marriage or *caritas*-driven communion between humans and God – a notion that would have been blasphemous to the Greeks, for whom the self-sufficient perfection of the gods meant they needed neither to love humans nor to be succoured by human love – the idea that the object of love may be a *person* also entered the Christian imaginary.

As Irving Singer (1984) discusses at length, there were clear tensions and contradictions in this Medieval worldview, not least between the supreme omnipotence of God and the degree of agency and creativity this realistically left to the faithful, who were enjoined to love other people but only as an instrument of God's love and of the believer's humble love of God. In practice, Singer points out, the infinite power and inscrutable wisdom of God often promoted 'the sickly desire to be accepted in one's own self-hatred instead of learning how to love oneself and others as oneself' (1984: 361). Nonetheless, a crucial step had been taken in the movement from the Greek idea of love as an 'appraisal' of the Good, to the idea of love as the 'bestowal' of value – these are Singer's preferred terms – and with this a vital seed had been sown. But for this seed to germinate – for Christian love to be transformed into a fully humanised romantic ethic – a further subversion in the Western history of love was necessary. And for this we had to wait until the twelfth century and the appearance of 'courtly love'.

3

Courtly love

'The men will do no more, – they have lost the capacity for doing', said the elder girl. 'They fuss and talk, but they are really inane. They make everything fit into an old, inert idea. Love is a dead idea to them. They don't come to one and love one, they come to an idea, and they say "You are my idea," so they embrace themselves. As if I were any man's idea! As if I exist because a man has an idea of me! As if I will be betrayed by him, lend him my body as an instrument for his idea, to be a mere apparatus of his dead theory. But they are too fussy to be able to act; they are all impotent, they can't take a woman. They come to their own idea every time and take that. They are like serpents trying to swallow themselves because they are hungry.' (XII, 288)

So says Winifred, explaining her interest in feminism to Ursula in D. H. Lawrence's *The Rainbow* (1915). Lawrence's opposition to the dead idea of love was driven by a sensual naturalism in rebellion against the sterile rationality of the machine age. Abstract individualism and alienation from the body was the cultural backdrop to the slaughter and maiming of millions: 'the human body is only just coming to real life', Lady Chatterley rebukes her 'professional corpse' of a husband who, wounded in action at Flanders, is now from his wheelchair pontificating about 'the inexhaustive realm of abstract forms' and the 'supreme pleasure' to be had from 'the life of the mind'. Connie retorts: 'With the Greeks it gave a lovely flicker, then Plato and Aristotle killed it, and Jesus finished it off. But now the body is coming really to life, it is really rising from the tomb. And it will be a lovely, lovely life in the lovely universe, the life of the human body' (XVI, 283–4).

I will return to consider Lawrence's philosophy of love later in this book, but in this chapter I want to look at the work of the non-conformist Swiss intellectual Denis de Rougemont, and specifically his historical account of the rise, and the modern consequences, of that version of *eros* known as 'courtly love'. Rougemont would have shared Winifred's and Connie's suspicion of love as a Platonic Idea. The highest form of love, Rougemont argued, is neither a state of being which is suffered or undergone nor a zealous intellectual passion, but rather an active, wilful doing. 'To be in love is a state; to love, an act' (Rougemont 1983: 310). But Rougemont also rejected what he saw as the reactionary glorification of 'bestial innocence' and the 'primitive flood of instinct' in Lawrence's writings. Love's purpose, he asserted, is not to gratify our animal desires, but to create enduring 'structures of active relations' – exemplified through marital fidelity (1983: 310–11, 236–7). While Paz, as we saw, distinguishes sexuality from eroticism and eroticism from love, Rougemont reminds us of a further distinction: between the 'divinising' amorous passion of *eros* and the 'humanising' love that is *agapē*:

> Sexuality is the instinct which directs the individual to the objectives of the species. Eroticism is sexual pleasure for its own sake and not as a means of procreation. Amorous passion is infinite desire which takes as its object or pretext a finite individual. And true love, active love, that which seeks the welfare of the Other, designates the supreme end, the fulfilment of the whole person in the act of giving. (Rougemont 1983: 6)

Most historians believe that the practices and ideals of romantic love in the West originated in the court society of eleventh- and twelfth-century Provence, and that this cultural 'revolution', in the words of C. S. Lewis, 'effected a change which has left no corner of our ethics, our imagination, or our daily life untouched' (1938: 4). Octavio Paz agrees with this assessment, which was also the central argument of Rougemont's classic study, *Love in the Western World* (1940). But on one important point Paz and Rougemont's thinking sharply diverges. Paz argues that courtly love cultivated and nourished the Christian idea of the 'sanctity of the person'. Rougemont, by contrast, claims that courtly love was essentially narcissistic and world-rejecting, the person of the beloved being but a 'pretext' for the lover's unhappy pursuit of the divine. As the Swedish theologian Anders Nygren had argued in the 1930s, there is a fundamental antagonism between the selfless benevolence of *agapē* and the greedy egocentrism of *eros* (Nygren 1953: 175–80). Unlike Nygren, Rougemont believed this antagonism could be managed, but only so long as *eros* – whose desire to 'elevate life above our finite and limited creature state' always makes the true lover a 'slave of death' – was channelled into a desexualised and mystical form (Rougemont 1983: 311). The 'breakdown of marriage' in the modern Western world, Rougemont argues, partly derives from the way the *amour passion* of twelfth-century courtly love ceased to follow its original path of mystical transcendence, first becoming a means for the intensification of emotional experience, and later being degraded into a frivolous and escapist doctrine of 'romance' which 'renders the marriage bond intolerable in its very essence' (1983: 17). Modern romantic love, in other words, is a pale replica of the spiritual form in which erotic passion was originally clothed, and the shedding of this spiritual veil has left us with something crudely egocentric and incapable of inspiring lasting bonds between people.

Tristan and Iseult

Rougemont's investigation into the feudal origins, and the fateful consequences, of romantic love begins with the most famous twelfth-century love story, *Tristan and Iseult*. This fable, along with other chivalric and Arthurian romances of the period, was popularised in the form of a rhyming narrative which was probably one of the staple songs of the southern troubadours sung in the courts of the French nobility. In the classic version of the troubadour love poem, a male lover would declare his painful yearning for a high-ranking, unattainable noblewoman, and his devotion would be rewarded with the Lady's edifying approval, but only so long as he displayed refinement and restraint (*mezura*). The three central elements of the poetic doctrine of courtly love, according to one early twentieth-century historian, were therefore the worship of women, the treatment of love as 'free' and subject only to the authority of desire, and the sublimation of this desire into courtesy, valour and chivalric action (Wilcox 1930).

The dissemination of this lyrical genre, which drew on both the content and form of earlier Arabic-Andalusian love poetry and on the Neoplatonism of the Middle East, owed something to Eleanor of Aquitaine, whose grandfather, William IX, was the earliest troubadour whose work has survived. It may also have spread to northern France thanks to the influence of Eleanor's daughter, Marie of Champagne, whose court in Troyes was an important literary centre, providing patronage for a number of romantic poets and *trouvères* (the northern songwriters who wrote in Old French rather than Occitan), including the author of *Lancelot*, Chrétien de Troyes. Eleanor had accompanied a crusade to Antioch at the age of 27, and her year-long acquaintance with the majesty of Byzantium and Jerusalem had sown in her a liberalising disdain for the monastic austerities of the traditional French court. In 1152 she secured the annulment of her marriage to Louis VII, then immediately wed Henry Plantagenet, taking with her the courtiers and poets, such as Bernard de Ventadour, who would help spread the popularity of the romantic courtly lyric.

Later, when she grew tired of Henry's infidelity, Eleanor restored her own ducal court in Poitiers. The celebrated treatise *De amore et amoris remedio* by Andreas Capellanus, who claimed to be a court chaplain and family tutor – possibly of Marie of Champagne – described the halls of Poitiers as a 'court of love', where the lessons of the chivalric romances were pressed into public service (Kelly 1937).[1] There, with the Queen as the presiding magistrate, high-born lovers brought their troubled relations to the judgements of a jury of refined ladies. An advocate would deliver the noble's petition to ensure his anonymity – a certain knight, for example, who had betrayed the code of secrecy by indiscreetly defending a certain Lady when his anger was inflamed by her detractors, wanted to know if her resulting repudiation of him was just – and the court would offer guidance, apportion blame and elucidate the duties and responsibilities of *fin'amors*.

The radical subversion of feudal gender relations suggested in these accounts is quite remarkable, even though there is still controversy among historians regarding the accuracy of these representations. John Benton (1961: 587, 590), for example, accepts that Marie of Champagne 'was one of the outstanding literary patrons of her day', but claims that 'the intentions of Andreas and Chrétien when they wrote about worldly love were conventionally moral and humorous or ironic'. Had Marie been so openly subversive of the attitudes and beliefs of the patriarchal world she inhabited, Benton argues, the many pious and literate men (and husbands) likely to have been scandalised by her public endorsement of adultery would have surely left a more prominent historical record of Marie's troublemaking. Even William Jackson, however, who mocks the idea that Andreas' humorous manual, *De Amore*, was related in spirit to the idealised love sung of by the troubadours, agrees that the historical documents reveal a 'startling change of attitude to woman in society' (Jackson 1985: 4). Howard Bloch (1991) also places courtly love in the context of the improving material situation of the female nobility in southern France, but claims that the rapid reversal of women's position in the second half of the twelfth century, while the culture of courtly love continued to flourish, demonstrates that the idealisation of women was an ideological ruse, a way of denying women's earthly

---

[1] *De Amore*, which was written in the 1180s, also appeared with the title *De arte honeste amandi*, which gave rise to the 1941 English translation, *The Art of Courtly Love*. Half of the book comprised dialogues, some between courtly lovers themselves, concerning matters of honour, entitlement and religious virtue. Rather than a treatise on the 'true' nature of (spiritual and emotional) love, as the early historians of courtly love interpreted it, *De Amore* is today often understood to have been a 'not too serious text-book' instructing the aristocracy in the social art of a sophisticated and elaborate game (Jackson 1985: 11).

desires and rendering them too pure and virtuous for participation in worldly affairs. This feminist critique of courtly love, already prefigured in Kate Millet's *Sexual Politics* (1970: 36–7) and Firestone's *The Dialectic of Sex* (1971), gains some support from Simon Gaunt's analysis of the lyrics of the female songwriters (the *trobairitz*), which often expressed disgruntlement at 'the trap male troubadours set for their *domnas* when they describe them as haughty and imperious, only to reproach them with this' (Gaunt 1995: 176).

Of the famous *Tristan* love story, five 'original' versions exist. The poems of Béroul, Thomas and Eilhart were written in the second half of the twelfth century, while the authors of the other two versions from the thirteenth century, one of whom converted the poem into prose, are unknown or disputed. Like all great myths, the original story has no definitive author. Both the origin and to some extent the meaning of the myth are obscure, the chief function of myth, Rougemont argues, being to articulate that which is too dangerous to speak of explicitly. *Tristan* is set within the courtly chivalric culture of the dominant social caste of Medieval Europe, and according to Rougemont it is the established rules and conventions of knightly chivalry which provide a 'container' for the fable's darker anti-social content, creating 'a framework within which it could be expressed in symbolic satisfactions' (1983: 22–3). This content is amorous passion, and this passion is a threat to society, Rougemont argues, because what it really wants is not, as we might imagine, human association, but rather a transfiguring, divinising *death*.

To explain this, Rougemont draws attention to a series of riddles in *Tristan and Iseult*. These, in turn, require some familiarity with the structure of the narrative. Tristan is orphaned as a boy and raised at Tintagel by his uncle, King Mark of Cornwall. When he comes of age, he fights and kills the invading Irish warrior Morholt, but is wounded in combat by a poisoned barb. Pushed out on a boat by his kinsman to die at sea, his vessel lands in Ireland. Keeping his identity secret, he is there treated by golden-haired Iseult using medicine from her apothecary mother, who is the Queen of Ireland and the sister of Morholt.

A few years later King Mark receives a golden hair from a bird. Resolving to marry the woman from whose head the hair came, he sends Tristan out to find her. Tristan's ship is blown by a storm and lands again in Ireland. He kills a dragon, is wounded and once more is nursed by Iseult. Learning that Tristan murdered her uncle, she threatens to kill him, but then relents at the prospect of becoming the Queen of Cornwall. On the boat she takes with Tristan back to England, Iseult's maid gives the young protagonists a drink, but mistakenly hands them a love potion prepared by Iseult's mother for the wedding couple.

They fall in love and consummate that love in what the rest of the narrative implies is their sole act of physical intimacy.

Despite having betrayed his king, Tristan returns to perform his knightly duty, and delivers Iseult to Mark. After the marriage, four 'felon' barons begin to suspect that Tristan and Iseult are lovers. Evidence is procured, Iseult is banished to a leper colony and Tristan is sentenced to the stake. The lovers manage to escape, however, and for three years live a 'harsh and hard' life in the depths of the Forest of Morrois. One day, while out riding in the forest, King Mark discovers them sleeping. But Tristan's sword lies between them – a sign of their chastity – so the king chooses to spare them, replacing the sword with his own.

According to the Béroul version of the story, which Rougemont treats as the common ancestor of the five versions, the love potion wears off after three years, and at that point the couple repent and Iseult returns to a forgiving Mark. Iseult asks Tristan to remain in the neighbourhood, however, and on their parting declares she will join him again if he asks her to. They continue to meet clandestinely, but are again witnessed by the felon barons. Iseult, protesting her virtue, asks for a 'Judgement of God', which requires her to grip a red-hot iron that will not burn a handler who speaks the truth. She survives the ordeal by subterfuge, saying that no man has held her except King Mark and the poor pilgrim – who is Tristan in disguise – who recently carried her off the boat.

Tristan then travels abroad on new adventures. He is overheard yearning for Iseult, who he believes no longer loves him. The brother of another Iseult, 'Iseult of the White Hand', thinks it is his sister that he desires. Being too honourable to correct this confusion, Tristan agrees to marry the second Iseult, but refuses to consummate the marriage. Subsequently wounded by a poisoned spear, he sends for Iseult the Fair, who alone knows how to treat the poison. Approaching by boat, Iseult hoists a white sail to signal her pending arrival. Tristan's wife is tormented by jealousy, however, and tells him the sail is black. Tristan dies. Iseult lands, lays down with her dead lover and dies too.

Rougemont draws our attention to some obvious puzzles in the *Tristan* narrative. After sailing back from Ireland, why does Tristan return Iseult to Mark, rather than carry her away from him? For Tristan's prowess in battle is unrivalled, and the conventions of knightly society always sanctioned the rights of the stronger, particularly when it came to men's rights over women. Why, after having first sinned under the effects of the love potion on the boat, do the lovers then resist any further carnal contact? Why, after the love potion has worn off and they have repented, do they continue meeting? Why, when they have resolved to continue meeting, and when the Judgement of God has 'proved' their innocence, does Tristan then voyage forth on adventures that separate him from his beloved? Why does he marry a woman he doesn't love or desire and who cannot make him happy? Why are Tristan and Iseult, the first betraying his king, the second betraying her husband and deceiving her god, depicted as heroes, while the barons who are faithful to their king are called 'felons'?

The answer to this final question, Rougemont suggests, holds the key to the others. Feudal morality would call a baron a 'felon' if he disobeyed his lord or failed to protect him. If a felon is someone who transgresses a social code, then the code implied by the authors of *Tristan* is not that of feudal law but of 'courtly' honour, in which anyone who 'discloses the secrets of courtly love is a felon' (1983: 33). Courtly love – or *fin'amors*, as the poets of southern Gaul actually called it, the later term *amour courtois* originating with the French literary historian Gaston Paris in 1883[2] – arose partly as a reaction against the brutality of feudal conventions, which allowed noblemen to take wives purely for the sake of strategic self-interest, and to dissolve the marriage when a wife's wealth dried up or a different political alliance proved more favourable. As depicted in the Arthurian romance and the songs of the Provençal troubadours, courtly love replaced the lord or *suzerain* with a Lady, such that the knightly hero, who in reality was a vassal of the lord, conceived of himself as the loyal servant of a woman – his *domina*.

The cautery of desire

Courtly love disparaged marriage as a barren legal convention, but while it glorified extramarital love it was also, Rougemont claims, opposed to sexual consummation. This helps explain why Tristan and Iseult must be repeatedly separated from one another, why the sword protects their moral purity while they sleep and why Tristan must take leave of his beloved and voyage overseas. Tristan returns Iseult to Mark not out of respect for Feudal norms – with his strength as a warrior he could have taken Iseult and still conformed to the code of knightly honour – but because courtly love requires tragedy and suffering. While traditional Celtic legends depicted disaster as an external force and an epic test of the hero's valour, it is the 'internal tragedy' of self-engendered obstructions which is distinctive of courtly love in the chivalric romance. Where

---

[2] Had Paris been unsuccessful in canonising the term 'courtly love', a more precise translation of *fin'amors* would have been 'true love' or 'pure love'.

no obstacles to the lovers' union exist, they must be invented; and not as an occasion for courage and conquering, but for a suffering that cannot, in this life, be overcome. Hence 'this preference for whatever thwarts passion, hinders the lovers' "happiness", and parts and torments them' (1983: 35). Initially, these obstructions serve to excite and magnify the passion: 'When Tristan wanders far away from her, his love for her waxes, and the more he loves the more he is afflicted' (1983: 147). But eventually obstruction becomes the goal itself, a purifying ordeal that parts the spirit from its mortal coil through the final divinising revelation that is death.

It could therefore be said that *Tristan and Iseult* is a story not about loving, but about being in love: 'the matter in question is the *passion* of love, and not love purely profane and natural' (1983: 149). The logic of this passion, Rougemont insists, is narcissistic. It is a spiritual magnification of the self rather than a relationship with a beloved; it is a neo-Platonic union with the divine made possible by the appearance of beauty. 'Tristan did not love Iseult for herself,' Rougemont asserts, 'but only on account of the love of Love of which her beauty gave him the image' (1983: 223). The beloved is but a pretext, a step on the ladder of love: 'Tristan wanted the branding of love more than he wanted the possession of Iseult. For he believed that the intense and devouring flame of passion would make him divine' (1983: 260). And this passion, which wishes the self to 'become greater than all things, as solitary and powerful as God', is necessarily agonising. It must ruin without respite all that is mortal and not divine, and must find in life only torture and suffering, truly achieving its aim only with the death of lover and beloved alike. 'Passion means suffering, something undergone, the mastery of fate over a free and responsible person. To love love more than the object of love, to love passion for its own sake, has been to love to suffer and to court suffering all the way from Augustine's *amabam amare* down to modern romanticism' (1983: 50). The famous seventeenth-century love letters of the Portuguese nun, Mariana Alcoforado – probably a work of fiction, but instructive nonetheless – illustrate this well: 'I thank you from the bottom of my heart for the despair that you have aroused in me and I abhor the peace in which I lived before I knew you … for it is better to suffer as I suffer than to enjoy the shallow pleasure that your French sweethearts give you' (cited in Ortega y Gasset 1933: 528). 'Tristan does not love Iseult in her reality,' Rougemont thus observes, 'but to the extent that she revives in him the delightful cautery of desire' (1983: 152).

When Tristan and Iseult visit the hermit Ogrin, they complain that they are not to blame for their act of physical indiscretion. 'If she loves me', Tristan is heard telling Ogrin, 'it is by the poison which holds me from leaving and her from leaving me'. And Iseult: 'Lord, by almighty God, he loves me not, nor I him; except for a herb potion which I drank and which he drank; it was a sin' (cited by Rougemont 1983: 39). The love potion provides an alibi for their passion, allowing its socially destructive consequences to be articulated without connection to human will and responsibility. But the alibi contains an essential truth, Rougemont argues, for the 'mutual love' of Tristan and Iseult is really a 'false reciprocity'; they do not, in fact, love each other 'for the other as that other really is' (1983: 52).

> Tristan and Iseult do not love one another. They say they don't, and everything goes to prove it. *What they love is love and being in love.* They behave as if aware that whatever obstructs love must ensure and consolidate it in the heart of each and intensify it infinitely in the moment they reach the absolute obstacle, which is death. Tristan loves the awareness that he is loving far more than he loves Iseult the Fair. And Iseult does nothing to hold Tristan. All she needs is her passionate dream. Their need of one another is in order to be aflame, and they do not need one another as they are. What they need is not one another's presence, but one another's absence. *Thus the partings of the lovers are dictated by their passion itself*, and by the love they bestow on their passion rather than on its satisfaction or on its living object. (1983: 41–2)

The religious origins of courtly love

In Rougemont's view, the roots of this passionate, narcissistic love lie in Iranian and Orphic antecedents to Plato, whose own doctrine of infinite transcendence through divinising desire was then transmitted to the medieval world by Plotinus. There it converged with Celtic myths and druidical beliefs, particularly regarding the immortality of the soul and the coexistence of gods of light and darkness. These in turn met and mingled with third-century Manichaeism, a religion named after the prophet Manes which spread from Persia to India and Europe, and which had some influence on early Arabic love poetry (Boase 1977: 79–80). Manichaeism shared with Celtic, Iranian, Hindu and Gnostic myths a dualistic worldview, holding that the human soul is divine, seeking to escape the terrestrial prison of the god of Night by ascending towards unity, in death, with the god of timeless Light.

Rougemont emphasises that this pagan dualistic doctrine stood in sharp contrast to Christianity. For the latter, the physical world is the incarnation of the Word – of Light that illuminates and expels the Darkness. The doctrine of incarnation, in which God takes a human form in the body of Jesus, inverted the flight from matter characteristic of Manichaeism, making the resurrection of the flesh after the Last Judgement a reminder of the essential unity of body and soul. In keeping with this, love, for Christians, pointed not only towards a purely spiritual hereafter, but also towards one's physical neighbour, whom Jesus showed how one should love. While Catholic orthodoxy thus made human love possible, Rougemont argues, but complete union with the divine an unhappy impossibility, Manichaeism 'assumed the possibility of union between God and soul, which implied divine felicity and the unhappiness of every *human* love' (1983: 166, my emphasis). Hence the importance to Rougemont of the distinction between *eros* and *agapē*.

> Eros, it will be recalled, requires union – that is, the complete absorption of the essence of individuals into the god. The existence of distinct individuals is considered to be a grievous error, and their part is to rise progressively till they are dissolved in the divine perfection. Let not a man attach himself to his fellow-creatures, for they are devoid of all excellence, and in so far as they are particular individuals they merely represent so many deficiencies of Being. There is no such thing as our neighbour. And the intensification of love must be at the same time a lover's *askesis*, whereby he will eventually escape out of life. (1983: 70)

Agapē, by contrast, does not ascend towards an ecstatic fusion that can only occur with death, but rather to a *communion*, a 'marriage' of believer and God which is made possible thanks to the latter's descent from heaven to earth:

> since *agape* is alone in recognising the existence of our neighbour – *Eros* failing to do so – and is the love of this neighbour, not as an excuse for self-exaltation, but as an acceptance of him or her in the whole concrete reality of his or her affliction and hope, it seems legitimate to infer that the kind of love called *passion* must have arisen usually among peoples who adored Eros, and that, on the contrary, Christian peoples – historically speaking, the inhabitants of the Western Continent of Europe – must have remained strangers to passion, or at least must have found it incredible. But history compels us to acknowledge that exactly the opposite has happened. (1983: 71)

'*Exactly* the opposite' is a bit of an exaggeration. Rougemont's point is simply that passionate love began to be cultivated with gusto in early twelfth-century Europe where Christianity was dominant. It was, he argues, essentially a reaction *against* Christianity 'by people whose spirit, whether naturally or by inheritance, was still pagan' (1983: 74). For such people, who had converted but who still lacked faith, the sacrament of marriage was merely a physical and material union that joined bodies even where there was not love, but only social and economic interests, between them. The eleventh- and twelfth-century troubadours of Languedoc were the first to aestheticise, in subtle and sophisticated forms, this protest against loveless marriage, singing of the poet's restrained and patient love for an already wedded and unattainable Lady, seeking to win her own chaste affection through the beauty of a recital. The fact that Provençal poetry allotted to women a status and esteem that was denied them in feudal culture proves to Rougemont that the values and ideals of courtly love cannot have been a direct reflection of material conditions. Instead Rougemont finds the explanation for this cultural subversion in a religious heresy: Catharism.

Catharism grew out of the neo-Manichaean sects of Asia Minor and the Gnostic religion of the Bogomils, which in the twelfth century spread westwards from Macedonia through the Balkans and into Italy, Germany and France. Catharism was known to its critics as the 'Abigensian heresy' – the city of Albi, near Toulouse, had the highest concentration of Cathars until they were massacred and dispersed by troops of the French crown, under the direction of the Abbot of Cîteaux and with the blessing of Pope Innocent III. To its supporters, however, it was known as the 'Church of Love', an apparent inversion of the 'Church of Rome' (*Roma=Amor*). For the Cathars, God is Love, and he created human spirits in his image. But Satan seduced humans to follow him in his descent from heaven, parting them from their heavenly spirits and ensnaring their souls in the profane and perverted lusts of terrestrial bodies.

The Cathar Church was divided into the Perfect (*perfecti*, or 'Goodmen') and mere Believers (*credentes* or *imperfecti*). Only the former had undergone the major rite of Catharism, a baptism or *consolamentum* by which initiates 'undertook to renounce the world and solemnly promised to devote themselves to God alone, never to lie or take an oath, never to kill, or eat of, an animal, and finally ever *to abstain, if married, from all contact with a wife*' (Rougemont 1983: 80). Produced by a wicked demiurge, physical matter was thus for the Cathars inherently evil. It therefore followed that the propagation of new living matter by sexual reproduction was to continue Satan's work. The sacrament of marriage was but an oath of fornication (*iurata fornication*), and suicide, since it released the soul from its imprisonment, was not a sin.

Rougemont argues that many of the southern French nobility subscribed to the ascetic doctrine of the Cathars, though they were mostly Believers rather than *perfecti*. In the songs of the troubadours, whom Rougemont describes as the 'poorly disciplined disciples' of the Cathars, the unhappy marriages of the feudal lords and ladies were brought into aesthetic relief, and the dangerous heretical beliefs of the Cathars found a lyrical form which 'secretly directed the yearnings of distressed mankind to the next world, and concentrated them there' (1983: 238). With the poetry's glorification of death over the prospect of earthly reward, its approval of the distance between lovers that stokes the flames of passion, and its account of the lover's chaste yearning for a single kiss – like the Kiss of Peace exchanged during the Cathars' *consolamentum* – the troubadours' courtly rhetoric was in Rougemont's view 'the lyrical and psalmodic development of the fundamental symbolism' of the Catharist faith.

The Catharist poetry of courtly love, Rougemont claims, provided a mythical framework which, it is important to note, restrained the lawlessness of erotic passion, fitting it symbolically into moral categories and codes of conduct that 'operated to the benefit of civilisation' (1983: 277). Although the myth was briefly resuscitated by *Romeo and Juliet*, and Wagner's *Tristan and Isolde* – Rougemont even refers to German Romanticism as a 'new Albigensian heresy' – its gradual profanation is for Rougemont the longer and more telling story of Western civilisation. With the disappearance of the myth, the search for spiritual transcendence was degraded and replaced by the thrill of terrestrial pleasures, exotic experiences and adulterous adventures. Stendhal's famous theory of 'crystallisation', presented in his 1822 treatise *De L'Amour*, seemed to give this coarsened version of courtly love some cultural credence. '*Amour passion*', Stendhal wrote, proceeds by finding 'new proofs of the perfection of the loved one' in the same way that a leafless branch, dropped into the depths of a disused Salzburg salt mine, is rediscovered months later 'covered with a shining deposit of crystals', a 'galaxy of scintillating diamonds' (Stendhal 1975: 45). 'Passion-love' is elicited by a fantasised perfection born of the *idea* of love, which, according to Ortega y Gasset, was all Stendhal knew. His life was a succession of false love affairs which failed because the crystallised objects of his fantasies could never stand the test of reality. 'Love dies because its birth was an error' (Ortega y Gasset 1957b: 29).

But for someone gripped by the love of love, the disillusionment of a fantasy merely revives the need for new illusions. Instead of the eternity of a transfiguring death, popular romantic love, Rougemont argues, came to offer a constantly renewed cycle of passion, conquest, disappointment and renewed passion. The once-in-a-lifetime, always tragic, '*grand amour*' is replaced with the amorous interlude known as the 'affair' – 'a cultural form that attempts to immobilise and repeat, compulsively, the primordial experience of "novelty"' (Illouz 1999: 176). Instead of the sublime self-sacrifice of the lover, we have the repetitive death and resurrection of love; the passion inevitably wanes, but every disappointment is an occasion for new hope, every failed relationship the opportunity to rediscover the vibration of a new passion. As Rougemont declares: 'whereas infinity in the eyes of Tristan was an eternity from which there could be no return and in which his lacerated spirit would at last dissolve, men and women today can look to nothing but the everlasting return of an ardour constantly being thwarted' (1983: 285).

Eros vs agapē

Rougemont's study is one of the most original and sophisticated critiques of the seemingly world-denying, and ultimately self-defeating, idealism of *eros*, and the spirit of his analysis has informed many attempts to link the instability of intimate life in contemporary societies to the baleful influence of the culture of romantic passion, with its unworldly sentiments, impossible fictions and luminous dreams. The familiar tropes, euphemisms and clichés of vernacular love – the 'distance' that lovers must travel to make the 'heart grow fonder', the yo-yo lovers who 'can't live with' and 'can't live without' each other, the devotees of romantic literature who are perpetually dissatisfied with, or else perpetually in denial of, the profane reality of their love lives – all offer some testimony to the contemporary pertinence of Rougemont's analysis. To the psychoanalyst in particular, Rougemont's description of the narcissism of love seems unnervingly accurate: 'From the very beginning the passion of love is incapable of objectively seeing another person or having any real empathy with that person,' Lou Andreas-Salomé observed. 'It is rather our deepest penetration into ourselves, a thousandfold loneliness' (cited in Beck and Beck-Gernsheim 1995: 191).[3] Erotic love is fanciful, imaginary and unworldly, and it cannot be reconciled with the demands of practical life, with pragmatic interests and the realities of habit, compromise, calculation and routine. 'Passion is a utopia', the French sociologist Jean-Claude Kaufmann emphasises. 'It is inevitably doomed to die, at least in its original radical form, as it can survive only if it rebels against the world.' What we really need, Kaufmann argues, is not erotic passion but 'conjugal *agapē* enriched with mutual trust and recognition' (Kaufmann 2011: 131, 118).

Yet one could also argue that the choice offered by Rougemont and Kaufmann, between passionate *eros* and benevolent *agapē*, is unjustifiably stark,

---

[3] Beck and Beck-Gernsheim attribute this quote to *Die Erotik* (1910), but I cannot find the passage in either the German or the translated English edition of Andreas-Salomé's book.

and that the assumed separation of desire and tenderness denies that passionate cherishing and attentiveness to the other that Thomas Mann alluded to in *The Magic Mountain* (1924): 'In the most raging as in the most reverent passion, there must be *caritas*' (VII, 600). The sober critics of romantic love also overlook the fact that an exclusive loving commitment to another person is rarely possible without precipitous change and metamorphosis, without self-abandonment and sacrifice, by which the rational self is overwhelmed and left at the mercy of another's will. Whether this model of passionate love is really consistent with contemporary popular understandings of courtship and intimacy – which may be more rational, egalitarian and circumspect than Rougemont and others have claimed – is something that requires further exploration.

Courtly love gave self-abnegation an aesthetic form; it offered moral clarity and insight, and promised to ennoble the lover by magnifying the delicacy and depth of his soul. Even jealousy was seen as edifying – for the lover, though not for the Lady's cruel and possessive husband – because it demonstrated the singularity and exclusiveness of the suitor's devotion. Chrétien de Troyes' Lancelot is continually required by Guinevere to sacrifice his knightly reputation and risk defeat and humiliation in battle in order to prove the all-consuming nature of his dedication to her. 'The distance between the twelfth-century text and our own values becomes apparent,' Catherine Belsey observes, 'if we try to imagine the hero of a Victorian novel or a Hollywood western so distracted by love that he cannot function properly. Such a figure would be pathetic or absurd, and not heroic at all. Modern heroism consists precisely in refusing to "surrender" to love, however deeply it is felt' (Belsey 1994: 101–2). Today's 'romantic' culture, Eva Illouz (2012) argues, is indeed more likely to be governed by an emotional contractualism which treats conflict and suffering in love as evidence of a 'flawed self' – a sign of emotional immaturity, 'neediness' and a failure to love reciprocally and with rational self-interest.

Even Kaufmann acknowledges that one cannot give oneself unconditionally to another person without letting go of what was previously held to be incontestably real and certain: 'There cannot be any commitment to love unless the old self is put to death' (2011: 111). Like fellow sociologist Illouz, Kaufmann notes with some alarm the culture of rational calculation and emotional restraint that pervades modern-day internet dating, and how the belief that one knows precisely what one wants, and that what one wants already exists in the complete form of another person, conceals the distance that must be 'fallen' if a person is to experience the transcendence and the epiphany of a new human bond. As

Simmel described it, love is 'an ungrounded and primary category' that creates what did not exist before:

> As one who loves, I *am* a different person than I was before … . In the same way, the beloved as such is also a different being, arising from a different a priori than the person as an object of knowledge or fear, indifference or esteem. There is an absolute connection, and not a mere association, between love and its object only in this way: *The object of love in its complete categorical significance does not exist prior to the love itself but only by means of it.* (Simmel 1984: 161, my emphasis)

The tendency to treat *eros* as a fanciful utopia, and *agapē* as a sober attentiveness to reality, also ignores the necessary role of imaginative idealism in all attempts to foster ethical bonds between people for whom the modern world is a source of both ever-deepening interiority and evermore instrumental and depersonalising anonymity. It overlooks the fact that love for a concrete other is love for that which is there as well as here, for that which is unknown as well as known and for that which, as time, chance and circumstance exert their influence, is destined to become strange, remote and unfamiliar. If love, as Rougemont says, is 'the admission of this other's alien life and ever distinct person' (1983: 323), then it is also admission of that which is unfamiliar and elusive, that which is opaque and inaccessible to another consciousness, and that which cannot be fully cared for without the ongoing work of a constantly renewed imagination. For the human person, however 'distinct', is always also an absence, a mystery and an uncertainty, and although an acknowledgement of the strangeness and incomprehensibility of the other is part of the realism of mature love, so is the effort to personalise that strangeness and make from it a deeper and richer human relation.[4] It is perhaps no coincidence that the love of nature so familiar to modern Romanticism was also a common element of the troubadour lyric. As Irving Singer (2009: 54) points out, the troubadours – who included a youthful Francis of Assisi among their number – 'were among the first to see the things of this world as objects to be enjoyed in the imagination and not merely used for the glorification of God'.

---

[4] In Žižek's Lacanian formulation, courtly love erects obstacles to its consummation not in order to elevate the value of the object (the Lady), but in order to sustain the illusion that, were it not for those obstacles, *the object would be attainable*. Starting with a recognition of the absolute otherness and inaccessibility of the loved object, Žižek argues that 'genuine love' emerges only when the object of love reaches back with her own subjective desire: 'when I experience the other, the object of love, as frail and lost, as lacking "it", and my love none the less survives this loss' (Žižek 1999: 164).

The feminism of love

In Rougemont's critique of Neoplatonic *eros*, 'a man gives evidence of his love for a woman by treating her as a completely human person, not as if she were the spirit of the legend – half-goddess, half bacchante, a compound of dreams and sex' (1983: 313). Octavio Paz argues, however, that 'the deification of woman' in the Western tradition of romantic love should be understood not as a narcissistic fantasy, nor, as Bloch (1991) argues, as a misogynist ruse, but rather as a humanising 'recognition'. What is recognised, in the woman who is loved, is the essential 'sanctity of the person', the roots of this insight being the Judaeo-Christian belief that 'each human being, not excluding the basest of them, is the embodiment of a mystery that it is no exaggeration to call sacred' (Paz 1995: 114). That this recognition, moreover, had literary antecedents in the ancient world throws some doubt on Rougemont's endorsement of La Rochefoucauld's maxim that 'few people would fall in love had they never heard of love' (1983: 173).

The poetry of Sappho is almost certainly the oldest surviving record of sexual love that aspired to mutual intimacy and reciprocal longing rather than male conquest and domination (Stigers 1981). Even here, however, Paz argues that the prevailing theme was eroticism rather than love, and we are hard-pressed to find in any Greek poetry 'the sentiments and emotions of the Other' (Paz 1995: 55). According to Paz, the 'first great love poem' was written by Theocritus in Alexandria in the third century BC. 'The Sorceress' (*Pharmaceutria*) tells of the fevered desire, anger and despair of Simaetha, abandoned by her faithless lover Delphis. In so far as it depicts woman as an amorous and erotic subject, Paz argues, it marked a break with Athenian misogyny, reflecting the growing public prominence of patrician women in the ancient world, as well as the subversion of the male association of passion with enslavement. Two centuries later, the Roman poet Catullus captured what Paz suggests are three key elements of modern love: 'choice – the freedom of the lovers; defiance – love is a transgression; and jealousy' (1995: 63–4). Catullus' love of Clodia, who was married, older and his social superior, prefigured the gynarchic dynamics of courtly love, and also gave expression to the emotional torture of the exposed and vulnerable lover – 'I love you and I hate you', he told Clodia, in what may be the first recorded expression of love's internal contradiction (Elias 1987: 299).[5]

---

[5] Because hate depends on an attentiveness to the other person, it is more likely to be a perversion of or an accompaniment to love than its opposite. In Simon May's formulation, the true antithesis of love is not hate but *disgust* (May 2011: 250–2).

In the following decades, the Augustan poet Propertius also made love of a single woman – a courtesan of the higher class, or possibly the wife of a wealthy patrician – the focus of his writings. Giving her the pseudonym Cynthia, Propertius' elegies convey what Paz describes as an extraordinary 'modernity', detailing, with uncanny realism, the betrayal and infidelity, jealousy and abandonment, passionate lust, grotesque possessiveness and anger, characteristic both of the madness and turmoil of erotic love, and of its sombre mortality. Perhaps most dramatically, Propertius captured the aspiration of love to reach beyond the world of the living, to conjure the amorous spirits of the dead and to consecrate the soul of the beloved by seeking togetherness for eternity. 'You will be mine', the ghost of the dead Cynthia promises to Propertius, 'and I shall mix the dust of your bones with the dust of mine' (cited by Paz 1995: 70).[6]

The attitudes of Propertius, Catullus, Tibullus and other poets of Alexandria and Rome are significant because they express a defiance of the Greco-Roman culture of political duty, preferring to sing of private passions rather than patriotic deeds, the glory of war and the heroism of the warrior-citizen. This 'prehistory of love' was, in Paz's view, 'an authentic precursor of what today we call civil disobedience' (1995: 87). The necessary condition of this more Aristophanean *eros*, which classical philosophy condemned for its withdrawal from public life and its enslavement to the passions, was what Norbert Elias (1987) says was a 'civilising spurt' in the late Roman Republic and early Empire which significantly altered the balance of power between the sexes. This was particularly apparent in marriage, where the custom that placed women and their property under the control of men gradually lapsed, and women were given the legal right to divorce. As Paz describes:

> The twilight of the democracies and the rise of powerful monarchies caused a general retreat to private life. Political freedom was replaced by inner freedom.

---

[6] The *Liebestod* idea that death finally overcomes the distance between lovers is a frequent theme in the history of the novel. In Goethe's *Werther* (1774), where it is the traditional separation of passion and marriage which stands in the way of a loving union, Werther shoots himself in order to ensure 'one eternal embrace' with Lotte, whose marriage to the sober Albert he cannot bear, and who then suffers from a possibly fatal broken heart (II, 118, 125–6). In Eliot's *The Mill on the Floss* (1860), it is Maggie's love for her brother which can neither be explicitly named nor practically fulfilled. When their boat resurfaces after the climactic flood, its emptiness is Maggie's erotic completion: 'brother and sister had gone down in an embrace never to be parted' (VII, V, 467). In *Wuthering Heights* (1847), Cathy's marriage to Linton conspires with the intensity of Heathcliff's passion to make profane reality an obstacle to the unity of the lovers. Like Propertius' Cynthia, Heathcliff looks forward to a cadaverous intermingling, bribing the sexton to agree to bury him next to the body of Cathy, with the touching sides of their coffins removed. He thus imagines that, by the time the adjacent coffin of her husband has disintegrated, Cathy and Heathcliff's skeletons will have combined into one and Linton 'will not know which is which' (XXIX, 355).

In this shift of ideas and customs, the new situation of women was a decisive factor. We know that for the first time in Greek history women began to engage in occupations and serve functions outside their homes. Some were magistrates, a thing that would have been unheard of for Plato and Aristotle; some were midwives; and some devoted themselves to philosophical studies, painting, poetry. Married women were quite free, as can be seen from the vulgar language of the gossips in Theocritus and Herodas. Marriage began to be seen as a matter that ought not to be arranged by the heads of families alone, but as an agreement in which the participation of the contracting parties was essential. All of which shows, yet again, that the emergence of love is inseparable from the emergence of woman. There is no love without feminine freedom. (1995: 84–5)

The poetry of the ancients shows, in Paz's view, the timeless psychological reality of erotic love, and the fact that the 'amatory sentiment' has existed in all times and places. But Paz stresses the fact that the ancients lacked a 'doctrine' of love, an embodied set of ideas and practices that made love a way of life and the shared ethic of a community. It was the Provençal poets of the twelfth century who created the romantic 'code of love' that Westerners are the heirs of today. These troubadours addressed their songs – which were written in the vernacular rather than in Latin – not to the exclusively male audience of a Greek symposium, nor to the libertines and courtesans of Roman antiquity, but to the refined and noble ladies of the medieval court. Germanic and Celtic influences, and some Christian beliefs, had endowed women of the nobility more dignity and freedom than they had ever known during the Dark Ages, and this coincided, Paz points out, with a political situation in which the feudal lords, being almost permanently at war or on religious crusades, regularly left their wives or sisters in charge of governing their realms. Admittedly, these freedoms would subsequently be co-opted and, for a time, lost. The spirit of singular devotion to a woman would be appropriated by the Catholic Church and converted into the cult of the Blessed Virgin ('*ma dame*' was henceforth pluralised, as '*Notre Dame*' became the masthead of countless churches and cathedrals). Among the male nobility the ritualised public adoration of ladies would also be absorbed into the game of class distinction, becoming a symbolic means for the feudal aristocracy to distance themselves from the ribald antifeminism of the bourgeoisie and clergy. But however short-lived, the renaissance was real, and for Paz it echoed the springtime of Alexandria and Rome.

Paz stresses the significance of the way the Provençal poets adopted the Arab-Andalusian custom of reversing the vertical relationship of the sexes, addressing their beloved Ladies with the masculine *midons* (*meus dominus* – 'my ruler').

'The masculinisation of the role of women emphasised the shift in the hierarchy of the sexes: the woman now occupied the superior position, and the lover was her vassal. Love is subversive' (1995: 96). There are echoes here of Socrates' deference to his female muse Diotima, and of course of Alcibiades' subsequent homage to Socrates who, like an exemplary Lady of the court, always spurned the younger man's sexual advances (Singer 2009: 40–2). Courtly love was, as Paz puts it, both an asceticism and an aesthetic; it extolled chastity, and made courtship an art form and a cultural rite. But Paz disputes Rougemont's claim that *fin'amors* was an expression of Catharism, that its desired object was as much a creation of the imagination (a Platonic Idea) as an actual person, and that it explicitly rejected physical love in favour of humility and reverential distance. What the troubadours condemned of marriage, Paz points out, was not the propagation of satanic matter, but the traducing of love to a political and economic contract in which the feelings and desires of the woman were discounted. 'The Cathar believer condemned love, even of the purest sort, because it bound the soul to matter; by contrast the first commandment of courtesy was love for a beautiful body. What was holy for the Provençal poets was a sin for the Cathars' (Paz 1995: 104).

The Catharist suspicion of the body was also shared by Catholicism, and does not therefore account very well for the cleavage between Church and court during this period. As C. S. Lewis (1938) pointed out in his study of courtly love, the wickedness of concupiscence was axiomatic to the Medieval Church, whereas romantic love treated carnal passion as an authenticating and purifying force. William Reddy develops this point with greater sophistication, arguing that the most important historical factor in the emergence of courtly love was the sexual asceticism of the Gregorian Reform movement, of which the Cathar heresy was, in his view, a spiritual 'offshoot' (Reddy 2012: 129). The influence of the Gregorian Reform, which discounted all attraction between partners that was not sexual, but which also reduced physical desire to a selfish animal appetite whose enjoyment, even in marriage, was a shameful sin, was spread by dozens of Cistercian houses in southern France as well as by Robert of Arbrissel at the celebrated monastery of Fontevraud. Reddy argues that courtly love emerged *in opposition* to this, and indeed can best be understood as a kind of 'queer performativity', a 'surreptitious dissent, a shadow religion' (2012: 387, 389). It was an attempt to reformulate the more diffuse longing for personal intimacy and togetherness in terms which were both sexually literate and morally and spiritually edifying, creating 'a heroic ethic of courage, self-denial, self-discipline, and devotion to the beloved every bit as demanding and rewarding as the spiritual career of Christian asceticism'

(Reddy 2012: 167). However, because *fin'amors* remained in dialogue with this asceticism – because it promised to resist, purify and render innocent those otherwise shameful appetites – it implicitly accepted the idea that the longing for human connection was primarily libidinal in essence. Although, as we saw in the discussion of Plato's *Phaedrus* in the previous chapter, there are undoubtedly precedents for this distinction dating back to Greek antiquity, Reddy argues that it was the troubadours who ironically played the paramount role in the cultural formulation of the hierarchical dualism between 'natural' sexual desire and 'true' romantic love. Among the troubling consequences of this dualism which we must not overlook was the way it was employed, 700 years later, to underwrite the colonial association of the 'exotic' with the primitively and unruly lustful, and Western 'civilisation' with the mastery of dangerous and degrading desires.

In reflecting on the sexual connotations of the troubadour love songs, Paz notes that the first Provençal poets were noblemen themselves, and there was no ambiguity in their professed longing for the physical consummation of their love. Only subsequently did a class of professional poets appear, many of whom did not belong to the aristocracy. For these, the poetic convention which turned the male lover into a vassal of his beloved reflected a social reality, since the ladies they courted were almost always of a superior rank. It was this gulf in social status, Paz suggests, which accentuated the artistry and symbolism of courtly love – that is, it was the impossibility of love's completion which made that love a poetic fiction, an aesthetic doctrine and an idealisation of social reality. For these men, the Lady was a muse, and poetry was unrequited desire transmuted into verse – immortality, in the original Socratic conception, was brought forth in beauty. But even here, there was a poetic genre called *alba*, which spoke of lovers whose passions had already been consummated. And the imperative of chastity and sexual restraint was also often articulated as an *assag* or *assai* – a sensual 'test of love', the successful passing of which would open the way not to tragic suffering and death, but to what the poets called *joi*, which Paz defines as 'the pleasure of carnal climax, though refined by long expectation and *mezura*' (1995: 112). Chrétien's *The Knight of the Cart* certainly leaves no doubt about the sexual consummation of Lancelot and Guinevere's love, nor 'the force of women's desire and their capacity for passion' (Belsey 1994: 103). As the culture of courtly love moved north to Aquitaine and then England, it certainly appears to have shed the asceticism of its Neoplatonic influences, becoming 'generally sexual in its obvious intent, and only rarely interested in the values of unrequited yearning' (Singer 2009: 34). For Singer, unlike Reddy, courtly love was rooted in 'natural' desires, but it channelled those desires towards moral and aesthetic ideals which humanised Platonic and religious conceptions of love, divorcing amorous relations from the spiritual path towards God or absolute beauty which was still discernible in the writings of the Arab Neoplatonists Avicenna and Ibn Hazm. However much they drew upon Muslim philosophy, by articulating the extraordinary idea of a self-sufficient love between persons, the protagonists of courtly love were, in Singer's words, taking 'one of the first steps in the modern search for a humanising relation between men and women' (2009: 58).

What the Church condemned as the idolatrous deification of women was for Paz, therefore, a 'revolution' in the relationship between the sexes. In this subversive transformation, 'woman's social inferiority was counterbalanced by her superiority in the realm of love', and women were finally granted dominion over 'their own bodies and souls' (1995: 113). The unashamedly lustful, impious letters from Heloïse to Abelard represent perhaps the summit of this twelfth-century recognition of female sexuality. 'Men call me chaste', Heloïse wrote to her estranged lover and husband from the convent at Argenteuil, but 'they do not know the hypocrite I am'.

> In my case, the pleasures of lovers which we shared have been too sweet – they can never displease me, and can scarcely be banished from my thoughts. Wherever I turn they are always there before my eyes, bringing with them awakened longings and fantasies which will not even let me sleep. Even during the celebration of the Mass, when our prayers should be purer, lewd visions of those pleasures take such a hold upon my unhappy soul that my thoughts are on their wantonness instead of on prayers. I should be groaning over the sins I have committed, but I can only sigh for what I have lost. Everything we did and also the times and places are stamped on my heart along with your image, so that I live through it all again with you.[7]

The sanctity of the person

Whereas Rougemont fiercely opposed the materialist outlook that seeks to explain the 'higher' by the 'lower', and thus love as a 'deflection' of sexuality, Paz insists that the 'double flame' of eroticism and love is fed by the 'original fire' of sexuality (1995: 257). Like the sublimation of sex into eroticism, love, for Paz, is cultural figuration, ritual and representation. But love also transcends eroticism,

---

[7] 'Letter 3. Heloise to Abelard', in B. Radice (ed.), *The Letters of Abelard and Heloise*. Harmondsworth: Penguin, 1974, p. 133.

ennobling the body of the beloved through a process of spiritual purification. It 'transforms the subject and object of the erotic encounter into unique persons. Love is the final metaphor of sexuality. Its cornerstone is freedom: the mystery of the person' (1995: 128).

This association of love with freedom and personhood gains some support from historian Colin Morris, who also highlighted the way courtly love contributed to the 'discovery of the individual' in the eleventh and twelfth centuries, a period distinctive for its humanist interest in inwardness, personal sincerity (this was when confession became an established sacrament), the expansion of self-knowledge and the art of self-expression. Morris (1972: 75) draws attention to the way Lancelot, in Chrétien's *The Knight of the Cart*, is spurned by Guinevere for a moment's hesitation before climbing on the cart of shame.[8] The scene shows how inner devotion and subjective intent were becoming more significant than the outward performance of reputable acts; it also shows Chrétien's awareness of the conflict between the two, of the splitting of the desiring self into the public voice of reason and the extravagant irrationality of love. Heloïse also appealed to the idea of self-realisation through the purity and authenticity of desire: 'Wholly guilty though I am, I am also, as you know, wholly innocent', she wrote to Abelard. 'It is not the deed but the intention of the doer which makes the crime, and justice should weigh not what was done but the spirit in which it is done.'[9] For Morris, however, the cultural significance of the romantic lyric, the earnest search, which he also documents, for authentic friendship among humanist scholars and monks, as well as the twelfth-century fascination with transgressive love, is not that they promoted a discriminating interest in the distinctive life and character of another person, but that together they accelerated the development of interiority and self-examination. 'The centre of interest was not the friend or the mistress, but one's own self, the thoughts inspired, the passions aroused, by the distant beloved.' Morris's analysis, therefore, is for the most part consistent with that of Rougemont. Self-preoccupation, not attentiveness to the Other, was

---

[8] The cart is used for the pillorying of criminals: 'Whoever was convicted of any crime was placed upon a cart and dragged through all the streets, and he lost henceforth all his legal rights, and was never afterward heard, honoured, or welcomed in any court.' The driver promises Lancelot, who is searching for the Queen, that he will find out what has happened to Guinevere if he is willing to be carried into town in the cart. A 'common sense' fear of 'shame and disgrace' leads to a moment's hesitation, after which the 'heart' triumphs over 'reason' and Lancelot mounts the cart. Though she eventually forgives him, Guinevere initially rebuffs Lancelot for hesitating those 'two whole steps', viewing his concern for his knightly reputation to be a 'crime' against the higher principles of love (Vv. 247–398, 4441–4550).

[9] 'Letter 1. Heloise to Abelard', in B. Radice (ed.), *The Letters of Abelard and Heloise*. Harmondsworth: Penguin, 1974, p. 115.

in Morris's view what really marked the historic birth of the individual: 'when Bernard of Ventadour looked into his lady's eyes, he saw himself' (Morris 1972: 118–19).

Unsurprisingly, Paz rejects the reduction of erotic love to narcissism. Love is always to some extent self-reflective, because to love is to recognise the beloved in her or his freedom and thus to be conscious of being at the uncertain mercy of that freedom. Love is always a surrender and a servitude, a wager that aspires to reciprocity but which hangs helplessly on the very free will that the lover recognises and calls into being. Love is spoken of as a wound or an injury, Paz notes, precisely because to love is to become a vassal – to relinquish one's absolute sovereignty, to acknowledge the beloved's autonomy and to be vulnerable to rejection and humiliation, as well as to the feelings of inadequacy and unworthiness that even reciprocated love must gamble with. This risk-taking is what makes love seem inherently foolish; but if no one was prepared to be a fool, no one would love – or, for that matter, feel loved. As Simmel points out, 'an excessively sharp accentuation of a feature of all love' is that it is 'undeserved':

> Even the same mutual love cannot simply be reckoned so that no unpaid balance remains. Love belongs among the quantitatively indeterminable values, those values which, in principle, are not to be 'earned'. This is why we cannot really have a 'claim' to love either. On the contrary, under all conditions, even where the most exalted liberality and equivalent values compel it and seem to give us a right to love, it still remains a gift and a blessing. (Simmel 1984: 190)

As the 'final metaphor of sexuality', love is impossible, Paz argues, without the erotic attraction to a body. Love, in this sense, means something quite different to the affection we might claim to feel for a country, or a religion, or a set of principles or ideas. It is also not the same as the reverence, honour, respect and charity we may feel for our friends or kin, which Paz believes is better understood by the term 'piety'. Paz rejects the Greeks' attempt to politicise *eros*, for love is always a violation of the social order, its exclusiveness separating lovers from society and making them its enemies. 'A republic of lovers would be ungovernable; the political ideal of a civilised society – which has never been realised – would be a republic of friends' (1995: 138).

Paz thus stresses that 'without physical, carnal attraction there is no love' (1995: 156), and in this respect he departs from Rougemont's defence of Christian *agapē* and his claim that 'it is Eros, passionate love, pagan love, that spread through the European world the poison of an idealistic *askesis*' (Rougemont 1983: 311). But for all their differences, both Rougemont and

Paz are seeking in love a route to the recognition of the person. Indeed, while Rougemont condemned the idea that a marriage could be found on passionate love, he also described it as a 'fatal mistake' to preclude passion from marriage. And while Rougemont bemoaned that amorous passion which at its best was a divinising mysticism and at its worst an egocentric cult of emotional and physical experience, Paz too sounds a grave note of caution about the fate of love in contemporary society. For Paz, the concept of the person is the premise, as well as the product, of amorous love, and although this love is always corporeal, it is inconceivable without 'a soul incarnated in the body'. The person we love, in other words, is the heavenly mystery that we see and sense only because it has as its earthly reality the palpable and comprehensible form of a mortal body. 'Flesh is essentially a physical body charged with psychic electricity', writes Ortega y Gasset, and it is only because 'the visual image we have of a person's body is simultaneous with our psychical perception of his soul or quasi-soul' that we can 'distinguish a stone and machine from body and flesh'. What the troubadours called 'courtesy' [*cortezia*] we might also know as 'tact' – a term which 'alludes to that sense of spiritual perfection with which one seems to touch someone else's soul, to feel its contours, the harshness or gentleness of its character' (Ortega y Gasset 1957a: 115–16). And this in turn requires a certain distance – we must step back a little to see the shape of the self, and must avoid excessive touch lest, in Nietzsche's words, overgenerous handling 'wears down the soul' (Nietzsche 2015: 49).

What for Paz has today brought about the 'twilight of love' is not, as Rougemont argues, a de-spiritualised idealism, but rather a crude and conceited materialism which has desacralised the human body and turned the miracle of interiority into what the scientists and philosophers of 'artificial intelligence' believe is a manufacturable machine. By ridiculing the idea of the soul, Paz argues, this culture has set in train 'a gradual but irreversible devaluation of the person'. Biological reductionism, and above all genetic determinism, is the apotheosis of this trend towards 'the ascendancy of the machine as the archetype of the human being'. 'Our tradition told us that every man and woman was a unique, unrepeatable being; the modern age sees not beings but organs, functions, processes' (Paz 1995: 207). We seek to remedy lovelessness by the surgical modification of aging bodies, or by the changing of one's anatomical sex, but it is the spiritual estrangement of persons which is the measure of our alienation, and changing our bodies, though easier in today's techno-scientific universe than changing culture and society, offers no remedy for the impoverishment of the soul.

Love is an inevitable casualty of the rational assault on the person, but in its grandeur and its foolishness love is also an ever-renewable act of defiance. Finding its only justification in the lover's conviction – which to outsiders always looks like blind, irrational faith – that the person who is loved is lovable in herself and without further reason, love is an irrepressible revolt against reality, a refusal to accept a universe in which the beloved does not exist. Already, in *Romeo and Juliet* (1595), love had been mocked as a decorative, cliché-ridden attempt to conceal the ignoble truth of a grasping, animalistic desire. (Friar Lawrence says of Romeo's initial infatuation with Rosaline, 'Thy love did read by rote, that could not spell' (2.3.88), and Romeo's love is repeatedly ridiculed by the cynical Mercutio, and even questioned by Juliet at first.) And yet, also already in *Romeo and Juliet* we see romantic love fighting back against patriarchal philistinism, divisive feudal loyalties and the power of naked violence. With the language of heavenly bliss transposed to the realm of earthly affairs, Shakespeare's star-crossed lovers make gods of each other – 'thy gracious self', Juliet declares, 'is the god of my idolatry'; the more love she gives, she says, the more she discovers its 'infinity' (2.2.113-4, 134–5) – and they finally embrace death not with thoughts of divine redemption but with the promise of their own undivided union.

Love in Shakespeare is a rebellion against social and political conventions. Two hundred years later, a new faith in love emerged to oppose the dehumanising forces of industrial capitalism. 'As Christian faith caused great Gothic cathedrals to rise', Robert Polhemus (1990: 3) writes, 'so did erotic faith, or the desire for it, bring into being great nineteenth-century novels'. I will discuss some of these novels in Chapter 5, but before doing so I want to explore their social and cultural context, and this requires, in particular, a closer historical examination of the changing nature of the Western family.

4

Affective individualism and the conjugal family

The path from the twelfth-century troubadours to modern conceptions of romantic love is a long and twisting one, and a more ambitious intellectual history of love would need to visit the Italian Renaissance, Shakespearean theatre, and the French and German Enlightenment. The more modest aim of this chapter is to shift the focus onto social history – specifically, the history of the modern European family – in order to provide some context to the birth of the romantic novel, which will be the subject of the next chapter. This, in turn, will enable me to bring the discussion around to a more sociological analysis of love, but to do so in a way that allows for an exploration of the role of fiction in the cultivation of the romantic imaginary.

The 'central zone of the modern family', the French sociologist Emile Durkheim observed in 1892, is the 'permanent' bond between 'the husband and the wife, since all the children sooner or later leave the paternal household'. For Durkheim it was a law of social evolution 'that the family must necessarily contract as the social milieu, with which every individual is in direct relationship, extends further'. As the social interactions required of individuals in a complex industrial society expand and become more anonymous, Durkheim argued, family ties shrink in number, the obligations of kinship networks slacken and diminish, and marital relations become more intimate. With the development of modernity, the social and psychological possibility of a loving union between private selves increases dramatically. Durkheim proposed to call this new configuration of domestic relations the 'conjugal family' (Durkheim 1978a: 230–2).[1]

---

[1] The word 'conjugal', from the Latin *coniugare*, meaning 'to join together', had been used in French since the sixteenth century to refer to marital union. By the eighteenth century, the term was commonplace in English literature, with titles like *Conjugal Duty* (1732), *An Essay on Conjugal Infidelity* (1727) and *Precepts of Conjugal Happiness* (1767) advising readers on the rules and expectations of marriage. In the racy *Madame Bovary* (1857), the charlatan pharmacist Monsieur Homais is scandalised to discover his pupil, Justin, carrying a book entitled *Conjugal Love*. Though deeming it grossly inappropriate for women and children, Homais is titillated by the illustrations and

A family state of mind

The claim that, as societies modernise, the structure of the family changes from an extended to a conjugal or 'nuclear' form went largely undisputed by sociologists and historians until a flurry of scholarship on the history of the Western family began, in the early 1970s, to question the accuracy of this account. Perhaps the most surprising finding came from demographic research led in Britain by the Cambridge Group for the History of Population and Social Structure. Collecting data from parish registers and other local records, Peter Laslett and his colleagues challenged the assumption that households in pre-industrial Europe were large and complex units, and that the nuclear family was a later product of the modernisation process. In England, Laslett (1972a, 1972b) argued, the three-generation extended or 'stem' family had never been common, with the mean household size of 4.75 remaining relatively stable from the sixteenth century to the end of the nineteenth.

Laslett was criticised for using a computational mean to gloss over the diversity of family forms, with data (including some of his own) showing that extended family households were still more common among the pre-industrial peasantry, the gentry, in certain regions and under the influence of specific inheritance rules, and during the phase in a family's natural life cycle when grandparents were still alive (Berkner 1972, 1975). The composition of a household in pre-industrial Europe would most likely have fluctuated over time, and its size would have expanded and contracted according to external circumstances and the changing needs of its members. Even where a nuclear unit was the stable norm, it was almost certainly embedded, as today's nuclear family more seldom is, in a wider network of ties with extended kin who did not live in the same household. In addition, and perhaps more relevantly, critics complained that demographic research on family composition tells us little about what *meaning* family relations, including sexual relations, had to household members in earlier times, and how these meanings may have changed over the centuries. 'Household size,' Perry (2004: 17) emphasises, 'does not necessarily tell us either who was in the household nor to whom the members of that household felt their deepest obligations.' It was an interest in exploring this issue of meaning and feeling that

approves of the book's pseudo-scientific approach to sexual health and morality. Flaubert probably had in mind here Nicholas Venette's *Tableau de l'amour conjugal* (1696), translated into English as *The Mysteries of Conjugal Love Reveal'd* (1720).

gave rise to what Anderson (1995) has called the 'sentiments approach' to the history of the family.

'The nuclear family is a state of mind rather than a particular kind of structure or set of household arrangements.' So said Edward Shorter, who argued that what distinguishes the modern Western family from its predecessors is that family members today 'feel that they have much more in common with one another than they do with anyone else on the outside – that they enjoy a privileged emotional climate they must protect from outside intrusion, through privacy and isolation' (1977: 205). This was, in fact, also partly the argument of Durkheim, who suggested that, with the growth in individuals' outward-looking functional associations with non-intimate others, the realm of domestic intimacy becomes more clearly demarcated, allowing 'the personalities of the family members to come forth more and more'. As the family transfers its productive functions to more specialised agencies governed by impersonal relations of exchange, the domestic unit is no longer preoccupied with reproducing itself as an economic system (an 'attachment to things'), but instead 'becomes entirely a matter of persons. We are attached to our family only because we are attached to the person of our father, our mother, our wife, or our children' (Durkheim 1978a: 233–4). The word 'family', indeed, only came to mean the unit of spouses and their dependent children in the late eighteenth century, whereas previously it simply referred to the diverse residents of a household, including servants, apprentices, foster children and any relatives who might be living under the same roof (Tadmor 1995). This transformed understanding of the family reflects the 'double adaptive capacity' which Niklas Luhmann argues is characteristic of social systems in a modern, differentiated society. We think of industrial capitalism as a gigantic association of anonymous and interchangeable atoms – 'mass society', as the levelling tendencies of the nineteenth and early twentieth century were so labelled. But this is only part of the story. The number of strangers we are capable of interacting with increases in line with an enhanced capacity for more *intensive* relationships, 'in which more of the individual, unique attributes of each person, or ultimately all their characteristics, become significant' (Luhmann 2012: 13).

Love before modernity

According to Shorter, the declining permeability of the family to external rules and obligations, and the growing emotional openness of family members to each other, is particularly apparent when we look at changes that started to occur in the seventeenth and eighteenth centuries in the domain of sexual relations. Here, Shorter claims, we can begin to see the first signs of a transition from 'instrumental' to 'affective' sexuality, whereby the size of a woman's dowry and the interests of family status came to have less impact on marital choices than the prospect of physical and emotional intimacy and the search for personal happiness.

Drawing on the records of medical doctors and minor officials, as well as the writings of parsons and schoolteachers who moonlighted as amateur historians, folklorists and antiquarians, Shorter paints a harsh and unsentimental picture of sexual relations among the popular classes in premodern[2] Europe. Courtship, he argues, was for the most part scripted by custom and devoid of emotional spontaneity. Social norms reduced erotic contact between non-married couples to a minimum (a French historian, for example, was unable to document the practice of open-mouthed, 'intrabuccal' kissing before 1880). When parents objected to a proposed union, the young couple would sensibly renounce each other, for to risk disinheritance in a society where wealth was family property was to flirt with destitution. Physical attraction between couples was less important to marriage choices than the maintenance of family alliances, the wealth of a woman's parents and, among the lower classes, a prudential concern for one's spouse's ability to endure strenuous work.

Once couples were married, Shorter claims, the enforcement of strict sex roles perpetuated an emotional isolation devoid of personal attentiveness, with hierarchical principles of authority and obligation dictating family members' behaviour, and sentiment and sensitivity treated with suspicion. Face-to-face exchanges between husband and wife were infrequent, so it seems, and, even among the rich, spouses were rarely in private together. Looking outwards in the direction of community bonds, norms and sanctions, rather than inwards to the domain of interpersonal feelings and attachments, couples in premodern Europe would not have recognised Cathy's all-consuming devotion to Heathcliff: 'If all else perished, and *he* remained, I should still continue to be; and, if all else remained, and he were annihilated, the Universe would turn to a mighty stranger' (IX, 99).

---

[2] 'Modernity' is a term used by sociologists to describe the period of economic, political and cultural development in the West that began with the American and French Revolutions and, arguably, ended in the twentieth-century world of 'late modernity'. For most historians, however, the modern begins with the end of the Middle Ages and the start of the Renaissance. What I have referred to here as the 'premodern' is by historians such as Shorter and Stone more commonly termed the 'early modern' (thus distinguishing it from the subsequent period of 'classical' modernity).

One might imagine that sex, in this unforgiving world, could have been an opportunity for more tender intimacies, but in practice it was, according to Shorter, a perfunctory and mechanical activity, with women's participation purely a matter of child-breeding. Though we should be cautious when extrapolating common practices from the recorded edicts and prescriptions of the ruling strata, the theological consensus of the sixteenth and seventeenth centuries preached that sensuality was sinful, with intercourse prohibited when conception was impossible (which prevailing wisdom, lacking a proper understanding of menstruation, limited to the nine months of pregnancy). While nineteenth-century moralists would later condemn sexual pleasure that was not consecrated by love, the medieval Christian Church treated sensuality as a sin 'against nature' rather than against human feeling. 'Every ardent lover', so it was said, 'is an adulterer with his own wife' (cited in Morris 1972: 108). What 'nature' demanded was that the woman lie passively on her back, a position endorsed because, in the words of the French historian Jean-Louis Flandrin (1979: 162), it 'was the most favourable to procreation, and, probably above all, because it symbolised masculine domination and the fertilising gesture of the tiller of the soil'. Although Lawrence Stone observes that English attitudes to sexuality in the sixteenth and seventeenth centuries, particularly among the upper classes, were more permissive than those of Southern Europe at the time, he also reminds us that poor hygiene, frequent illness and, for the majority of the labouring classes, sheer physical exhaustion, would not have made sex an attractive prospect, even in less devout, and less patriarchal, relationships (Stone 1990: 304–7).

In terms of the division of labour, many historians have noted that women exercised considerably more autonomy within their own clearly demarcated domain – in the peasant economy this was domestic production and work in the adjoining farmyard and commons – than in the modern era, where, as Shorter sanguinely describes it, 'husband and wife consult about and co-operate on everything imaginable' (1977: 73). In Seccombe's (1992: 86–7) account, peasant housewives were, through their sex-specific labours, sufficiently integrated into the household economy to make them valued members of a 'patriarchal partnership', their formal legal subordination to their husbands existing alongside an unsentimental relationship of mutual dependency and accommodation that Seccombe suggests could be regarded as a premodern version of 'companionate marriage'. 'Between the farmer and his wife,' Houlbrooke says of the need for marital cooperation in the agrarian household, 'there had to be complete mutual trust and confidence'. Marriage may have been an unequal partnership, he concludes, but it was 'less unequal, and less different from marriage today, than might at first sight appear' (Houlbrooke 1984: 107, 119).

In urban areas as well, other historians have argued, 'women of the popular classes had a vital economic role which gave them a powerful and recognised position within the household' (Tilly, Scott and Cohen 1976: 454). But Shorter's analysis of gender relations in the premodern household is far less salubrious. He emphasises the callousness of the traditional patriarch, who demanded submissiveness from his wife and who often treated her as little more than an economic resource, sometimes less valuable than livestock. In peasant households in eighteenth-century France, Shorter writes, it was customary for the wife to stand behind her husband while he ate, only taking food for herself after he had finished. 'In the Deux-Sevres, wives were more the *premières servants* than the *compagnons* of their husbands' (Shorter 1977: 67).

The sexual revolution

Rocketing rates of out-of-wedlock pregnancies in the period between 1750 and 1850, although undoubtedly influenced by falling abortion rates and improved female health, are the most important statistical indicator, Shorter argues, that sexual attitudes and practices underwent a major transformation during the Industrial Revolution and the rise of capitalism. This statistical trend was apparent throughout Northwestern Europe and North America, 'from interior Massachusetts to the Alpine uplands of Oberbayern' (1977: 89). Community supervision of social interaction between the sexes had begun to weaken, with the peer group increasingly taking the place of parental, ecclesiastical and manorial authorities. The decline in monthly variations in premarital conceptions also showed how seasonal fluctuations in premarital intercourse – normally dictated by the calendar of festivals and by the privacy afforded by summer weather – was being replaced by a more even distribution of sex throughout the year. For the small proportion of the population living in cities, social control over sexuality was already laxer, and it is here, Shorter suggests, where the sexual revolution began. As urban life was denser, faster and more diverse, young men and women, particularly among the rapidly expanding proletarian class, found it easier to meet in settings where they were unknown or unsupervised, and where chance encounters, made more frequent by the development of a national labour market, played a greater role in mating choices. Higher recorded rates of bridal pregnancy in the cities suggest that urban couples were more inclined to sleep with each other before marriage, while higher rates of illegitimacy may reflect the ease with which a seducer could escape and disappear into the fog of a big city. While economic and geographical endogamy were scrupulously enforced in traditional rural communities, ensuring that wealth stayed within families and villages, the nineteenth-century growth in marriages between people from different places and, less prominently, different classes suggests, according to Shorter, 'the advance of true love: the sacrifice of community approbation for personal happiness, the sacrifice of money for self-realisation' (1977: 154).

'Love' and 'passion' are terms that then started to appear in accounts given by unmarried women to officials investigating their pregnancies, and observers began to record men renouncing handsome dowries in order to follow their heartstrings, as well as seducers choosing not to flee but to woo their pregnant conquests out of wedlock. Lawrence Stone describes the report of a surgeon working at a London hospital in 1751. A young woman from the country had been sent to London by her father, who was determined to sabotage her relationship with a lowly farmer's son. By the time her suitor had tracked her down, she was in hospital recovering from the amputation of a leg. The young man's love was blind to her physical disability, however, and the pair were married the next day on the hospital ward. The surgeon recorded how his clinical superior referred with awe to 'this strange, intoxicating distemper of love' which is 'surely one affection above all others that one would pray to be inoculated with' (cited by Stone 1990: 198–9).

The pain of love unrequited or betrayed also became a subject of social and psychological commentary in this period. According to Stone, England was seen by foreign observers as the place where marriage was increasingly founded on mutual affection and companionship rather than political and economic interest. Sophie von La Roche, after visiting London in 1786, was apparently 'not at all surprised to learn at the lunatic asylum of Bedlam that most of the young female inmates had been unhinged by thwarted love' (Stone 1990: 219–20). The sexual revolution, for Shorter, was therefore also a romantic revolution: 'a rush of sentiment swept over mating and dating, replacing familial and prudential considerations with "inclination", "affection", and finally "romance"' (Shorter 1977: 125). The growing desire for spontaneity and empathy in sexual relations – this, for Shorter, is the essence of modern romantic love – further dissolved the divisions, constraints and barriers of tradition: 'spontaneity, because it involves substituting extemporaneous dialogue for traditional scripts; and empathy, because it beats down the sex roles, the entire sexual division of labour that had customarily separated the lives and emotions of men and women' (1977: 152).

The transition from instrumental to expressive family relations also affected childcare practices, particularly among the middle classes. It was they, along with the nobility, who according to Ariès (1962) first 'discovered' childhood as a distinctive period of sweet innocence and vulnerability, and set about making the health, education and character development of the child the central preoccupation of the modern family. Improved incomes and living conditions reduced the need for bourgeois women to work and allowed the welfare of their children to increase in importance. The growth of maternal tenderness may have also broken that vicious circle described by Stone, in which the brutal treatment of children 'contributed to a "psychic numbing" which created many adults whose primary responses to others were at best a calculating indifference and at worst a mixture of suspicion and hostility, tyranny and submission, alienation and rage' (Stone 1990: 80). As the bond between parent and child became closer, parents were also likely to have better trusted their offspring's mating choices, or believed that they had successfully transmitted to them their values, and were therefore more relaxed in the supervision of their courtship practices.

While Shorter agrees with Philippe Ariès that the rise of expressive parenting, and with it the idea of the family as a moral and spiritual institution, was led by the middle classes, he argues that the growth of romantic love was primarily a lower-class phenomenon: 'The new proletarians of the eighteenth century were the vanguard of the sexual revolution' (Shorter 1977: 255). His argument here echoes Engels' claim that marriage for mutual affection was unheard of among the propertied classes, dominated as they were by economic interests, whereas among the working class, where there was no family wealth to protect and fortify, 'these marriages are the rule' (Engels 1942: 63–72). Historians generally agree that the rise in pregnancies outside marriage – the rate of which, in the course of the eighteenth century, surged everywhere in Western Europe, doubling, and sometimes quadrupling, according to country and region – was essentially a working-class trend. But Shorter's explanation for this – that the proletarianisation of men, and especially women, exposed them to an egocentric logic of self-gratification whose values then spread beyond the economic domain, so that 'the sexual and emotional wish to be free came from the capitalist market-place' (1977: 253–4) – is highly problematic. Eros is crudely naturalised – the romantic revolution of the eighteenth and nineteenth centuries, Shorter says, 'meant taking the lid off' sexual desire (1977: 261) – and there is limited acknowledgement of the way sexual relations are shaped and sublimated by culture, custom and material constraint. What is also overlooked from this Rousseauian standpoint, which even Engels seemed to share, is the extent to which the rise in extramarital childbirth reflected not the sexual emancipation of newly wage-earning women, but rather their growing vulnerability. Not only was this a consequence of the process of proletarianisation, but it also reflects a critical reconfiguration of gender relations.

Women in early capitalism

In the peasant economies of premodern Europe, men needed to marry early in order to acquire help managing their landholdings as well as to produce legitimate heirs. In Northwestern Europe, according to Seccombe (1992), the surveillance of sexual intimacy between publicly betrothed couples was more relaxed than we are often given to believe, and the supervision of courtship was certainly less repressive here than it was in the Mediterranean countries. The estimate that in early modern England around a quarter of all marriages involved women who were already pregnant suggests that prenuptial sex may have always been a socially accepted test of the couple's fertility, 'a silent counterweight to the moral wrath of the Church in a society where such importance was placed on the preservation of the family bloodline' (Seccombe 1992: 115). Indeed, the custom of sex before marriage in order to confirm a couple's reproductive viability must have survived sufficiently long in some rural areas for it to feature as a plot device in Thomas Hardy's *The Well-Beloved* (1897). The power of community sanctions against local men who reneged on their obligations and the practical need for men to find a wife are probably the most important factors explaining why roughly 80 per cent of prenuptial pregnancies during this early modern period led to marriage.

The dissipation of patriarchal and community control over courtship brought about by the structural and compositional changes of industrial capitalism, combined with the better short-term economic prospects of a proletarian male who chose to live independently rather than marry and support a family, placed women in a more precarious position, however. It is possible that premarital sex did indeed increase, perhaps because of men's greater freedom from moral regulation, and perhaps also because the value of a woman's virginity as a nuptial bargaining chip plummeted once male suitors were proletarianised and had no inherited property to offer in exchange (Stone 1990: 401–3). But these are speculations, and they are to some extent overshadowed by the fact that the statistical likelihood of an out-of-wedlock pregnancy being converted into a 'legitimate' birth declined from 79 per cent in 1670 to 63 per cent in 1800, according to Seccombe's analysis of English data, falling more precipitously in other regions of Europe. 'Proletarianisation', Seccombe (1992: 222) points out, 'generally made it easier to engage in premarital sex and for men to evade the obligation to marry in the event of conception. For women, on the other hand, proletarian "freedoms" often entailed an increased vulnerability – both economic and sexual – inducing them to seek out marriage partners at an early age.'

In Tilly, Scott and Cohen's (1976) analysis, Shorter's account of the eighteenth-century sexual liberation of women is a fairy tale which mistakes the changing social and economic *context* of premarital sexual practices for changes in the values and practices themselves. Increasing numbers of women worked outside the home, they point out, not because the market economy met their newly discovered self-interest, but because their traditional obligations to their families, whose resources were dwindling due to land enclosures, the decline of domestic industry and an increasingly polarised rural class system, forced them into wage labour.[3] Added to this was the impact of a cultural shift in English society from a bilateral lineage system, which was relatively symmetrical with regard to gender, to one which traced descent through the male line, allowing first-born sons to monopolise the rights of inheritance. The spread of primogeniture, which according to Perry (2004: 40) accelerated in England in the seventeenth century, effectively disinherited daughters from a share in their family's property, making the economic situation of increasing numbers of women, including those from more prosperous families, much more precarious. It is ironic that, as the domestic economy collapsed, and women lost their recognised place in the reproduction and inheritance of property, their displacement from the family status and production system put them at the forefront of the turn towards free-standing subjectivity, inwardness and the heightened consciousness of the self: 'the modern individual was first and foremost a woman' (Armstrong 1987: 8). Although women may have become, as a result, the pioneers of that mental and emotional reflexivity which was inseparable from the rise of the novel, the demise of bilateral and matrilineal household and kinship structures

---

[3] Around a fifth of England's arable land was enclosed and claimed for private ownership in the second half of the eighteenth century, with 40,000 small farms disappearing during this period. The landless proletariat of England increased from around 25 per cent of the population at the beginning of the century to 60 per cent by the end. Enclosures disproportionately affected the common fields, forests and 'waste' land which rural women in particular depended on for grazing domestic livestock, collecting firewood, catching wild rabbits and pigeons, and scavenging for wild nuts, berries and fruit. The contribution which women's access to the commons made to the survival of rural households, including those proto-industrial households already dependent on the money economy, cannot be overestimated (Perry 2004: 9–10, 62–4).

also left women – particularly newly proletarianised women – dangerously exposed to sexual exploitation.

As more and more women were thrown onto an occupationally restricted labour market – domestic service was their most likely destination, while smaller numbers found themselves dressmaking, laundering, in petty sales and victualling – competition for jobs depressed women's wages to between a third and a half of their male comparators. When productive labour was transferred from the home to the private premises of a capitalist where it was exchanged for a wage, many women were prohibited from following their husbands and fathers into the trades and professions that they were nonetheless experienced at. Barred, mostly by male guilds and labour organisations, from at least half of the trades in which women had previously worked (Perry 2004: 57), and excluded from medical, educational, political and other public associations, women were not only disqualified from formal access to better paid work, but also saw the cultural devaluing of their vernacular knowledge and wisdom as skilled metalworkers, midwives, weavers, bookbinders, teachers and healers. As the wage relation tightened its grip, 'the wife of the prosperous capitalist tended to become idle, the wife of the skilled journeyman lost her economic independence and became his unpaid domestic servant, while the wives of other wage earners were driven into the sweated industries of that period' (Clark 1919: 235).

In the rural economy, women were increasingly used as a reserve army of labour, hired on a seasonal basis, typically for low-skilled and low-paid work such as weeding, planting and gathering. Being badly paid, and often irregular, women's work in the eighteenth century provided little scope for them to live independent and self-gratifying lives. At best, they could contribute their meagre earnings to a family that was increasingly dependent on the cash economy for survival; at worst, they were an economic burden on their family of origin, for whom a daughter's swift marriage meant one fewer mouth to feed. Many young women were, in these circumstances, compelled to seek more assiduously a marital mate, not out of romantic choice but with economic security foremost in mind.

As women's material situation worsened relative to men, asymmetrical gender roles also began to take precedence over the commonalities of class. Bourgeois liberalism delivered *de jure* freedoms to men of all social ranks, but women were left marooned in a no-man's-land between feudalism and capitalism. 'The universities were open to the male offspring of brewers and haberdashers', Perry (1986: 104) reminds us, 'but closed to the daughters of the oldest noble families in England'. Dispossessed of class membership and solidarity, women were instead increasingly defined by their capacity to bear and raise children, and to provide sexual services to men. At the same time, however, men among the lower and middle classes were delaying marriage until their own economic circumstances were more favourable to supporting a family. Without the presence of the woman's family to enforce her lover's promises, and with working-class men also forced, by the vagaries of a national labour market, to place the search for work ahead of sexual loyalty, women's vulnerability to illegitimate pregnancy inevitably increased.

Affective individualism and bourgeois romanticism

Shorter's claim that the working classes led a sexual revolution in the eighteenth century must therefore be treated with circumspection, for higher rates of out-of-wedlock pregnancy are evidence not necessarily of changing sexual values and practices – which historians such as Louise Tilly suggest remained largely unaltered – so much as changing social relations and economic conditions. Lawrence Stone, on the other hand, argues that the development of Western modernity did indeed see a moral and cultural revolution in conjugal relationships, but that the 'leading sectors of value-change' were not the poor but rather 'the professional and gentry classes' (1990: 24). Sexual intrigue and romance, Stone points out, had been a latent preoccupation of the nobility since the period of the troubadours, becoming a prominent theme in the poetry and theatre of Elizabethan England, and later in the court of Queen Henrietta Maria and her husband Charles I. Although these currents subsided after the 1640s, in Stone's view they softened up the landed classes to the bourgeois denunciation of arranged marriages, a protest which became increasingly vocal in the eighteenth century. First the novelists, playwrights and moralists of the middle classes argued that children of both sexes had a right to veto the matches proposed by their parents; then the roles were reversed and it was parents who could veto the autonomous choices of their children. After that, the surge of what Stone calls 'affective individualism' asserted the right to personal happiness and self-realisation through 'companionate marriage': 'for the first time in history romantic love became a respectable motive for marriage among the propertied classes' (Stone 1990: 190).

As with our knowledge and understanding of love in the ancient world, Stone acknowledges the inevitable class bias that arises from the historian's dependence on the diaries, letters and memoirs of the literate classes to study something so universal, and so universally hidden, as sexual intimacy. But his argument is that this bias is mitigated by the evidence that the upper classes 'were the pacemakers of cultural change', and that they 'more or less successfully imposed their values on their social inferiors' (1990: 26, 339). The ethos and values of affective individualism, Stone suggests, were formed out of a number of cultural, intellectual and motivational practices. These included introspective interest in the self and its inner motives and desires, as well as a thirst for personal autonomy and a belief in the right, against the traditional demand for unthinking deference to social authorities, to greater privacy, self-expression and individual happiness. It was the Reformation which encouraged a preoccupation with one's inner self, and it was the Puritans, deprived of salvation through sacraments and desperate to master the fear of irreversible damnation, who were the experts in self-scrutiny. Consistent with this was the way the English Puritans of the seventeenth century pioneered a new genre of autotelic writing, cultivating their soul-searching sensibility through diaries, autobiographies and love letters. Letter writing became more common among women separated from their husbands and fathers during the English civil wars, and this period of conflict also handed many women greater independence and responsibility than they had previously enjoyed, not unlike the female nobility in war-torn Medieval Europe.

The paradox, of course, is that Puritanism involved a renunciation of the ethic of brotherliness, as well as demanding emotional sobriety and suppression of affect. How did a religion that fostered suspicion and inquisition result in an 'affective individualism' that bound husband and wife together in a spirit of reciprocal generosity and mutual love? Stone's answer implicitly invokes what Raymond Williams called a 'structure of feeling' – emergent meanings and values that are 'thought as felt and felt as thought', and which 'do not have to await definition, classification, or rationalisation before they exert palpable pressures and set effective limits on experience and on action' (Williams 1977: 132). Stone argues that late seventeenth-century England witnessed a hedonistic reaction against the Puritan experiment of 1640–60, a widespread hostility towards all forms of dogmatic enthusiasm combined with an ethic of tolerance that derived 'as much from indifference as from principle'. This spirit of indifference – 'extrovert, easy-going, and willing to tolerate diversity, if only for the sake of peace' – was ironically what allowed Puritanism itself to survive after the Restoration (Stone 1990: 152). Eighteenth-century political ideas about freedom of contract and voluntary consent also fed into this less fanatical, more liberal outlook, permeating Puritan culture itself. So did a growing humanist ethic of 'civility' and 'manners' which advocated more modesty, concealment and restraint in the exposure of the body and its waste products, and which encouraged the upper classes to claim more domestic privacy by introducing corridors into houses so that bedrooms could be accessed without passing through adjacent chambers. A burgeoning confidence in humans' ability to control nature and eliminate scarcity was also making it more credible to desire comfort and pleasure in this life, rather than the next, invalidating the 'siege mentality' of the preindustrial age and eventually turning the pursuit of happiness into a constitutional right.

A second factor contributing to the rise of affective individualism in the family was, Stone argues, the Puritan interpretation of 'holy matrimony'. Ironically for a religion so scrupulously utilitarian, early Puritan clerics such as William Perkins had argued against the Roman Catholic view that sex was an evil to be tolerated only in the service of human propagation. Instead sex within marriage was defined as a gift from God, an act of mutual intimacy which each party owed to the other as an expression of their blessed union. From this arose the idea of marriage as a unique emotional covenant requiring mutual respect and sharing, a relationship that was impaired, argued reformers such as Daniel Defoe as well as a number of French Cartesians, by women's lack of education and their inability to join with their husbands as intellectual equals. Protestant-inspired ideas of conjugal likeness and concord, sometimes informed by Italian Renaissance writers who had rediscovered Aristophanes' allegory in the *Symposium*, then began to influence wider cultural understandings of marriage, and of its possible relationship to selfhood and happiness.

When Richard Baxter's wife died in 1681, he paid tribute by writing her biography, and in the process painted a picture of their relationship that diverged from the standard patriarchal conventions of marriage. She was, he wrote, a woman who was 'quicker and more discerning' than himself, and he declared that he had been 'ruled by her prudent love in many things'. 'The Baxters', Stone (1990: 234–5) notes, 'clearly enjoyed a most intimate spiritual, intellectual and emotional relationship'. A century later it was US Founding Father, John Dickinson, who formulated, in an undated letter to his wife, the most memorable slogan for the cult of companionate marriage: 'I love you dearly – best of women, best of wives and best of friends' (cited in Stone 1990: 240). The love letters of William and Mary Wordsworth suggest that there were other men and women who had successfully united passion and friendship in their conjugal relations (Gay 1986: 57), and indeed MacFarlane (1986: 174–208) cites ample evidence of companionate marriages and romantic sentiments in England dating back as early as the sixteenth century. In Stone's view, it was the original Puritan belief that marriage could and should be a bond of reciprocal respect and affection which made possible a 'psychological relaxation' that opened personal life to greater emotional and sexual intimacy (Stone 1990: 175–6). This was, he argues, one unintended legacy of Puritanism that survived the process of secularisation, spreading upwards from the bourgeoisie to the gentry and then the aristocracy, and much later to the working class.

Finally Stone refers to a 'basic personality' change, most prevalent among the upper bourgeoisie and squirearchy, which may have been a mutually reinforcing product of more affectionate styles of parenting. Its ideal type was the 'Man of Feeling', a term popularised by Henry Mackenzie's 1771 novel of the same title, which, Stone wryly observes, offered its readers 'an outburst of weeping (by either sex) on average every ten-and-a-half pages' (1990: 163). This eighteenth-century 'new man' was more capable of personal intimacy and emotional expressiveness, both in marriage and with children, and was more 'easily moved to outbursts of indignation by cruelty and to tears of sympathy by benevolence' (1990: 180). The Man of Feeling, whether real or ideal, was influential enough to strengthen support for legislative reforms aimed at preventing cruelty to animals, abolishing the slave trade, ending brutish punishments like public flogging, and improving the treatment of prisoners and the mentally ill. His popularity may also have accelerated the trend towards more intimate styles of address, such as nicknames and endearments, between spouses, and between children and their parents, and towards a waning of the stiff reserve that characterised family relations among the middle and upper classes in earlier times.

Although Stone has little definitive to say about the precise origins of these proto-Romanticist personality traits, Colin Campbell (1987) argued that the ethic of feeling arose out of a pietistic strand of Protestantism which survived the general decline of Calvinism. Exported to the Puritan colony of New England, and subsequently reintroduced to Britain, this 'other Protestant ethic' fostered in its believers a desire to make the 'visible' church of their members approximate as closely as possible the 'invisible' church of those whom God had predestined for salvation. Although only God knew for sure whom among the church were truly members of the elect, these separatist sects believed that an anguished sensitivity to their own and others' suffering was a divine quality implanted by God, and they looked for emotional displays of grief, melancholy, pity and self-pity, as possible outward signs of candidates' inner state of grace. What arose from this, according to Campbell, was an emotional hedonism that found expression not only in romantic love but also in the day-dreaming practices of modern consumerism.

Marriage and the double standard

Most historians who have criticised the narrative of social change advanced by Shorter and Stone have argued that these skilled and entertaining authors 'exaggerate', as Houlbrooke says of Stone, 'the speed, extent and uniformity of change' in the values and practices of family life, paying insufficient attention to economic differentiations and overestimating the correlation between official doctrines and actual practices. Houlbrooke insists that there is sufficient evidence from surviving diaries and letters to indicate that in the sixteenth and seventeenth centuries love in marriage was already a valued ideal, and that 'expectations were high, emotional demands extensive, mutual involvement deep, and shared interests and sense of humour very important' (Houlbrooke 1984: 15, 104). Notwithstanding this dispute, the other obvious criticisms to be made of the theory of affective individualism is that its exaggeration of change, rather than misrepresenting traditional (or 'early modern') society, is the result of an inaccurate depiction of *modernity*, since it sentimentalises relationships that in practice remained stubbornly patriarchal. Thus, just as sexual permissiveness is casually conflated by Shorter with romantic love, so too have historians tended to overlook the coexistence of romantic love with compulsory female domesticity. Even in the courtly love tradition, the worshipped Lady had to wait passively at home while her lover proved himself through ennobling adventures and valiant deeds. In some imaginative variations – such as Chrétien de Troyes' *Erec and Enide* – the practices of knightly courtship persisted even after the lovers had married, but this division of the sexes into separate spheres of public adventure and private domesticity did not light an obvious path to a culture of mutual desire, sharing and companionship.

Stone, it is true, does acknowledge that the late eighteenth and early nineteenth centuries saw a wave of sexual prudery spread down from the lower-middle classes to the poor, and indeed he explicitly rejects a unilinear theory of family modernisation, speaking instead of 'huge, mysterious, secular swings from repression to permissiveness and back again' (Stone 1990: 422). Mark Poster, who is interested in the relationship between family organisation and personality formation, suggests that bourgeois youth was, 'almost from the beginning', driven by ideas of romantic love, but that these passionate sentiments rarely survived the middle-class norms of marital respectability and delayed gratification (Poster 1978: 168–9). These norms imposed a separation of sex from love, and they were especially repressive for women.

Bourgeois men viewed women of their own class as saintly, asexual creatures whose natural virtues of modesty, chasteness and passivity made them perfectly suited for affective domesticity but incapable of sensuality, independent imagination and desire. In a curious reversal of the Greeks' understanding of male and female sexualities, it was now men who were believed to be the helpless servants of their natural appetites, and women who, lacking their own sexual desire, were tasked with the moral vocation of taming their husbands and channelling the men's baser instincts into the orderly transmission of wealth, blood and reputation. Bourgeois women gained a certain degree of moral superiority from the association of feminine virtue with sexual chastity, and it is argued by some historians that the desexualisation of women in Victorian society ironically made enduring relationships of passionate love *between women* a respectable complement to their heterosexual marriages (Smith-Rosenberg 1975; Seidman 1991: 50–5). But the requirement that women sublimate their desires into socially acceptable forms came at considerable personal cost. Canonised by Coventry Patmore's poem, 'The Angel in the House' (1854), the oppressive impact on women of the Victorian model of femininity was memorably denounced by Virginia Woolf in 1931, in a talk she gave to the Women's Service League on the subject of women's employment. Her first published article, she told the assembled audience,

was about a novel by a famous man. And while I was writing this review, I discovered that if I were going to review books I should need to battle with a certain phantom. And the phantom was a woman, and when I came to know her better I called her after the heroine of a famous poem, The Angel in the House … . She was intensely sympathetic. She was immensely charming. She was utterly unselfish. She excelled in the difficult arts of family life. She sacrificed herself daily. If there was chicken, she took the leg; if there was a draught she sat in it – in short she was so constituted that she never had a mind or a wish of her own, but preferred to sympathise always with the minds and wishes of others. Above all – I need not say it – she was pure. Her purity was supposed to be her chief beauty – her blushes, her great grace … . And when I came to write I encountered her with the very first words. The shadow of her wings fell on my page; I heard the rustling of her skirts in the room. Directly, that is to say, I took my pen in my hand to review that novel by a famous man, she slipped behind me and whispered: 'My dear, you are a young woman. You are writing about a book that has been written by a man. Be sympathetic; be tender; flatter; deceive; use all the arts and wiles of our sex. Never let anybody guess that you have a mind of your own' .... I turned upon her and caught her by the throat. I did my best to kill her. My excuse, if I were to be had up in a court of law, would be that I acted in self-defence. Had I not killed her she would have killed me. (Woolf 1966a: 285–6)

Men, by contrast, may have had a recognisable mind of their own, but they too were injured by the doctrine of separate spheres. For bourgeois men in particular, the act of sex, with its incontinent lust and unprofitable climax, was the antithesis of middle-class family sobriety and the utilitarian prudence demanded by their economic identity, as well as being a shameful stain on their wives' moral purity and on the spiritual union of husband and wife. One result of this was the sexual double standard, which pardoned men for adultery – typically with lower class women from whom they did not expect bourgeois standards of feminine delicacy – but at the same time condemned sex before or outside marriage by bourgeois women as an offense of utmost gravity. In England the Matrimonial Causes Act of 1857 made divorce a lawful option for a man whose wife had strayed from the marital bed; but it was only in 1923 that the law recognised a husband's adultery alone as sufficient grounds for a woman to file for divorce. In Chrétien's romances, love was in conflict with the chivalric code of knightly honour, but there was no guilt attached to the betrayal of a loveless marriage. By the time of Tennyson's *Guinevere* (1859), in contrast, a new patriarchal 'morality' was apparent: the Queen's adulterous relationship with Lancelot has become the most ignoble act of treachery, and she is cast aside by King Arthur who, as Belsey (1994: 122) puts it, 'executes his own divorce'. The industry of prostitution was another product of this moral asymmetry, for the splitting apart of men's sexual and affectionate ties – sex, for a typical bourgeois man, could be had with a degraded object but not with a respectable person – meant that 'a class of fallen women was needed to keep the rest of the world pure' (Thomas 1959: 197).

It was Freud who, in a 1912 essay, famously extrapolated from bourgeois men's predilection for prostitution a 'universal tendency to debasement in the sphere of love'. Childhood libido, he argued, is first drawn towards people – normally the opposite-sex parent or siblings – who are involved in the child's care. When this early 'affective' libido is subsequently sexualised by the more powerful 'sensuous' libidinal currents of puberty, it then encounters the incest taboo and is repressed. In ideal circumstances, Freud suggests, the repressed desires find a satisfactory outlet through sexual contact with an adult who resembles the tabooed object, and who, in the course of time, attracts the 'affection' – not just the sexual appetite – that was originally tied to the earlier infantile attachments.

According to Freud, however, two factors impede this healthy resolution to the persistence of infantile desires, the one internal and the other external. First, there is the intensity of the original affective bond, since the more powerful this attraction, the less likely it is to find a corresponding substitute in the real adult world, and the more likely that the young adult's sexuality will instead remain repressed and fixated on unconscious incestuous fantasies. The second factor, Freud claims, is the 'frustration in reality' deriving from the absence of, or impermissible access to, suitable substitute object-choices. As a consequence of the moral prohibition on adolescent and premarital sexual activity – 'the long period of delay, which is demanded by education for cultural reasons, between sexual maturity and sexual activity' – young adults suffer further sexual repression. The outcome of this is a condition of 'psychical impotence' that Freud claimed was a 'universal affliction under civilisation' (Freud 2001: 187, 184).

In this psychological condition, the association of sexual pleasure with the satisfaction of forbidden incestuous desires makes sex seem degrading and polluting, and therefore something incompatible with the moral respectability of marriage. That this is a psychical, not a physical, impotence is proven by the fact that sexual gratification is still obtained (by men) through contact with people who are 'debased' into pure sexual objects (prostitutes being the most obvious example). 'The whole sphere of love in such people remains divided in the two directions personified in art as sacred and profane (or animal) love. Where they love they do not desire and where they desire they cannot love. They seek objects which they do not need to love, in order to keep their sensuality away from the objects they love' (Freud 2001: 183). Stone's lengthy summary of James Boswell's startlingly frank and guilt-ridden sexual diaries illustrates this well. Boswell, Stone (1990: 374) observes, was tormented by a 'failure to link *Eros* and *Agape*: lust and love', an affliction that became particularly problematic for him after his marriage in 1769 to a woman he was deeply attached to. Insatiably promiscuous, Boswell often suffered from impotence when he was seducing women of his own social class, but always recovered his virility with prostitutes, servants and lower class mistresses. According to Stone's count, Boswell contracted gonorrhoea at least seventeen times in his sexual career, yet he never infected his wife. She in turn showed remarkable forbearance of his sexual exploits – which he always confessed to her – as long as he did not confuse them with love.

Freud's attempt to universalise the double standard is obviously flawed, since what he described was clearly the product of specific class and gender conditions. To be able to satisfy their sexual desires through contact with women from a lower social class – 'a woman who is ethically inferior, to whom he need attribute no aesthetic scruples, who does not know him in his other social relations and cannot judge him in them' (Freud 2001: 185) – these men logically could not be from the lower classes themselves[4]; and for bourgeois women to not engage in the same practices, either their character formation had to involve different psychological dynamics, or, more pointedly, the moral rules governing sexual relations had to be far more repressive for them than they were for men. It is hardly surprising, then, that Freud saw complete 'sexual anaesthesia', rather than simply sexual inhibition in marriage, to be the more common symptom among women 'who have never got over their parents' authority and have withdrawn their affection from them either very incompletely or not at all' (Freud 1991: 150). Such is the condition of father-loving Maggie Verver in Henry James's *The Golden Bowl* (1904).

Historically, the conventional sociological explanation for the double standard was that it arose from the economic interests of propertied men who, in order to prevent the fragmentation and dispersal of their wealth, needed to stop their daughters and wives from producing illegitimate children with a legitimate claim to their wealth. But since the double standard has long survived the contraceptive pill, this explanation is clearly inadequate. Patriarchy seems to be more responsible than class, with the policing of women's premarital virginity, or their sexual monogamy, a direct expression of male domination and control. The explanation, in other words, is 'to be found in the desire of men for absolute property in women, a desire which cannot be satisfied if the man has reason to believe that the woman has once been possessed by another man' (Thomas 1959: 216).

That said, we should not discard too hastily Freud's insights into the psycho-sexual development of the child, not least because the bourgeois family whose effects he took to be universal soon became the most prevalent family form in modern Western societies. This family brought with it greater emotional

---

[4] This should probably be qualified, as the 'tendency to debasement' could also take the path of *self-debasement* before women of a higher social class. Dickens, in *Great Expectations* (1861), imagines this in Pip's self-degrading infatuation with the cold and imperious Estella, while Biddy, whom he recognises as a model of moral decency and intelligence, is too 'wholesome', and too much his class equal, to arouse his erotically aspirational desires. Another literary representation of the splitting of *eros* and *agape* is apparent in the Oedipal narrative of Lawrence's semi-autobiographical *Sons and Lovers* (1913). William and especially his brother Paul are clearly in love with their mother, whose emotional investment in their lives has enabled her to survive an abusive marriage. Both sons develop a misogynistic streak, and have faithless relationships with women whom they disparage for not possessing the virtues of their mother.

intimacy, with women expected to use their supposedly natural instinct for maternal love to fashion deep, morally cultivating bonds with their children, and to provide an oasis of tranquillity and affection for their work-weary husbands. In its classic nineteenth-century form, polarised gender identities were thus mapped onto a strict division between public and private spheres, whereby the nuclear family was constructed as a comforting sanctuary from the callous and impersonal world of male politics, commerce and rational self-interest. Though the home was a feminine sphere of nurturance and affection, the husband remained the head of the household, with the privacy of the family, and its freedom from interference by state and community authorities, meaning there were few external restraints on his power, and few opportunities for women to assert their own needs.

If Freud was right that the strength of an infant's emotional attachment to a caregiver, as well as the strength of moral prohibitions on sexual desire, make 'psychical impotence' more likely, then this was certainly a risk in the nineteenth-century bourgeois family. Here exclusive emotional intimacy was combined with scrupulous standards of hygiene, a repulsion towards waste and incontinence, and strict weaning practices designed to foster self-control, such as strapping the child to the potty. Emotional affection, and particularly maternal love, was earned by the bourgeois child only in exchange for showing ruthless self-mastery and denial of sensory pleasure, with the threat of a withdrawal of parental love, rather than physical punishment, being the preferred parental sanction. As the nineteenth-century moral and medical war on childhood masturbation seems to illustrate, enormous pressure was placed on the child 'to give up bodily pleasure in favour of parental affection', and 'learn the difficult emotional lesson that its own body was disgusting' (Poster 1978: 173–4). The insularity of the bourgeois nuclear family, the untrammelled power – and affection – of the parents, and the tendency for children, in the absence of other role models, to emotionally identify with the parent of the same sex, all made rebellion against sexual repression a traumatic prospect for the child. The latter was, instead, encumbered by a punitive superego, a pervasive fear of guilt and, in the case of many men, an apparent inability to feel affection, respect and desire for the same person.

Troubled pleasures

The growth of affective individualism in modern societies, and the development of a more emotionally literate form of selfhood centred on the domain of conjugal relations, is today an established tenet of the history of the Western family. We have seen that questions have nonetheless been raised about the scale and depth of these changes, as well as their uneven relationship to gender and class hierarchies. A reductively linear account of the progressive growth of affective individualism is also problematic if it underplays the significance of the transformations in social and personal life that appear to have occurred in the last 50 years. Eva Illouz (2012) argues, for example, that the romantic sensibility of the early nineteenth century would be unrecognisable to our own more radical culture of sexual freedom and emotional authenticity, and that we need to acknowledge this historical contrast in order to make better sociological sense of the doubts, instabilities and sufferings that today seem so endemic to personal relationships in the contemporary world.

If Jane Austen's fictional heroines are uncannily self-possessed, Illouz argues, it is because they remind us how courtship practices among the English gentry of the early nineteenth century followed well-known sequences of ritual courtesy and endearment that progressively tested a suitor's moral character, and incrementally advanced a relationship in reciprocal ways without exposing the woman, in particular, to emotional rejection or psychological humiliation. For all that has been written about the history of affective individualism, Austen's novels are cultural testimony to a world in which the ardour of expectation, the hopes of happiness and the erotic force of desire were not intrinsic properties of the self to be disclosed and exchanged in risky relations of potentially overwhelming intimacy, but rather socially sanctioned emotions that were produced and fashioned through normatively regulated practices. Feelings of love took gradual shape, in other words, in the moral crucible of social rituals and roles. Instead of being an uncontrollable emotion that 'idealises the object of love to the point of blindness', love, for Austen, was the education of the passions through the modest expression and discernment of publicly recognised virtues. The embeddedness of romantic practices and sentiments in a common moral universe meant that, at least for middle-class women of the eighteenth and nineteenth centuries, 'the self was less vulnerable to others' gaze and to their validation, precisely because the actors' sentiments did not radiate from the interiority of their self' (Illouz 2012: 23, 40). It is with this contrast in mind that Alasdair MacIntyre described Austen as 'the last great effective imaginative voice' of Aristotelianism, and why he regarded the popularity of Irving Goffman's interactional theory of identity management to be symptomatic of a demoralised world in which objective standards of character, merit and honour have been eclipsed by an 'emotivist' dependence on the presentation of self (MacIntyre 1985: 240, 115–17).

Illouz not only recognises the historical role that was played by eighteenth-century ideals of romantic love in recognising and promoting the emotional autonomy of women, but also wants to draw attention to the contrast between the ethical codification of early modern courtship rituals, and the later culture of emotional self-scrutiny and self-management of bodies and feelings that only really began to develop in affluent Western consumer societies in the second half of the twentieth century. In the former case, new ideals of companionate love were still largely articulated within familiar economic and normative structures, whereas what occurred in the twentieth century was the radical disembedding of romantic choices from moral regulation and class endogamy. The eventual outcome was 'a self-regulated market of encounters' between highly individualised actors, for whom volatility, uncertainty and emotional turbulence in the realm of love is the price paid for detaching sexual desire, and sexual attractiveness, from the socially constructed – and socially exclusionary – virtues of moral character and personhood.

I will return to the contemporary sociology of love later in this book, but as we have ended this chapter with a reference to nineteenth-century fiction, I now want to look in more detail at the role of the novel in the cultivation of the Western tradition of romantic love. Feminist critics of the novel have often viewed the discourse of affective individualism as an ideological ruse that conceals the gender asymmetries inherent in the patriarchal family, and even Austen's more sophisticated moral vision has not escaped censure for praising feminine self-abnegation and marital domesticity as the only respectable career for women. There are exceptions to, and subversions of, the dominant patriarchal discourse of the romantic novel, however, and many of the classic Regency and Victorian novelists found skilful ways of acknowledging female sexual desire and advancing more subtle, unconventional and ambivalent treatments of matrimony. It is to the troubled pleasures of the nineteenth-century love story that we now turn.

5

Novel passions

Given the conflicts and tensions characteristic of the bourgeois nuclear family, it is perhaps unsurprising that the eighteenth- and nineteenth-century romantic novel has been regarded as a key ideological mechanism for stabilising, in the minds of an increasingly literate public, the contradictions and uncertainties of love in early capitalist modernity. The novel played a crucial role in developing the narrative element that today is often regarded as a definitive ingredient of romantic love, in which lovers tell a story about themselves, aestheticise their relationship and construct a past and a future together that speaks of identity, self-realisation and an Aristophanean fusion of souls. The romantic novel was also founded on the feminisation of love, however, and this entailed a gendered discourse that held a woman's life to be perfected in virtuous wedlock, while men, their sexual impulses softened by marital morality and feminine tenderness, were better able to fulfil their social identities and responsibilities in the rational world of politics, commerce and civilisation.

By the middle of the eighteenth century the novel was already competing with religious and political writings for a share of the reading public, and by the end of the century, according to some estimates, as much as 80 per cent of the population of England were reading novels (Perry 2004: 25, 7). With demand sustained by the establishment of circulating and subscription libraries, as well as book review sections in popular magazines and journals, around 2,500 or more novels were published in Britain in the classical period studied by Ruth Perry, from Richardson's *Clarissa* (1748) to Jane Austen's *Persuasion* (1818).

Perry agrees with the critics of the demographic approach to the study of the history of the family, noting that statistics on household composition, even if they indicate continuity of family structure, fail to register a 'transformation in the psychological meaning of kin relations'. What is critical for her is a cultural shift in the understanding of what constituted the primary kinship group: 'a movement from an axis of kinship based on consanguineal ties of blood lineage to an axis based on conjugal and affinal ties of the married couple' (Perry 2004: 2–3). The conflicts this created between traditional obligations to parents and siblings (as well as to family property, status and lineage) and more personal responsibilities for one's spouse and dependent offspring were especially disorientating to women. In the new literary form of the novel, Perry notes, these conflicts were articulated and managed through an 'obsessive concern with defining family membership' combined with a preference for sentimental endings which tried to reconcile, if only through nostalgic remembrance, marital obligations with more extended family ties.

These conflicts may also have fostered complex erotic attachments among family members. Oedipal desires, for example, were believed by Freud to be an inevitable consequence of close parental affection and care, and marital choices may have been both an expression of and an attempted solution to the fears and longings of children reared in a culture of affective individualism. A woman might feel that she could emotionally honour her duty to her father, for instance, by marrying a man in his likeness, or she could remedy her orphaned identity by finding a spouse with the dispositions of a loving parent. While the transition from consanguineal to conjugal ties marked, at the level of culture, a historical break with the past, ontogenetically – that is, at the level of individual psychological development – it was a rupture that had to be experienced anew by each generation of offspring. As the family became, in Foucault's words, the 'obligatory locus of affects, feelings, love', its emotional inwardness fostered in children an attraction to their parents that was psychologically deeper and more personalised than the more traditional ties of consanguineal loyalty, and which made their own adult search for love and intimacy a troubled journey plagued by the memory of older attachments. Since 'sexuality has its privileged point of development in the family', Foucault (1990: 108–9) observes, it 'is "incestuous" from the start'.

Freud had argued that overcoming incestuous fantasies and securing 'detachment from parental authority' was 'one of the most significant, but also one of the most painful, psychical achievements of the pubertal period' (Freud 1991: 150). With this in mind, it was an interesting paradox of early Victorian fiction, Robert Polhemus points out, that the prohibition on explicit references to sex actually allowed novelists to paint more complex erotic landscapes serving these otherwise discordant and unconscious needs. In his view the 'cultural purpose' of the 'incestuous bias' implicit in much of this literature was 'to promote marriages of positive filial feeling and kindred responsibility', allowing lovers to break with their families of origin and at the same time preserve an emotional connection to them (Polhemus 1990: 182). We should not overlook the darker side of the changing emotional nexus of the family, however, for the growing eroticisation of domestic relationships, combined with a weakened appreciation of the family as a unit of collective welfare, was stripping daughters and sisters of the protective cloak of family blood and honour, and increasingly turning them into objects of male possession. This was, Perry notes, also reflected in the novel:

> As daughters were redefined as strangers-in-the-house and commodified as "chickens for other men's tables", fathers took less responsibility for them and mothers began to feel competitive with them. Perhaps that is one meaning of the plots in which stepmothers and even occasionally biological mothers, envious of the heroine's beauty, intelligence, or learning, denigrate or neglect her until she is forced to leave home. Brothers identified increasingly with their fathers rather than their sisters as evolving gender definitions dismantled sibling unity. Thus, both fathers and brothers began to see their female relatives less as extensions of themselves or members of their own clan, and more as possessions in their power and hence possible sexual objects, close at hand and available. (Perry 2004: 377).

'Reader, I married him'

The construction of women as displaced and orphaned souls needing to find their identities completed in marital domesticity and motherhood is one of the ideological devices deplored by feminist critics of the novel, which was fast becoming a powerful outlet for some of the dominant myths of bourgeois society. In the era of courtly love, the troubadour lyric and the *trouvère* romance placed *eros* at the motivational centre of the narrative, and although this passionate and subversive love was resolutely opposed to the false institution of marriage, it could still be deflected into the service of the social order: 'political enemies as well as dragons could be overwhelmed in the name of one's lady' (Boone 1987: 37). In the eighteenth and nineteenth centuries, similarly, the romantic novel became the chief ideological repository of the marital ethos, typically promoting wedlock, especially for women, 'as *the* ultimate signifier of personal and social well-being' (Boone 1987: 66). As the more inward-looking nuclear family took shape, the enfeeblement of community supervision not only raised the prospect of greater sexual and emotional intimacy, however, but also 'increased the possibility of unchecked exploitation of wives by their husbands'. The veneration of wedlock in literature was, Joseph Boone argues, the veneration of 'gender dichotomisation, hierarchy, and largely separate spheres of activity' (1987: 50). Companionate marriage was clearly not an equal one; Milton hailed the sensual and spiritual union of marriage in *Paradise Lost* (1667), but he still saw Eve as inferior to Adam: 'Hee for God only, shee for God in him' (4.299). The contradictions this necessarily implied were concealed in the novel, most commonly by making marriage the end rather than the beginning of the story, with the curtain closing before the rancour and inequities of marital life could be revealed to and recognised by the reader. Popular romantic fiction in the centuries that followed rarely departed from this formula, with marital domesticity magically resolving the torrid divide between body and mind, sensuality and morality, whose struggle typically generated the central narrative tension of the story. Once the tempestuous and unreliable flame of desire was mastered and subdued, lovers would find the proof of their eternal love in an affectionate look of mutual recognition exchanged across the breakfast table. 'I hold myself supremely blest – blest beyond what language can express; because I am my husband's life as fully as he is mine.' Thus Jane Eyre declares her final state of marital happiness. 'All my confidence is bestowed on him, all his confidence is devoted to me; we are precisely suited in character – perfect concord is the result' (XXXVIII, 519).

At the time of publication, *Jane Eyre* (1847) was received with hostility as an 'anti-Christian' attack on the conventions of female subservience, and today it is still recognised as a pioneering work of feminist individualism. The image of marital perfection with which the novel ends, however, compromises its radical message, a message that was already distorted by the constraints of a class-bound and colonially disposed imagination. In Terry Eagleton's analysis, the struggle for female self-assertion in Charlotte Brontë's novels, and the 'contradictory amalgam of smouldering rebelliousness and prim conventionalism' that is the manifestation of this, reflects the contradictory class location of the archetypical Brontë governess, whose intellectual and emotional literacy as a teacher is accompanied by economic dependency and subordination to a male employer. 'She lives at that ambiguous point in the social structure at which two worlds – an interior one of emotional hungering, and an external one of harshly mechanical necessity – meet and collide' (Eagleton 1988: 16). Brontë's 'smouldering rebelliousness' and 'emotional hungering' are evident in a letter she wrote to W. A. Williams in 1859 which criticises the fiction of Jane Austen for its lack of emotional depth: 'what throbs fast and full, though hidden, what the blood rushes through, what is the unseen seat of life and sentient target of death – *this* Miss Austen ignores' (cited in Armstrong 1987: 191–2). But in Nancy Armstrong's Foucauldian analysis, the treatment of female desire by Victorian novelists like the Brontës naively depoliticised its subject by imagining a 'natural' sexuality independent of the novel's own historical work of cultural and psychological construction.

> Underlying the rhetoric of nineteenth century literary realism is the assumption that middle-class respectability doomed the woman to a kind of half-life within society because by definition respectability required her sexual repression ... . I would like to suggest that novels themselves generated our modern conviction that social conventions systematically suppressed forms of sexuality which existed prior to those conventions and made them necessary. In place of the theory of repression ... . I will assume that these extra-social depths in the self were themselves products of Victorian culture. (Armstrong 1987: 165)

For postcolonial critics of the Victorian novel, on the other hand, the feminist individualism of novels like *Jane Eyre* was compromised and distorted by an imperialist narrative which excluded non-white women from the struggle for emancipation, or else defused the conflict between the sexes by conceptualising it in terms of a 'savagery' imported from the primitive world of the colonies. Rochester's West Indian wife, imprisoned in his attic for 10 years, provokes Jane's sympathy and identification – she is, Gilbert and Gubar (2000: 359–62) suggest, the 'dark double' or 'avatar' of Jane, whose animalistic rage against her captor is the acting out of Jane's own repressed rebellion against patriarchy. The tendency for male writers familiar with the Arabic Orient to associate North Africa and the Near East with 'sexual promise (and threat), untiring sensuality, unlimited desire', and then to use the imagery of the Orient to paint pictures of illicit sexuality that Western readers would otherwise find unpalatable, was first noted by Edward Said in *Orientalism* (1979), his neglect of the homoerotic elements of orientalism notwithstanding (Boone 1995). The libidinal fantasies of Emma Bovary and Frédéric Moreau, for instance, are 'packed with Oriental clichés: harems, princesses, princes, slaves, veils, dancing girls and boys, sherbets, ointments, and so on' (Said 1979: 190). Jane Eyre's struggle, of course, is not so much for erotic fulfilment as for personal autonomy and loving respect. Nonetheless, Brontë's tendency to use non-Western characters to signify not just Jane's angry desire for freedom but also the coarse spirit of male domination – Rochester, for example, is at one point resentfully compared by Jane to a 'sultan' bestowing gifts and favours on her as if she were his degraded 'slave' (XXIV,

310) – suggests an uncomfortable collusion with racism that has been referred to as 'feminist orientalism': 'by figuring objectionable aspects of life in the West as "Eastern", these Western feminist writers rhetorically define their project as the removal of Eastern elements from Western life' (Zonana 1993: 594). Charlotte Brontë may have opposed the inhumanity of colonialism, but her position 'arises not out of concern for the well-being of the "dark races" subject to British colonisation', Susan Meyer argues, 'but primarily out of concern for the British who were, as the novel's figurative structure represents it, being contaminated by their contact with the intrinsic despotism and oppressiveness of dark-skinned people' (Meyer 1989: 261). The contamination is eventually eliminated by means of Bertha's self-immolation, a sacrificial act that recalls the Indian custom of sati, as well as the British colonial administrators' initial sanctioning of it (Spivak 1985). In the purified marital world that the reader is finally left with, we should also note the praise that Jane, at the end of the novel, generously extends to the pious missionary St. John Rivers who is busy martyring himself to the advancement of Christian civilisation: 'Firm, faithful, and devoted, full of energy, and zeal, and truth, he labours for his race; he clears their painful way to improvement' (XXXVIII, 520–1).

Colonial acts and prejudices haunt the pages of Victorian literature, but in matters of romance it was the mythical tranquillity of the bourgeois family that had the greatest rhetorical appeal. In the typical courtship plot of the eighteenth- and nineteenth-century novel, the heroine was initially in thrall to an unscrupulous or tyrannical male, and either had to be weaned from this oppressive relationship by a more admirable and devoted wooer (Darcy, for example, must free Elizabeth from the spell of Wickham), or else rescued by the original seducer's own reformed generosity and appreciation (Mr. B. becomes Pamela's husband and protector). The idea that masculine brutishness can be tamed by feminine innocence – a narrative that became a staple of popular romance in fiction and film in the centuries that followed the birth of the novel – also constructed marriage as an ingenious private solution to the inescapable reality of a patriarchal society, for the husband, however much reformed, must always retain sufficient menace to protect his wife's virtue from the other brutal men who will inevitably rule this world. The message here explains the feminist account of the integral connection between male violence against women and the 'protective' marital compact. 'Female fear of an open season of rape', Susan Brownmiller (1976: 16) wrote, 'was probably the single causative factor in the original subjugation of woman by man, the most important key to her historic dependence, her domestication by protective mating.'

Pamela (1740) established the moral contours of this now familiar dynamic, with love 'first eroticised as an antagonistic struggle between "feminine" virtue and "masculine" vice, and subsequently as a complementary alliance of male "master" and female "servant" in the socially approved sexual hierarchy of marriage' (Boone 1987: 86). A 'schizophrenic image of femininity' was one result of this narrative trope, Boone argues, as bourgeois women were praised for their chaste domesticity and feminine grace, but were still 'expected to exude the sexual attractiveness necessary to lure those "unregenerate Adams" to the path of righteousness and matrimony' (1987: 60–1).

In the gothic seduction plot, aggression against a woman's virtue was a moral scandal, but the general social conditions of male dominance and female passivity were rarely challenged, with the tragic death of the female victim often conceived as the woman's only possible liberation from unhappiness. This was the fate of brave *Clarissa* (1748), as well as that of *Anna Karenina* (1878), *Tess of the D'Urbervilles* (1892) and, though hers was a psychic rather than physical death, of Sue Bridehead in *Jude the Obscure* (1895). Walter Scott's *The Bride of Lammermoor* (1819) dramatised the growing conflict between romantic love and the religious and patriarchal values of family loyalty. Though in this novel the heroine rebels against an arranged marriage by murdering her husband on their wedding night, Lucy internalises the impossibility of her situation, is gripped by violent confusion and succumbs to a grotesque, convulsive death.

Treated as the tranquil but essentially unremarkable successor to the love story's narrative climax, married life itself was rarely a sustained subject of novelistic commentary. When the problems and conflicts of marriage were indeed addressed, they were typically depicted with comic sexist stereotypes – one thinks here of the Bennetts in *Pride and Prejudice* (1813), for example, or the Tullivers in *The Mill on the Floss* (1860) – or else reduced to the delusions and deficiencies of individuals, rather than being a reflection of the institutional organisation and values of heterosexual wedlock. Bleaker portraits of marriage were also inclined to locate the source of suffering in an organic or metaphysical realm beyond human control. An atmosphere of 'cosmic doom' pervades *Jude the Obscure*, Boone highlights by way of illustration, which conveys 'an ultimately pessimistic view of *all* sexuality as tragic, and of flesh and spirit, man and woman, humanity and universal malignity, as irreconcilable binary oppositions' (1987: 129). Tolstoy's short story 'The Kreutzer Sonata' (1889) makes the conflict between flesh and spirit a sadistic sex war, reflecting the author's ultimate conviction that sensuality is a sordid vice and that 'love in its various developments is not a fitting object to consume the best energies of men' (Tolstoy

2004a: 202). In the *Liebestod* and *amour passion* traditions more characteristic of Continental fiction, on the other hand, sadness and pain were idealised as the only true testament of love's authenticity, bespeaking a profundity of desire and a longing for romantic oneness that could only be realised – as exemplified by *The Sorrows of Young Werther* (1774), *Madame Bovary* (1856) and *Wuthering Heights* (1847) – in a Wagneresque death. If the passionate delirium of love cannot, after all, resist routinisation and defilement by the demands of practical and patriarchal life, only the annihilation of that love can save it from disgrace.

Romance and the slave narrative

Novelistic representations of love are not exhausted by their ideological functions, however, and we must not lose sight of the more progressive and subversive themes in Victorian fiction, and the way literary idealism fostered disaffection as well as reconciliation with the status quo. The romantic imaginary, as Herbert Marcuse wrote of the 'affirmative' character of bourgeois aestheticism, expresses 'not only the justification of the established form of existence, but also the pain of its establishment'. 'By making suffering and sorrow into eternal, universal forces, great bourgeois art has continually shattered in the hearts of men the facile resignation of everyday life.' With its exalted sense of tragedy and its exorbitant idealism, romanticism 'has planted real longing alongside poor consolation and false consecration in the soil of bourgeois life' (Marcuse 1968a: 98–9).

Literary historian Rudolph Binion argues, in any case, that the years 1879–1914 saw an unprecedented cultural campaign *against* the romanticisation of the bourgeois family, with mainstream European novels and plays attacking the possessiveness, authoritarianism and patriarchal violence characteristic of a family form that conjugal birth control had made smaller and more emotionally toxic (Binion 1994). Other literary theorists have stressed the importance of reading the nineteenth-century romantic novel with a closer attentiveness to the historical context in which it was written. The first generation of African American novelists, for example, have often drawn criticism from modern historians of black literature for the way they passively replicated the ideological structure of the white Victorian marriage plot. They were also reproached for using black women characters to demonstrate and defend the purity and virtuousness of all African Americans, thus causing 'black female sexuality', as Gloria Naylor (1989: 22) writes, to be 'whitened and deadened to the point of invisibility'. William Wells Brown's *Clotel* (1853), the first published novel by an

African American, included a light-skinned mulatto as its heroine, a formula that would be copied by black feminist novelists like Pauline Hopkins and Frances Harper, allegedly to make novels about black people more appealing to a white readership for whom slavery was more tragic if the victim was nearly white. Although Brown's protagonist, Clotel, eventually drowns herself to escape being returned to slavery, the story also ends in standard fashion, with the marriage of Clotel's daughter. This use of the sentimental romance narrative by black authors appeared to carry on well into the twentieth century, with Jessie Fauset's novels in the 1920s and 1930s criticised by Barbara Christian for featuring 'light-skinned women who unquestionably claim propriety as the highest ideal', and who 'pursue the values of material success through marriage and inevitably believe that refinement is a reflection of spirituality' (Christian 1980: 43).

Overlooked by many critics, however, is the distinctive meaning that marriage had to the former slave population of America. 'While modern minds are inclined to view marriage as an oppressive, self-limiting institution,' Ann duCille points out, 'for nineteenth-century African Americans, recently released from slavery and its dramatic disruption of marital and family life, marriage rites were a long-denied basic human right – signs of liberation and entitlement to both democracy and desire' (1993: 14). Brown thus begins *Clotel* by reminding his readers that marriage, 'the oldest and most sacred institution given to man by his Creator, is unknown and unrecognised in the slave laws of the United States' (I, 44). And although he also ends the book with a marriage, this is a marriage between fugitive slaves (as he himself was), who can enjoy legal wedlock only if they remain exiled in Europe. The way the narrative deals with the sexual exploitation of black women by white married gentlemen also exposes the moral hypocrisy of the white gentry classes, and with it the irony that marriage is 'a fundamental civil and moral right denied black men and women, for whom holy wedlock is a more "sacred obligation" than it is for the white men who abuse it' (duCille 1993: 22).

Harriet Wilson's *Our Nig* (1859) – the first published novel by an African American woman – also reads, superficially at least, like a sentimental seduction plot, but the narrative clearly exposes the way marriage was for many nineteenth-century women a pragmatic economic necessity rather than a romantic choice. In making the initial protagonist, Mag Smith, white, and her husband black, Wilson was also able to write about the infamy and disgrace of miscegenation. Although the final section of the story involves the marriage of Mag's daughter, her husband proves untrustworthy and soon deserts her. A conventional romantic ending would have been the tragic death of the abandoned wife, but instead Wilson closes with Frado's attempt to support herself and her child by turning her experience into the novel that is being narrated. Harriet Jacobs's *Incidents in the Life of a Slave Girl* (1861), despite being dismissed by one historian of American slavery for being 'too melodramatic' and concluding with an implausible 'all live happily ever after' ending (Blassingame 1979: 373), also famously eschewed the standard finale of the Victorian wedlock plot: 'Reader, my story ends with freedom; not in the usual way with marriage. I and my children are now free!' (XLI, 164) Through the voices of their long-suffering but independent-minded female protagonists, both Wilson and Jacobs 'accept the ideology of home and motherhood, but they demand their own power of definition, and of self-dependency, by insisting on the right to support their children and themselves within their own domestic and woman-centred economy' (Foreman 1990: 323).

DuCille also draws attention to the fact that both Hopkins and Harper wrote primarily for a black readership, and how the use of light-skinned, mixed-race characters was a political device by which black authors aimed not to pander to white readers' prejudices but rather 'to insinuate into the consciousness of white readers the humanity of the people they otherwise constructed as subhuman – beyond the pale of white comprehension' (1993: 8). The tendency for nineteenth-century African American novelists to desexualise their mixed-race heroines is also interpreted by duCille as a deliberate rebuttal of planters' myths about the natural sexual promiscuity of black women. The passionless mulatto maiden was 'a rhetorical device and a black political strategy designed to link black and white womanhood under the protective umbrella of chastity and virtue, even as dominant discourses sought to separate them' (1993: 31). The sexually pure and virtuous woman is a commonly criticised trope of Victorian culture, but it 'necessarily takes on a different political meaning when written in the face of centuries of institutionalised rape and sexual coercion. For early black women writers, literary passionlessness negated a negative: it endowed virtue to the historically virtueless' (1993: 32).

The improbability of love

Examples like these remind us that nineteenth-century literature needs to be read with historical sensitivity if its ideological forms are not to conceal its more progressive achievements. While love in the African American slave narrative was partly a protest against the brutality of the bondage system, European romantic fiction was playing an important role in fostering new understandings adequate to the 'double contingency', as Niklas Luhmann phrases it, that arises when individuals begin to assert their independence from social powers and rules, and start to place their trust in one another's freedom. The accelerating dynamic of individualisation in urban Europe and North America was by the nineteenth century creating conflicts and uncertainties that were not always reducible to the structures of sexuality, gender, class and ethnicity. As the prescriptive categories and constraints of the traditional order were loosened, knowledge of one's self and one's life experience became more singular, and this inevitably made it harder, as well as more appealing, to find one's existence affirmed and understood by another person. According to Luhmann, the semantics of romantic love evolved to address this problem, bringing into being a private world of intimate relationships that was communicatively coherent and in principle available to all, yet which was also licensed to depart from public opinion. Although the historical growth of intimacy first required concessions to the established order – by admitting, for example, that love was a malady or an irrational passion – the spread of individualism ultimately reinforced the need for a romantic code that legitimised attentiveness to the freedom and uniqueness of another, and which valorised the lover's affirmation of what the beloved finds of deep personal relevance. In Luhmann's words, 'in order for a commonly shared private world to become a differentiated entity, each person must be able to lend his support to the world of the other (although his inner experiences are highly individual), because a special role is accorded to him in it: he appears in the other person's world as the one who is loved' (2012: 17).

Being able to affirm the unique standpoint of the other is an improbability which the code of love functions to make possible. Thanks partly to the development of the novel, this code became increasingly reflexive, and it was the reflexivity of love which helped free sexual intimacy from the imperatives of social stratification, and started to bring love within the reach of everyone. For as long as love addressed itself to external, objective characteristics – to beauty, wealth, virtue or social standing – it was destined to remain a gift of the privileged, and there could be no commonwealth of love. Yet it was built into the code of romantic love to regard all codes, rules and calculations as a betrayal of love's authenticity. Excess and immoderation, extravagant devotion as well as unconditional submission, total joy as well as abject suffering, differentiated love from practical and economic interests, preventing social elites from rationalising and monopolising love as a moral or legal entitlement. Indeed in the very act of sexual reciprocity, the reflexive nature of love was also able to assert itself:

> In physical interplay one discovers that, beyond one's own desire and its fulfilment, one also desires the other's desire and thus learns that the other wishes to be desired. This makes it impossible for 'selflessness' to provide a foundation for one's actions and the form they take; rather the strength of one's own wish becomes the measure of what one is able to give. As a result of this, sexuality breaks out of the schematism of egoism/altruism and the hierarchisation of human relationships according to sensuality/reason. (Luhmann 2012: 28)

But this breaking out of reason and convention, this magical marriage of sense and nonsense that characterises the emotional coupling of bodies and desires, needed a language to prove its existence, a language that could appease the interests of moral respectability while also giving form to the mystery of sexual communion. For sex is an uncanny unity of sensory arousal and mental expansiveness, in which physical sensitivity to the smallest of touches is combined with an oceanic consciousness that is too elevated and all-encompassing to be able to know and name the details. When Robert Jordan, in *For Whom the Bell Tolls* (1941), lies with his lover Maria beneath the pine trees of the Sierra de Guadarrama, Hemmingway describes a metaphysical journey which 'led to nowhere, then to nowhere, then again to nowhere, once again to nowhere, always and forever to nowhere' (XIII, 166) – because the sexual act, in its dream-like transit of thought, fantasy and feeling, is the wilful intensification of precisely that which is out of place and time.

But place and time, nonetheless, must make their appearance. Life and its mortality dictate that the excessiveness of love cannot last. Desire exhausts itself, passions fluctuate and decline. Our bodies age and decay, absorbing the deadly inertia of passionless things. And mind itself asserts its irrepressible solitude, as individual perspectives diverge and clash. Even the most devoted lovers must also live in, and relate to, a world of erotic threats and rivals – of former lovers, suspected suitors, of tempting alternatives real and imagined – as well as inhabiting a world of non-loving and unlovable people and things, in which desire must be turned off for the sake of practical interests, profane projects and instrumental attachments. Love must battle with insufficiency as well as excess – and often with both at the same time, for an equal balance of passion in any love affair is rarely more than a fleeting equilibrium. The absolutism of love must therefore also accommodate the experience of difference, incongruity, doubt and separation, must assimilate these tensions and find in them the reason and the proof of love's existence. If love is an impossibility, then this impossibility must be reimagined as the very reason for love, its tragedy as well as its redemption.

'Precisely for this reason one had to hold resistance, detours or obstacles to one's love in high regard, because only through them does love endure. The word served as the medium for this duration,' Luhmann writes, 'in that words divide more clearly than do bodies, turning differences into information and thus also into the cause for continued communication' (2012: 71).

Luhmann is referring here to the French literary tradition, in which writing and reading were typically built into the texture of the narrative. 'Language,' Flaubert parenthetically remarks, describing Emma Bovary and Léon's exchange of confidences, 'is indeed a machine that continually amplifies the emotions' (III, I, 218). *Madame Bovary* is partly a mocking commentary on the foolishness of a feminine imagination that has fed too greedily on the illusions of romantic literature. But there is enough moral ambiguity in the novel for the reader to share without shame Emma's erotic hopes, fantasies and sufferings, and to grasp the exquisite partnership of love and suffering, imaginative expectation and inevitable disappointment, erotic yearning and necessary estrangement. Language doesn't just 'amplify' the emotions but, through the poetry of its texture, rhythm and form, it enchants the senses and excites a longing for that which reason cannot fully name. In this sense literary escapism is never as conformist as the cultural critic might assume: 'Desire, even when it is profoundly conventional, is at the same time the location of a resistance to convention. It demonstrates that people want something more' (Belsey 1994: 7).

But to want more is to flirt with disappointment, and thus erotic love found in the romantic novel a resource to endure privation through the cultivation of faith. In *Far from the Madding Crowd* (1874), Oak tells Bathsheba, while she suppresses a yawn: 'I shall do one thing in this life – one thing certain – that is, love, and long for you, and keep wanting you till I die' (IV, 26)[1] When Eustacia confides to Clym Yeobright in Hardy's *Return of the Native* (1878) that she fears her own passionate love for him will wane, Yeobright responds: 'When we see such a time at hand we will say, "I have outlived my faith and purpose", and die'

---

[1] In today's more utilitarian understanding of sexual partnerships, as Illouz (2012: 64–7) points out, such a willingness to surrender oneself to another, without any prospect of reciprocated affection, would be regarded as evidence not of strength of character and depth of feeling, but of psychological immaturity and lack of emotional independence. Although we are more likely to associate this surplus of love with women – in *For Whom the Bell Tolls*, for example, Maria responds to being rebuffed by her lover during a moment of physical danger by reaffirming her devotion: 'if thou dost not love me, I love thee enough for both' (XXI, 279) – Illouz (2012: 104) notes how the twentieth century saw a reversal of gendered courtship rituals, especially among the gentry class, which traditionally required men to display the strength and constancy of their affections while 'women were more likely than men to be emotionally reserved'.

(III, IV, 168). Every doubt, delay or decay of love is a test of faith: a foretaste of forsakenness and a presentiment of death.

Love is in the head

Women were unprecedented participants in the growth of the novel – as authors, readers and characters – and we must remember that romantic love could never have become a popular faith without women being recognised, and recognising themselves, as desiring subjects answerable to an inner world of thought and fantasy, as well as to an outer world of matrimonial convention. Robert Polhemus finds this recognition conveyed in Vermeer's *A Lady Writing* (circa 1665). The painting depicts a woman pausing in the act of writing, 'an individualised woman in the midst of life, the artist's contemporary, who possesses the power of thought and pen – the inner room of her own consciousness'.

> The painting joins the act of writing and the emotion of love. It leads us to imagine that love gives the lady occasion to write, but that writing, as she looks away from the page into the space of her consciousness, directs and feeds her thoughts .... Reflecting, sifting through images, memory, and experience, choosing words and syntax, one takes on authority – becomes an author. To write is to examine, extend, and populate an inner space, to preserve consciousness, to mediate experience and thought ... . In Vermeer's picture, the lady writing means individualism, means the desire to communicate intimately, means the projected, subjective drama of the erotic self – means, in short, love. The picture has an aura of passion about it, but the passion is private. We cannot see the forms that it takes, we can only see the expression of the woman who sees and feels inwardly. The deliberation over a letter makes it possible for a woman to be clothed, alone, and still, and yet to engage herself fully in a passionate act of love. (Polhemus 1990: 18)

To be able to enter that 'state of trance' which Virginia Woolf said was the precondition of the writer's vocation implies, of course, the possession of wealth, privacy and time. Woolf (1966b: 143) herself drew attention to the fact that 'of the four great women novelists – Jane Austen, Emily Brontë, Charlotte Brontë, and George Eliot – not one had a child, and two were unmarried'. Comparing the inwardness of the novelistic imagination to the meditative state of a fisherman, Woolf also highlighted the struggle of the female writer to carry on dreaming when the dream inevitably encountered the forbidden world of female desire. Her arresting image gives Vermeer's painting another layer:

I want you to figure to yourselves a girl sitting with a pen in her hand, which for minutes, and indeed for hours, she never dips into the inkpot. The image that comes to my mind when I think of this girl is the image of a fisherman lying sunk in dreams on the verge of a deep lake with a rod held out over the water. She was letting her imagination sweep unchecked round every rock and cranny of the world that lies submerged in the depths of our unconscious being. Now came the experience that I believe to be far commoner with women writers than with men. The line raced through the girl's fingers. Her imagination had rushed away. It had sought the pools, the depths, the dark places where the largest fish slumber. And then there was a smash. There was an explosion. There was foam and confusion. The imagination had dashed itself against something hard. The girl was roused from her dream. She was indeed in a state of the most acute and difficult distress. To speak without figure, she had thought of something, something about the body, about the passions which it was unfitting for her as a woman to say. Men, her reason told her, would be shocked. The consciousness of what men will say of a woman who speaks the truth about her passions had roused her from her artist's state of unconsciousness. She could write no more. (Woolf 1966a: 289)

In the novelistic tradition the idea that love is in the head is rightly associated with Jane Austen's romantic sensibility. Darcy declares that he loves Elizabeth for her 'liveliness of mind', and it is her emotional sophistication, sharp wit and moral discernment which, by singularising the heroine of *Pride and Prejudice* (1813), make her both highly attractive and, eventually, someone capable of her own discriminating love. Elizabeth's playful intelligence and generally perceptive appreciation of human character give her a depth that defies the typical male suitor who would confuse love with possession. This interiority is contrasted with the shallowness of her sisters, particularly the matrimonial strategising of Charlotte and the hormonal greed of Lydia. The conventional reading is that Lydia embodies the kind of crude, careless, unscrupulous sensuality that is anathema to the rationalism of both Elizabeth and her creator (it is notable, for example, that once she has accepted Darcy's marriage proposal, Elizabeth, Austen writes with deliberate emphasis, 'rather *knew* that she was happy, than *felt* herself to be so' (III, XVI, 352)). Austen, however, also uses Lydia to present a surprisingly convincing account, given the prevailing standards of morality, of a lustful woman's erotic imagination, which like Molly Bloom wants nothing but an anonymous and undifferentiated *more*. Fantasising about visiting the military camp in Brighton, Lydia pictures the 'earthly happiness' of streets 'covered with officers', sees herself as 'the object of attention, to tens and to scores of them at present unknown' and imagines being 'seated beneath a tent, tenderly flirting with at least six offers at once' (II, XVIII, 224). 'No one who pays close attention to this prose would say that Jane Austen did not know the flash of sexual fantasy and the pull of eroticism,' Polhemus (1990: 44) observes, 'and only someone insensitive to language could miss the appeal of Lydia's version, ironic and insidious as it turns out to be.' The novel may have delicately toyed with illicit desires in order to invoke the corrective authority of the conjugal family, but who really knows what female readers were doing with *Pride and Prejudice*, how selectively they may have engaged with the text and how attentive, or inattentive, they were to Austen's edifying message? 'Very often the novel writes of contracts but dreams of transgressions, and in reading it, the dream tends to emerge more powerfully' (Tanner 1979: 368).

Subverting gender

Patriarchal gender conventions are also overturned in other nineteenth-century novels. The double standard is subverted in Charlotte Brontë's *Villette* (1853), for although her desire for Dr John is not reciprocated, the reader is never in doubt that Lucy continues to love him even as she falls in love with Paul. Though Cathy's feelings for Edgar Linton pale beside her passion for Heathcliff, she still professes to love both men, and her erotic identity comprises both attraction to sameness ('I am Heathcliff!') and attraction to difference (Linton offers wealth and class status, but is also a model of gentlemanly affection and restraint that is in marked contrast to Cathy's own turbulent passions). In *The Mill on the Floss* (1860), faithful Maggie Tulliver is in love with three different men, including her brother and the handsome and charismatic Stephen. The subtly erotic, sensuous boat journey she shares with the morally suspect Stephen was condemned by some literary critics, who complained that her third suitor, the cultured and sensitive, though physically disfigured, Philip Wakem, was virtuous Maggie's true romantic match. Polhemus (1990: 185) detects a note of male chauvinism in these commentaries: 'Why must these feminine icons of sympathy, idealism, and faith have bodies and libido?'

In *Far from the Madding Crowd* (1874), Bathsheba runs her own farm with technical competence and emotional autonomy. Like Emma Bovary, Anna Karenina and Natasha Rostov, she is not content to be the passive object of an affluent gentleman's desire. She taunts and then politely rejects the repressed fetishist Boldwood, and she rebuffs Gabriel Oak for his rustic simplicity and primitive idealism. The real object of her passion is the brash and flashy pseudo-soldier, Troy. Troy teases and menaces with his virile, swashbuckling sword-play, and Bathsheba is captivated by his flamboyant shows of male prowess, his indifference to the voice of morality and his absolute determination to be, and to be for, solely himself – 'simply feeling, considering, and caring for what was before his eyes' (XXV, 130–1). The test of a stronger adversary arouses the independent-minded heroine, and she is thrilled by images of risk and transgression. Even when she has learned the extent of his betrayal of her, she is still consumed by paroxysms of jealousy and self-abasement. Pleading with Troy to kiss her, his wife, rather than the corpses of his lover and their illegitimate child, Bathsheba's desperation – 'a long, low cry of measureless despair and indignation, such a wail of anguish as had never before been heard within those old-inhabited walls' (XLIII, 237) – shows both the agonising vulnerability and the self-destructiveness of being in love.

In *David Copperfield* (1850), it is the morally upright Agnes who slowly reveals to David the folly of his youthful romantic idealism. Agnes is David's spiritual 'sister', as perfect a model of companionate marriage as we are likely to find in the canon of Victorian fiction. Yet Agnes' quasi-Platonic, perpendicular arm gesture, which is a leitmotif for her rational sensibility and saintly nature, appears in the book alongside the more insouciant posture of another love interest, the congenial rogue James Steerforth, who, even when his corpse is washed up on the shore at Yarmouth, is found lying in his signature pose, with his head still resting languidly on his arm. Martha Nussbaum suggests that David's love of Steerforth is more credible, and more erotic, than his loving appreciation of Agnes, despite the fact that David and Agnes end the novel happily married and with children. The reason for this is that Dickens' description of Steerforth captures, in a way that is never apparent in the character of Agnes, the unique singularity of an embodied person. In contrast to Agnes' impersonal gesture of reason and morality, Steerforth's deportment, Nussbaum writes,

> signifies nothing publicly communicable. It's only meaning is that he is there. It is mysteriously, sensuously, his, his beyond explanations and reasons. Its power to haunt comes not from the public world of reason-giving (in fact, it distracts David from that world, making moral judgement upon Steerforth's actions impossible), but from the private world of personal emotion and personal memory. It is irreducibly particular, characteristic of him and no other. It is what David recognises him by. And its easy charm and erotic grace are for David part of a world of shadows and moonlight, not of the world of reasons and justifications. He cannot explain its power. He can only repeat the description, in

> haunting and almost incantatory language, as if the description, and the gesture,
> were, for him, for us, a magic spell. Above all, the gesture, and the language used
> to describe it, are erotic. Agnes uses the body as an instrument of the moral … .
> In Steerforth's gesture we feel the mystery and excitement of a body animated
> by a unique spirit, pointing to nothing but itself and the bed on which it rests.
> (1990: 350)

Adam Smith had argued in *The Theory of Moral Sentiments* (1759) that sexual desire and romantic love are passions with no moral significance, because, being idiosyncratic, inscrutably exclusive and prone to excess, they cannot be imaginatively shared and judged by the rational spectator. We can identify and sympathise with sentiments that are the products of a person's reflective awareness – such as fear, anger, hope, gratitude or shame – but according to Smith the incontinence of the lover is too 'gross' and 'offensive' to permit moral identification: 'our imaginations can more readily mould themselves upon his imagination, than our bodies can mould themselves upon his body' (Smith 1982: 32, 29). Nussbaum disputes this, arguing that novels can enable the reader to experience the physical love felt by particular characters – including those besotted with morally deficient figures – and that the imaginative role play of the reader also enriches her or his own capacity to love. In *David Copperfield* there is, moreover, a reflexive dimension to the representation of love, for David is also written into the story as the imagined author of the book, someone who delighted in novel-reading from an early age, and who ends the book with a hint of sorrow at having to leave the imaginative activity of storytelling and soberly return to the moral reality of his family. David is primarily a writer rather than a reader, but this is still a subtle departure from the standard feminisation of the romantic imagination in Victorian literature, where it is the capricious and adulterous mind of an excitable woman – Emma Bovary, or Clare Newcome in Thackeray's *The Newcomes* (1855) – that is most likely to be found feeding on the racy pages of a French novel.

In one important scene, when the two men meet by chance after several years of separation, David has just been to see *Julius Caesar*, and his mind is so animated by the melodrama and fantasy of the theatre that, at the sudden sight of Steerforth, 'my old love for him overflowed my breast so freshly and spontaneously, that I went up to him at once, with a fast-beating heart' (XIX, 233). What David experiences here, Nussbaum argues, is what we all experience as lovers who read love stories, for in cultivating our imaginations these stories enable us to reach beyond reason and evidence in the same kind of 'generous fiction-making' that David expressed in his passion for the flawed and unreliable Steerforth. 'All love, is, in that sense, love of fictional characters; and literature trains us for that element in love' (Nussbaum 1990: 356). Or as Singer puts it, the amorous imagination functions like the dramatic imagination, enabling us to 'believe' in a character or person even though we know what we are seeing is only a fleeting and contingent reality. 'Love is the art of enjoying another person, as theatre is the art of enjoying dramatic situations' (Singer 1984: 20).

Conjugal love disrupted

As mentioned earlier, there is another erotic theme that we may be surprised to find in the pages of nineteenth-century fiction, and this is the spectre of incest. Heathcliff and Cathy are *de facto* siblings, even if they are not related by birth. Elizabeth's separation from her father is first rehearsed through her initial rejection and punishment of Darcy, and when she finally transfers her loving feelings from her father to someone who is, as Polhemus puts it, 'more deserving but also much less inhibiting to her self-realisation' (1990: 37), she wins her father's consent only because he sees in Darcy his own fatherly qualities: 'you could be neither happy nor respectable,' Mr Bennett tells his daughter, 'unless you truly esteemed your husband; unless you looked up to him as a superior' (III, XVII, 356). Feminist icon Maggie Tulliver loves her brother because she wants to be like him, wants to appropriate his masculinity and to enjoy the freedom and opportunities of his sex. But she is also in masochistic thrall to his bullying male chauvinism, and his power is a fatal aphrodisiac that can only be enjoyed – and destroyed – when they are drowned together in a climactic embrace. Pip is as infatuated with Miss Havisham as he is with Estella. Estella turns out to be his adopted sister (the daughter of his father-substitute, Magwitch); Miss Havisham is the mother he never had. When Pip extinguishes Havisham's burning body by embracing her, it is a moment of physical and spiritual purification that Polhemus describes as 'one of the great visionary erotic passages in literature' (1990: 155). In the second, less melancholy ending of *Great Expectations* (1861) that Dickens was persuaded by his friends to publish, Pip and Estella are reconciled in what some critics felt was too conventional a conclusion, and which Boone argues perpetuates the idea that romantic wedlock eventually yields 'a seemingly stable identity that will resist future vacillations' (1987: 98). Yet there is an understated atmosphere of nostalgia and lamentation that hangs over the final scene, as well as a note of ambiguity in their declaration of 'friendship' and Estella's pledge that they 'will continue friends apart' (LIX, 412). Only a superficial reader would call this a happy ending.

Romantic ambivalence and narrative uncertainty also accompany the female protagonists at the close of Charlotte Brontë's *Villette* and Eliot's *Middlemarch* (1872). Emma Bovary's death seems like a moral punishment for adultery, but the reader is left in no doubt that her sexual exploitation by Rodolphe is the hidden face of the same bourgeois marital sterility she was fleeing from. It was probably Henry James, however, who had the greatest reputation for mastering the unresolved ending. 'His books end as an episode in life ends', Joseph Conrad observed. 'You remain with the sense of life still going on' (cited in Boone 1987: 189). James' world is one of strategising egos and half-communicated truths, in which his characters attempt to manoeuvre each other with feints and allusions and with the ever-so-delicate language of moral respectability and beautiful appearances. Their motives are sometimes splendid, sometimes base, but rarely do they say precisely what they mean, and they always seem to know too little, or else too much, about what they are really doing, to achieve the power, felicity or perfection that is frequently their goal. For this reason alone it is hardly surprising that James' lovers do not find harmony in wedlock.

Isabel Archer, for example, falls victim to the magnificent tyrant and collector of beautiful things, Gilbert Osmond, and although she decides in the end to return to face the consequences of her ill-chosen marriage, James concludes *The Portrait of a Lady* (1881) with deliberate ambiguity, refusing to disclose whether Isabel is resigning herself to captivity, or returning to rescue Osmond's illegitimate daughter from the clutches of her scheming father. Maggie Verver, the pretty but asexual protagonist of *The Golden Bowl* (1904), finally realises that, through the prim and perfect fidelity she has successfully shown her father, she has colluded in the sexual affair of their respective spouses. But though she is physically reunited with her husband at the novel's end, the last sentence, in describing her 'pity and dread' and the way she averts her eyes from his face by burying them in his chest (XLII, 443), conveys a reconciliation that is uneasy, mistrustful and which stops short of mutual understanding. The same is true of *The Wings of the Dove* (1902), which has Kate Croy persuading her lower class lover, Merton Densher, to court a terminally ill American heiress with the hope that she might leave her estate to him and in so doing remove the barriers of class-stigma and money that are impeding the prospect of the young lovers' own marriage. Milly learns of the plot, and of her betrayal by a trusted friend, but still generously names Densher in her will. Ashamed at their connivances, Densher renounces the bequest he receives after Milly's death, and offers to Kate the choice either of the money or of him, but not both. Kate's reply, which concludes the book, makes her decision ambiguous and leaves the future of their relationship unresolved: 'We shall never be again as we were!' (XXXVIII, 422).

Perhaps, in any case, the preoccupation with the ending of novels does an injustice to the experience of their reading. Certainty is the death of desire; the ending of any enthralling book is a tragedy for the reader, whose return to reality must be a recognition that what was so thrilling was also so unreal. 'The one desire that dreams themselves cannot finally satisfy is the desire to stay asleep, to go on dreaming and so prolong the narrative' (Belsey 1994: 208). This helps explain, Belsey points out, why modern enthusiasts for romantic fiction are often such avid consumers of the genre. No matter how perfect the novel's conclusion, the story is never fully gratifying, and the reader must forever be starting again.

> Desire is predicated on lack, and even its apparent fulfilment is also a moment of loss. Similarly for the reader of romance, the fulfilment of desire in a happy ending is also the unhappy end of the story, since the characters now move on to that transcendent domestic plane where they live happy ever after, immobilised by their own reciprocal happiness. 'Happy love has no history' [de Rougemont]. No more events are scheduled to happen to the protagonists, and there can therefore be no more story – and in consequence no more delightful, fearful, uncertain, desiring reader-subject. (Belsey 1994: 38–9)

Love and nature

A final theme in the nineteenth-century love story that I want to highlight is the way the censorship of sex invited Victorian novelists to diffuse sexuality into the broader narrative texture of their tales. 'If there were no acceptable "site" for sex,' Polhemus (1990: 180) suggests, 'then libido, as in a "harmless" dream, might be anywhere and everywhere. The boundaries between sexual and nonsexual activities become blurred when all physical eroticism must be implied and inferred.' Eliot begins *The Mill on the Floss* with an erotic paean to nature: 'A wide plain, where the broadening Floss hurries on between its green banks to the sea, and the loving tide, rushing to meet it, checks its passage with an impetuous embrace' (I, I, 5). In the next paragraph the narrator declares that she is 'in love with moistness', and dreamy images of liquidity, flow and dispersion permeate the text, expressing the sensuality and receptiveness of the body – particularly the female body – as well as conveying, as Polhemus argues, the only trajectory which sexual desire can take if it is to preserve itself against the opposing force of civilisation: 'relationship, renunciation, dispersion' (Polhemus 1990: 169).

Simone de Beauvoir argued that the exertion required by women writers to break free of patriarchal entanglements often meant 'they do not have enough strength left to profit by their victory and break all the ropes that hold them back'. Lacking the confidence and lucidity to 'face nature in its non-human freedom', women novelists, she suggested, were more inclined to represent nature as a placid and tamed object, as 'what woman herself represents for man: herself and her negation, a kingdom and a place of exile; the whole in the guise of the other' (Beauvoir 1972: 718–20). When in love, of course, the natural world glitters with divine luminosity and unquestionable goodness, and it is hardly surprising that in romantic literature nature readily becomes both a metaphor for and mirror of the merciful innocence of love. Loving, Andreas-Salomé writes,

> means knowing someone whose colours all things must wear if they are to reach us whole, to the extent that things cease to be indifferent or frightening, cold or empty, and that even the most threatening, like the wild beasts when we enter the Garden of Eden, fall tame at our feet. In the most beautiful love songs, something of this irresistible feeling survives, as if the object of love were not only itself, but also the leaf quivering on the tree, the sunlight flaming on the water – metamorphosed into all things, and a magician that metamorphoses all things: an image split into a thousand shards through the infinity of the All, so that, whereever we go, it is always the sweet land of our birth. (Andreas-Salomé 2014: 66–7)

In Thomas Hardy, however, we may find something closer to what Beauvoir wanted women writers to achieve. Perhaps more than any other nineteenth-century novelist, Hardy used nature and landscape as props and metaphors for human existence, combining a lovingly detailed observation of the vicissitudes of the natural world with a reverent appreciation of its unmastered mystery and destructive power. Just as bodily desire is cultivated, sublimated and inspired by our dialogue with romantic literature, so too there is a constant linguistic traffic in Hardy's novels between organic nature and the human world, whereby each borrows the guise of the other to dramatise and make visible their common features. Hardy did this in bleak as well as uplifting ways. In *The Return of the Native* (1878) the heath is introduced as a 'ballast to the mind adrift on change, and harassed by the irrepressible New' (I, I, 7), whereas beneath the pastoral charm of *The Woodlanders* (1887) we find a Darwinian world of merciless struggle, growth and decay, where the competition between lichen, ivy and sapling mirrors the restless antagonisms of human beings.

The ongoing interchange between humans and nature also allowed Hardy to dramatise love and sexuality in interesting ways. Sometimes the sexualising of nature is so explicit it borders on the pornographic: 'We read a description of the countryside and suddenly we are seeing a woman's body; a sheep is shorn, and Hardy makes us think of a sexual deflowering' (Polhemus 1990: 231). But Hardy is more subtle than this implies. Though he always wrote of love, Hardy's novels rarely linger on the interiority of the human heart, preferring to set that heart, and sharpen its contours, against the backdrop of earth and stars. 'The talk between the lovers when it is not passionate is practical or philosophic, as though the discharge of their daily duties left them with more desire to question life and its purpose than to investigate each other sensibilities,' Virginia Woolf wrote of Hardy's fiction. 'If we do not know his men and women in their relations to each other, we know them in their relations to time, death, and fate' (Woolf 1968: 261–2). Hardy's tendency to set most of the interactions between his characters outdoors also frees them of emotional claustrophobia, permitting an expansiveness that is at once passionate and contemplative.

We know Hardy's characters in their relations to the world, but it is also in relation to their world that his characters know each other. By inserting the physical world as a mediating link between lovers, Hardy was able to displace the harmonious unity desired by the fervent romantic imaginary ('I am Heathcliff!'), and instead envisage a more organic, and more sustainable, love, which grows through dialogue, companionship and shared vocation. 'Theirs was that substantial affection which arises (if any arises at all) when the two who are thrown together begin first by knowing the rougher sides of each other's character, and not the best till further on, the romance growing up in the interstices of a mass of hard prosaic reality' (LVI, 314). This was Hardy's concluding account of Bathsheba and Oak's romance, which begins to blossom in Bathsheba's consciousness when she notices his lack of interest in himself, his turning outwards to his environment – 'among the multitude of interests by which he was surrounded, those which affected his personal well-being were not the most absorbing and important in his eyes' (XLIII, 232) – and how this suggests to her the possibility of a richer life and vision than a love which would enclose her in a submissive or narcissistic world.

A similar theme is apparent in the more tragic *Two on a Tower* (1882), where Hardy has struggling landowner Viviette Constantine fall in love with budding astronomer Swithin St Cleeve, eight or nine years her junior and her social inferior. Swithin has his sights set on the heavens, and his emotions run from 'dignity' and 'grandeur' through 'solemnity' to 'ghastliness' when he contemplates the magnitude of a universe that he recognises was 'not made to please our eyes' (I, IV, 33–5). His instant attractiveness to the eyes of the older woman derives partly from the outward reach of his consciousness. She first encounters him, squatting uninvited on the roof of a commemorative tower in her late husband's family cemetery, with his eye cemented to his telescope, his body 'immutable as that of a bust, though superadding to the serenity of repose the sensitiveness of life'. He is, Hardy says, quite literally in love with the sun – a 'place where nobody had ever been or ever would be' (I, I, 9). With his attentions firmly fastened on a slowly dying universe, his 'mental inaccessibility' is both a sexual magnet and a force capable of destabilising the hierarchies of age and class that would otherwise make romance between these two characters inconceivable: 'He had never, since becoming a man, looked even so low as to the level of a Lady Constantine' (I, V, 47).

The gendering of science and mental abstraction cannot be denied here, and the death of the disgraced Lady Constantine at the end of the novel, which recalls the sacrificial fate of Tess, suggests the victory of oppressive social convention over the exhilarating freedom which acknowledgement of humans' cosmic insignificance might bring. 'The simple fact is,' Swithin explains, 'the field of astronomy reduces every terrestrial thing to atomic dimensions' (III, V, 247). But in Swithin's case, his telescopic consciousness ultimately corrodes his romantic faith, and having been generously released by Viviette for five years of travel and astronomical research, he returns with his affection for her dulled, and only a lingering sense of moral obligation to honour their pledge to be married. But in Viviette, ironically, the magnitude of the starry universe continues to expand and recalibrate her soul – she switches from passionate joy to an equally loving and self-denying altruism, but in each case she is 'warm and impulsive to indiscretion'. For she has done what Beauvoir says women must do: 'to undertake, in anguish and pride, her apprenticeship in abandonment and transcendence' (1972: 720). Her thirst for freedom repeatedly hits the barriers of a patriarchal society, and yet while fear of social ostracism makes her insist on the secrecy of their relationship, her sensual appetite for life is plain to see. In one scene, while she entertains the visiting Bishop, Hardy humorously implies a moment of post-coital tranquillity: her 'recently gratified affection lent to her manner just now a sweet serenity, a truly Christian contentment' (II, XI, 178). Earlier in the novel she had mischievously cut a lock of hair from Swithin's sleeping head, taking for herself what he was not yet ready to give, delighting in her enjoyment of his terrestrial body while he was lost in his heavenly dreams. Her playfulness opposes, but also presupposes, the ghastly abyss of nothingness on whose precipice we totter. 'Woman,' Beauvoir (1972: 719) says, 'exhausts her courage dissipating mirages and she stops in terror at the threshold of reality.' In *Two on a Tower* it is the woman more than the man who holds her nerve. Though Hardy, unfairly, does not let her survive the novel's climax, Viviette retains her faith in love to the end. She is a long way from the neurotic and sinister kleptomania of Boldwood, as well as from the psychological self-absorption of Sue Bridehead.

Undoubtedly Hardy's most famous love scene is when Bathsheba and Oak race against an approaching storm, thatching the sheaves on top of a stack of barley so as to create a sealed roof capable of protecting the crop from ruin. The lightning springs across the sky in a 'perfect dance of death', yet 'they could only comprehend the magnificence of its beauty'. Oak's thatching tool is struck by a bolt and he is almost blinded, but the elemental sense of awe and fear, and the practical necessity of their physical contact, create a thrilling atmosphere of acute sensory awareness and almost naked intimacy. The lightning is the Promethean spark that kindles their desire, but the storm also warns the protagonists of their vulnerability and insignificance: 'love, life, everything human, seemed small and trifling in such close juxtaposition with an infuriated universe' (XXXVII, 197–8). Sexuality finds both its catalyst and its antagonist in the superhuman enormity of nature; nature is a metaphor for the formless power of human passion, but also casts the individual as abandoned and alone in a cosmos of unfathomable power and scale. This scale exceeds the tools of measurement and calculation; 'grandeur' and 'ghastliness' evoke a biblical universe of heaven and hell, even though the subtext of all Hardy's novels is a dying religious world.

Hardy saw an older society disappearing, and a new and harsher world of violent social forces coming into being. His treatment of social change, class, gender, the industrialisation of agriculture and the rationalisation of rural life made him in many people's eyes the most sociological of the Victorian novelists. But Hardy consciously resisted the temptation to write political tracts or arguments, believing his craft was to record the impressions of the world as we experience it, not to supply readers with ready-made theories of reality. In Woolf's words, Hardy 'saw with intense irony and grimness that no reading of life can possibly outdo the strangeness of life itself, no symbol of caprice and unreason be too extreme to respect the astonishing circumstances of our existence' (1968: 265). In this respect, where love is concerned, his stories were always a test as much as a testament of romantic faith.

6

Lawrence's love

But the awakened one, the knowing one, saith: 'Body am I entirely, and nothing more; and soul is only the name of something in the body' .... Behind thy thoughts and feelings, my brother, there is a mighty lord, an unknown sage – it is called Self; it dwelleth in thy body, it is thy body. There is more sagacity in thy body than in thy best wisdom. (Nietzsche 1997: 30)

How can one truly love a person, in her physical reality and distinctiveness, while at the same time sharing a romantic faith, with its common rituals, values and conventions? How can one give a person one's own singular voice of love when the language of romantic liturgy has already been written? If love is a revelation, then for this very reason it must also be a repudiation of all that has been said and known about love. At the heart of the modernist project of love is clearly a tension: between the individual – joyful, vital, uniquely creative and self-possessed – and society, with not only its ennobling collective memories and ideals, but also its irresistible logic of social reproduction, sexual depersonalisation, cultural repression and conformism. D. H. Lawrence wrote from the centre of this contradiction. He condemned the stereotyped, sentimentalised, 'counterfeit love' that, once it has run its natural course, takes its revenge, he argued, in the predictable form of mutual hatred between erstwhile lovers. But he also denounced the trivialisation of love to mere physical enjoyment, as if sex was akin to a tasty meal, like eating and drinking with one's genitals. What was missing, Lawrence believed, was 'a proper reverence for sex, and a proper awe of the body's strange experience' (Lawrence 1961: 96–7, 90).

> In contrast to the puritan hush! hush! which produces the sexual moron, we have the modern young jazzy and high-brow person who has gone one better, and won't be hushed in any respect, and just 'does as she likes'. From fearing the body, and denying its existence, the advanced young go to the other extreme and treat it as a sort of toy to be played with, a slightly nasty toy, but still you can

get some fun out of it, before it lets you down. These young people scoff at the importance of sex, take it like a cocktail, and flout their elders with it. (1961: 91)

'Doing as she likes' was clearly not what Lawrence had in mind when he thought of sexual liberation. For Lawrence, the body was the soul, and an instrumental or hedonistic handling of the body would therefore always be a spiritual degradation. Self-possession, rather than self-indulgence, was the first premise of human flourishing, which is partly why Lawrence was interested in the novels of Thomas Hardy. In the summer of 1914 he had declared in a letter to Edward Marsh his intention 'to write a little book on Hardy's people'. By the autumn it was clear that his study had become more a device to articulate his own personal creed, with Lawrence telling his other early mentor, Edward Garnett: 'I have been writing my book more or less – very much less – about Thomas Hardy' (Lawrence 1932: 209, 213–14). Lawrence's 'little book' on Hardy certainly ended up less about Hardy than its title indicates, but it is valuable, nonetheless, for the light it shines on Lawrence's own philosophy of love. This philosophy can be better elucidated by first noting the surprising kinship between Lawrence's social outlook and the more rigorous political theory of one of the twentieth century's great thinkers, Hannah Arendt.

The individual against society

In *The Human Condition* (1958), Arendt had launched a withering critique of 'the social'. This was a term she used, sometimes interchangeably with 'society', to categorise the routinised forms of thought and behaviour whose purpose was, she argued, not to elevate human existence, but simply to perpetuate it, as if both individual and society were just organic systems demanding to be reproduced. In Arendt's view, the ever-expanding realm of the social was stifling individual autonomy and degrading humans' capacity to create, initiate and bring into being that which is new and unexpected. Politics, whose ideal form was, for Arendt, the doing and saying of memorable things, was in her view the most serious casualty of this process, being progressively transformed from the public performance of memorable words and deeds into a technocratic service dedicated to the reproduction of life at ever-higher levels of abundance. 'Society is the form in which the fact of mutual dependence for the sake of life and nothing else assumes public significance and where the activities connected with sheer survival are permitted to appear in public' (Arendt 1958: 46).

Lawrence was no political philosopher, but his posthumously published *Study of Thomas Hardy* begins with a condemnation of our 'over-blown and extravagant' obsession with 'self-preservation' that could easily have come from the pen of Arendt:

> Man has made such a mighty struggle to feel at home on the face of the earth, without even yet succeeding. Ever since he first discovered himself exposed naked betwixt sky and land, belonging to neither, he has gone on fighting for more food, more clothing, more shelter, and though he has roofed-in the world with houses and though the ground has heaved up massive abundance and excess of nutriment to his hand, still he cannot be appeased, satisfied. He goes on and on. In his anxiety he has evolved nations and tremendous governments to protect his person and his property, his strenuous purpose, unremitting, has brought to pass the whole frantic turmoil of modern industry, that he may have enough, enough to eat and wear, that he may be safe. (Lawrence 1986: 3)

For Arendt, the principle of reproduction that drives the sphere of 'the social' is the radical antithesis of the human condition of 'natality' – the miracle of an entirely new existence coming into being. The social is also at war with the highest faculty of human existence – 'action' – which is when a 'natal' being actualises the mystery and newness of its very constitution by initiating something unique and unforeseen. Instead of making and protecting a public space for action, Arendt argued, modern industrial societies treat the dull compulsion of labour as the most honourable of human activities. Even when workers fabricate things whose durability could point beyond the ongoing struggle for survival, these things are, in the throwaway culture of the affluent societies, typically regarded as perishable goods that must be produced and replaced anew in order to perpetuate the endless, quasi-organic cycle of work and consumption (Arendt 1958: 124–6).

Arendt would have been uncomfortable with Lawrence's veneration of nature and his apparent neglect of that attachment to human-made things which Arendt called 'worldliness'. But Lawrence, like Arendt, also condemned 'the tight economical bud of caution and thrift and self-preservation', describing it as an assault on the will to human flourishing. In some ways prefiguring the later arguments of Bertrand Russell, whose ill-fated friendship Lawrence had enjoyed for a period in 1915–16, and whose essay 'In Praise of Idleness' (1932) became a rallying call for those disenchanted with the hypocritical fetishism of work, Lawrence argued that work is 'nothing more holy' than 'the producing of the means of self-preservation', and 'a state which every man hopes for release from'.

But released for what, exactly? 'Let him rest and amuse himself, and get ready for tomorrow morning', Lawrence says sardonically. ' "We must work to eat, and eat to – what?" Don't say "work", it is so unoriginal' (1986: 28–30).

A logical desire to make necessary work quick, precise and efficient has in turn elevated the idea that the most accomplished form of work is that which best resembles the perfectly functioning machine. From this perspective, which is today echoed in popular psychological discourses that promote a utilitarian, risk-averse model of love purged of unhealthy self-sacrifice, that which is not useful or productive is wasted effort. In Lawrence's view, however, 'waste' and 'excess' are precisely 'the thing itself at its maximum of being. If it had stopped short of this excess, it would have not been at all. If this excess were missing, darkness would cover the face of the earth' (Lawrence 1986: 6–7). We court this darkness when our appreciation of living things stops at an understanding of their function or usefulness. It is in the glorious red of its petals, Lawrence writes, not in the fruit or the seed, that the poppy fulfils its aim.

> Seed and fruit and produce, these are only a minor aim: children and good works are a minor aim. Work, in its ordinary meaning, and all effort for the public good, these are labour of self-preservation, they are only means to the end. The final aim is the flower, the fluttering singing nucleus which is a bird in spring, the magical spurt of being which is a hare all explosive with fullness of self, in the moonlight; the real passage of a man down the road, no sham, no shadow, no counterfeit, whose eyes shine blue with his own reality, as he moves amongst things free as they are, a being; the flitting under the lamp of a woman uncontrovertible, distinct from everything and from everybody, as one who is herself, of whom Christ said 'to them that have shall be given'. (Lawrence 1986: 8)

The anti-sociologism of both Arendt and Lawrence is evident in their respective writings, though for a working-class miner's son Lawrence's suspicion of social reform, at least in his early writings, is perhaps the more surprising. 'The working man is not fit to elect the ultimate government of the country', Lawrence opined in a letter to Lady Ottoline Morrell in 1915, insisting on the need for a new philosophy to address the madness of a continent sinking into war. 'Last time I came out of the Christian camp. This time I must come out of these early Greek philosophers' (1932: 239). Like Arendt, Lawrence favoured a Council system rather than the direct democracy of the Athenian *polis*. 'I think the artisan is fit to elect for his immediate surroundings, but for no ultimate government. The electors for the highest places should be the governors of the bigger districts – the whole thing should work upwards, every man voting for that which he more or less understands through contact – no canvassing of mass votes' (1932: 247).

Lawrence seemed to care as little for the mass of the poor as he did for the ruling elite; and although he said the wealthy were, thanks to their actual acquaintance with wealth, likely to be 'sadder and wiser', he believed that a liberated mind could deliver the same truths, and there were 'sufficient people with sound imagination and normal appetite to put away the whole money tyranny of England today' (1986: 33). What Lawrence was looking for was a true 'individualist', by which he meant 'not a selfish or greedy person anxious to satisfy appetites, but a man of distinct being, who must act in his own particular way to fulfil his own individual nature. He is a man who, being beyond the average, chooses to rule his own life to his own completion, and as such is an aristocrat' (1986: 45).

Lawrence's interest in Hardy's fiction becomes explicable here. He approved of Hardy because his characters were true *individuals*, caring little for their own self-preservation and willing to risk safety and contentment in the brave and unscripted struggle to 'come into being'. 'These people of Wessex are always bursting suddenly out of bud and taking a wild flight into flower, always shooting something out of a tight convention, a tight, hide-bound cabbage state into something quite madly personal … . They are people each with a real, vital, potential self' (1986: 16). And for Lawrence, as for Hardy, *love* is the most intense and authentic articulation of this bursting into life. Thus when he wrote from Germany to his old neighbour Sallie Hopkin during his elopement with Frieda Weekley in the Summer of 1912, he emphasised the glorious, 'god-like' revelation of love, almost as if love were the archetype of the new and unforeseen: 'Never, never, never could one conceive of what love is, beforehand, never' (1932: 43). Two years later he felt able to advise Thomas Dacre Dunlop – the English consul at Spezia, whom Lawrence had befriended during his stay in Lerici in 1913–14 – on what was required for the success of his own marriage:

> One must learn to love, and go through a good deal of suffering to get to it, like any knight of the grail, and the journey is always *towards* the other soul, not away from it. Do you think love is an accomplished thing, the day it is recognised? It isn't. To love, you have to learn to understand the other, more than she understands herself, and to submit to her understanding of you … . Your most vital necessity in this life is that you shall love your wife completely and implicitly and in entire nakedness of body and spirit. (1932: 207)

Frieda, too, had written of the struggle to love in their own relationship:

> It was a long fight for Lawrence and me to get at some truth between us; it was a
> hard life but a wonderful one … . Whatever happened on the surface of everyday
> life, there blossomed the certainty of the unalterable bond between us, and of
> the ever present wonder of all the world around us. (Cited in Moore 1960: 222)

It was because Hardy made 'the struggle into love and the struggle with love' the centrepiece of his novels that Lawrence so admired him. Yet he also complained that Hardy's characters leaned away from the truly tragic towards the pathetic, since they were always 'unfaithful to the greater unwritten morality' that would have given them the strength to defend their love against the dictates of the community. For love naturally runs against the moral demands and expectations of the 'great self-preservation system'. It transgresses the claims of money, status and social success, and thus it always courts tragedy. To 'be passionate, individual, wilful, you will find the security of the convention a walled prison, you will escape, and you will die, either of your own lack of strength to bear the isolation and the exposure, or by direct revenge from the community, or from both' (1986: 17).

Utopia and disappointment

Lawrence had begun talking to the Bloomsbury's set about forming a utopian society, perhaps in Florida, or on an island, or on the 500-acre Oxfordshire estate of the Liberal MP Philip Morrel, whose wife Lawrence had befriended. He called the project 'Rananim', after a Hebrew song translated to him by the Russian émigré Samuel Koteliansky. For a short period he believed he could find enough genuine 'individualists' to form such a pastoral community, people capable of defying the prison of moral respectability as well as the degrading forces of money, work and war. He wrote to Willie Hopkin in January 1915, sketching out his 'pet scheme':

> I want to gather together about twenty souls and sail away from this world of war
> and squalor and found a little colony where there shall be no money but a sort
> of communism as far as necessaries of life go, and some real decency. It is to be a
> colony built up on the real decency which is in each member of the community.
> A community which is established upon the assumption of goodness in the
> members, instead of the assumption of badness. (1932: 219)

A month later, to Lady Morrell, he reiterated his desire to form a community of people bonded in their freedom and in their unwavering confidence in their own desire:

> I want you to form the nucleus of a new community which shall start a new life amongst us – a life in which the only riches is integrity of character. So that each one may fulfil his own nature and deep desires to the utmost, but wherein tho', the ultimate satisfaction and joy is in the completeness of us all as one. Let us be good all together, instead of just in the privacy of our chambers … . And this shall be the new hope: that there shall be a life wherein the struggle shall not be for money or for power, but for individual freedom and common effort towards good … . Let us have *no* personal influence, if possible – nor personal magnetism, as they used to call it, nor persuasion – no 'Follow me' – but only 'Behold' … . It is communism based, not on poverty but on riches, not on humility but on pride, not on sacrifice but upon complete fulfilment in the flesh of all strong desire, not in Heaven but on earth. (1932: 224–5)

Katherine Mansfield tried to humour Lawrence by collecting practical information about possible sites for his project, but the tone of her suggestions was mocking, and as the Cambridge-Bloomsbury crowd began to turn against him, Lawrence became increasingly discouraged (Moore 1960: 230, 245). In the collection of travel essays he published in 1916, *Twilight in Italy*, his declining faith in the self-organisation of individuals was already apparent. There he describes a lengthy encounter, while walking through Switzerland to Italy – probably in September 2013 – with a group of exiled Italian anarchists. 'Why should we have a Government?', their leader asked rhetorically. 'Here, in this village, there are thirty families of Italians. There is no government for them, no Italian Government. And we live together better than in Italy. We are richer and freer, we have no policemen, no poor laws. We help each other, and there are no poor.' The man paused, waiting for Lawrence's reply. Lawrence recalls:

> I did not want to answer. I could feel a new spirit in him, something strange and pure and slightly frightening. He wanted something which was beyond me. And my soul was somewhere in tears, crying helplessly like an infant in the night. I could not respond: I could not answer. He seemed to look at me, me, an Englishman, an educated man, for corroboration. But I could not corroborate him. I knew the purity and new struggling towards birth of a true star-like spirit. But I could not confirm him in his utterance: my soul could not respond. I did not believe in the perfectibility of man. I did not believe in infinite harmony among men. (Lawrence 2007a: 113–14)

The sensuality of woman

By 1922, Lawrence had also begun to revise his previous belief in the primacy of the sex instinct. Although Lawrence's work continued to be received as sexually subversive and aggressively hedonistic, there was a conventionalism to Lawrence's outlook – as feminist critics like Kate Millett (1970) would later point out. The heterosexual bond Lawrence now saw as a dynamic polarity founded on difference, sexual intimacy providing a fleeting union whose greatest significance was that it prepared the lover – more particularly, the *male* lover – for the higher, but also more primordial, purpose of collective world-building.

We now know that it was Frieda who inspired Lawrence's original appreciation of the importance of sexual love. After the traumatic death of his emotionally possessive mother – a loss he feared he would never recover from – it was Frieda who convinced him that he could find a deeper and more mature love that connected him, without reservation, to the life and body of another person. It was Frieda's aristocratic courage for living which gave Lawrence the confidence to make physical passion his own creed. 'She gave him sensual happiness', Maurice Green (1974: 131) writes of Frieda in his study of the von Richthofen sisters, 'but she also gave him – by the same gift – his mission as a writer. She gave him her identity, *her* idea – which became his idea'. Lawrence always subscribed to the traditional dualism of gender, but under Frieda's influence he also believed that men could be fundamentally transformed by what he increasingly saw as the natural sensuality of women. In a letter sent from Italy in the summer of 1914 to A. W. McLeod, a former colleague and friend from his three-year stint as a schoolteacher in London, he wrote:

> I think the *one* thing to do, is for men to have courage to draw nearer to women, expose themselves to them, and be altered by them: and for women to accept and admit men. That is the start – by bringing themselves together, men and women – revealing themselves each to the other, gaining great blind knowledge and suffering and joy, which it will take a big further lapse of civilisation to exploit and work out. Because the source of all life and knowledge is in man and woman, and the source of all living is in the interchange and the meeting and mingling of these two: man-life and woman-life, man-knowledge and woman-knowledge, man-being and woman-being. (1932: 198)

It is 'the desire of every man', Lawrence said in his *Study of Thomas Hardy*,

> that his movement, the manner of his walk, and the supremest effort of his mind, shall be the pulsation outwards from stimulus received in the sex, in the

sexual act, that the woman of his body shall be the begetter of his whole life, that she, in her female spirit, shall beget in him his idea, his motion, himself. When a man shall look at the work of his hands, that has succeeded, and shall know that it was begotten in him by the woman of his body, then he shall know what fundamental happiness is. (1986: 52–3)

It was, indeed, Frieda who gave him 'his idea, his motion, himself'. 'Do you know how much liberating I did for Lawrence', Frieda said after his death. 'It was given to me to make him flower.' Erotic love was *her* creed, not his: 'don't forget that this religious (if you can call it so) approach to physical love is my feeble contribution', she wrote to another correspondent after the publication of *Lady Chatterley* (cited in Green 1974: 130, 135). But by the 1920s, Lawrence had in fact begun to stake out the terms of his opposition to his wife's proselytising. This is perhaps surprising to anyone familiar with the history and controversy of *Lady Chatterley's Lover* (1928) – suppressed for over 30 years for its supposedly pornographic content, and eventually celebrated by many critics and readers for its ingenuous descriptions of authentic physicality and guiltless, guileless desire. Didn't Tommy Dukes give voice to Lawrence's doctrine when he advocated a 'democracy of touch' and the 'resurrection of the body' (VII, 89)? Didn't Mellors declare to Connie at the end of the novel that sex is the font of all life: 'Even the flowers are fucked into being' (XIX, 370)?

One can certainly read a kind of erotic de-sublimation in the novel's refusal to symbolically diffuse sexuality into nature, as the more hesitant Victorian novelists had done, and Lawrence's tendency to treat nature not as a metaphor for sex, but rather as the extension and adornment of a more primal, more fleshy, more self-confident reality. Lawrence had acquired from Nietzsche a contempt for the Platonic 'crusade for "ideals", and for this "spiritual" knowledge in apartness' – which he saw perpetuated in the 'sharp knowing' of Jane Austen's 'snobbish' characters (Lawrence 1961: 122–3). When Mellors and Connie decorate their naked bodies in flower stems, petals and leaves, Lawrence is certainly not using nature to eroticise the body by concealing it; when Mellors winds a 'creeping-jenny round his penis' (XV, 275), this is no Kantian fig leaf.[1] George Bernard Shaw 'says clothes arouse sex and lack of clothes tends to kill sex', Lawrence wrote, but in Lawrence's view this sex-in-the-head is 'counterfeit sex', far removed from 'the deeper sex of the real individual' which has eluded

---

[1] The fig leaf, Kant (1963: 57) argued, by removing the object of sexual attraction from sight, 'was the feat which brought about the passage from merely sensual to spiritual attractions, from mere animal desire gradually to love, and along with this from the feeling of the merely agreeable to a taste for beauty'.

almost everyone. 'If there is no sex to muffle up, it's no good muffling' (Lawrence 1961: 99, 101). Lawrence thus appeared to repudiate the classic Kantian aesthetic, that contemplative ascesis by which bodily urges are held in check in order to facilitate more sublime mental satisfactions (Bourdieu 1984: 486–7). His novels would therefore be categorised as 'improper art' by the standards of Stephen Daedalus in Joyce's *A Portrait of the Artist as a Young Man* (1916). Designed to excite what Joyce's alter-ego dismisses as 'kinetic' feeling (V, 204), Lawrence's art, it seems, is there to make you want to fuck.

The sacrament of marriage

But that is clearly an inadequate and inaccurate formulation that doesn't do justice to the complexity of Lawrence's outlook. Lawrence was much more of a traditionalist than is sometimes imagined, and certainly more of a traditionalist than his wife, whose extramarital affairs were legendary. Lawrence was dismayed at the description of his work as 'pornographic'. His aim, in writing about sexual love, was to instil a spiritual reverence for the sexual bond, and to show how physical intimacy with another person could be a religious calling. The naked flower scene in *Lady Chatterley*, for all its comic light-heartedness, is clearly a playful allusion to pagan marriage, the flower stalks and petals being the garlands that sanctify and commemorate the lovers' communion. For all his graphic openness about bodies and desires, Lawrence also wanted to guard the sacrament of sex, to protect its essential mystery by marking out a perimeter of peaceful chastity and temperance which was not only the after-effect of the sexual flame but also 'the unnamed god that shields it from being blown out'. As Mellors continues in his closing letter to Connie: 'it is so good to be chaste, like a river of cool water in my soul. I love chastity now that it flows between us. It is like fresh water and rain. How can men want wearisomely to philander? What a misery to be like Don Juan, and impotent ever to fuck oneself into peace' (XIX, 370). In 'À Propos of Lady Chatterley's Lover' (1930), Lawrence reiterated his belief in the unnaturalness of free love:

> All the literature of the world shows how profound is the instinct of fidelity in both man and woman, how men and women both hanker restlessly after the satisfaction of this instinct, and fret at their own inability to find the real mode of fidelity. The instinct of fidelity is perhaps the deepest instinct in the great complex we call sex. Where there is real sex there is the underlying passion for fidelity. (1961: 103–4)

'Christianity's great contribution to the life of man', Lawrence argued, perhaps surprisingly, is therefore the sacrament of marriage. This is not because marriage ensures a person's eternal salvation, but rather because the soul, to be fulfilled, must be developed and nourished for the whole of a person's life, and the rhythm of this life, both cyclical and sequential, is knitted into the fabric of the natural world. In Lawrence's view, the Christian Church, to the extent that it retained the pagans' sensitivity to the rhythms of the cosmos, also protected and consecrated the pattern and tempo of sexual life, allowing the changing cadences of the sexual relation – the fallow season, the dormancy, the periods of contemplation, expectation and action – to contribute to and sustain a deeper, longer and more glorious sense of existence. Lawrence is not, like Brontë, Eliot or Hardy, diffusing sexuality into nature as a means of its sublimation; but he is using the majesty of nature, and the awe it inspires in us, to articulate and promote a mystic reverence for sex.

> Sex is the balance of male and female in the universe, the attraction, the repulsion, the transit of neutrality, the new attraction, the new repulsion, always different, always new. The long neuter spell of Lent, when the blood is low, and the delight of the Easter kiss, the sexual revel of spring, the passion of midsummer, the slow recoil, revolt, and grief of autumn, greyness again, then the sharp stimulus of winter of the long nights … . Oh, what a catastrophe, what a maiming of love when it was made a personal, merely personal feeling, taken away from the rising and the setting of the sun, and cut off from the magic connexion of the solstice and the equinox! (1961: 109–10)

The variance of the seasons, the cycle of the moon and the passage of light from the dawn to the dying of a single day are, Lawrence continues in a memorable passage that is all the more poignant given his premature death, phases of 'harmony and discord' that echo the 'secret music of life'.

> And is it not so throughout life? A man is different at thirty, at forty, at fifty, at sixty, at seventy: and the woman at his side is different. But is there not some strange conjunction in their difference? Is there not some peculiar harmony, through youth, the period of child-birth, the period of florescence and young children, the period of the woman's change of life, painful yet also a renewal, the period of waning passion but mellowing delight of affection, the dim, unequal period of the approach of death, when the man and woman look at one another with the dim apprehension of separation that is not really a separation: is there not, throughout it all, some unseen, unknown interplay of balance, harmony, completion, like some soundless symphony which moves with a rhythm from phase to phase, so different, so very different in the various movements, and

yet one symphony, made out of the soundless singing of two strange and incompatible lives, a man's and a woman's?

This is marriage, the mystery of marriage, marriage which fulfils itself here, in this life. (1961: 110–11)

We can perhaps see from this why Aldous Huxley preferred Lawrence's 'new mythology of nature' to the Rousseau-inspired endorsement of natural impulses by nineteenth-century romanticism. Love requires restraint as well as passion, but this restraint must find both its power and its pattern in the form and rhythms of nature. Lawrence's 'realistic mythology of Energy, Life, and Human Personality' was 'untranscendental', in Huxley's words; it 'will provide, it seems to me, the inward resistance necessary to turn sexual impulse into love' (1929: 142).

Lawrence's worldliness

Perhaps more striking than Lawrence's lyrical veneration of marriage is the explicit opposition to sexual reductionism which he articulated in the early 1920s. Psychoanalytic ideas had certainly informed his earlier thinking, with *Sons and Lovers* (1913) exploring Oedipal themes as well as the splitting of love and lust that Freud had described in his 'Universal Tendency to Debasement' (1912) article. In *Fantasia of the Unconscious* (1922), however, Lawrence argued against the psychoanalytic doctrine of the sex instinct, and reasserted the fundamental mystery of man to woman and woman to man. 'Women will *never* understand the depth of the spirit of purpose in man, his deeper spirit', Lawrence declared. 'And man will never understand the sacredness of feeling to woman' (2005: 138). While conceding that the 'magic and dynamism' of the 'vital sex polarity' depends on this 'otherness', Lawrence also wanted to make a statement of male supremacy and independence – a statement that Kate Millett found so ubiquitous in his novels that in her view Lawrence 'turned his back on love' because really 'it is power he craves' (Millett 1970: 269).

There is, Lawrence wrote, a 'greater impulse' than the female sex impulse, which is 'the desire of the human male to build a world':

Even the Panama Canal would never have been built *simply* to let ships through. It is the pure disinterested craving of the human male to make something wonderful, out of his own head and his own self, and his own soul's faith and delight, which starts everything going. This is the prime motivity. And the motivity of sex is subsidiary to this: often directly antagonistic.

That is, the essentially religious or creative motive is the first motive for all human activity. The sexual motive comes second. (Lawrence 2005: 60)

Here we are closer to Arendt's theory of 'worldliness' than to the sexual naturalism for which Lawrence is renowned. Here we are also reminded of the novelty of human 'action', as well as the condition of 'plurality' which Arendt (1958) defended against the egocentric principle of 'sovereignty'. 'We have got to get back to the great purpose of manhood, a passionate unison in actively making a world', Lawrence writes in *Fantasia of the Unconscious*. 'This is a real commingling of many. And in such a commingling we forfeit the individual' (2005: 144). Instead of sex being sublimated into non-sexual ends, Lawrence says that sex is a vehicle for higher ends, but only insofar as the consummation of the sex drive creates the scene for a new beginning. Like the evanescent embrace of darkness and light before the break of dawn, or the momentary marriage of fire and water in the overhead arc of a rainbow, sex delivers a personal and emotional recalibration that resembles the aftermath of a thunderstorm: 'The air is as it were new, fresh, tingling with newness' (2005: 141). And then, as if reborn,

> The heart craves for new activity. For new *collective* activity. That is, for a new polarised connection with other beings, other men ...
>
> This meeting of many in one great passionate purpose is not sex, and should never be confused with sex. It is a great motion in the opposite direction. And I am sure that the ultimate, greatest desire in men is this desire for great *purposive* activity. When man loses his deep sense of purposive, creative activity, he feels lost, and is lost. When he makes the sexual consummation the supreme consummation, even in his *secret* soul, he falls into the beginnings of despair. When he makes woman or the woman child the great centre of life and of life-significance, he falls into the beginnings of despair. (2005: 142–3)

Was Lawrence 'feeling lost', having abandoned his working-class roots to share his life with a sexually liberated aristocratic 'individual'? Had he given too much of himself in order to satisfy his wife's lustful appetites? 'You treat me as if I were a piece of cake, for you to eat when you wanted' (I, 99), Peter complains to his wife in Lawrence's thinly veiled autobiographical short story, 'New Eve and Old Adam' (1934), posthumously published but written during the first months of their relationship. What was at stake, for Lawrence, in this turbulent and quarrelsome marriage? Lawrence was certainly making a personal complaint, but it was not directly, or at least not exclusively, targeted at Frieda. 'The psychoanalysts, driving us back to the sexual consummation always,' he writes almost bitterly, 'do us infinite damage' (2005: 144). To make better sense of this statement we need to introduce another character, for while Lawrence saw himself as a dogged and devotional 'priest of love' – 'I'll preach my heart out', he wrote to Sallie Hopkin, 'sticking up for the love between man and woman' (Lawrence 1932: 90) – he was up against the powerful influence of a more charismatic figure: not a priest, but a revolutionary 'prophet' of love.

'Repress nothing!'

Otto Gross was a renegade Freudian whose radical critique of bourgeois sexual morality prefigured the later ideas of Wilhelm Reich, Herbert Marcuse and R. D. Laing. The son of an eminent Austrian criminologist and magistrate whose work was influential enough to be translated and used by Scotland Yard, Otto had initially followed his father's wish that he study psychiatry, which Professor Gross believed was the future of criminal investigation and policing. Continuing his medical studies at the University of Munich, he graduated in 1899 as a doctor specialising in neurology and psychiatry. His first job seems to have been as a naval doctor, which took him on a ship to Patagonia. While at sea he developed a taste for cocaine, enabling him to maintain a nocturnal working rhythm which he sustained for the rest of his life. As a doctor he had easy access to drugs, and he soon combined cocaine use with a morphine addiction. Back in Europe he gained a post as an assistant at a famous psychiatric hospital in Munich, but his leanings towards psychoanalysis were incompatible with the neuro-psychiatric approach of his employer, and his clinical work was also disrupted by periodic self-admissions for drug withdrawal treatment.

Shabby and erratic in appearance and lifestyle, but naturally handsome, precociously intelligent and clearly charismatic, he was initially recognised by Freud as, along with Jung, one of the only two of his followers whom the father of psychoanalysis believed had original minds (Green 1974: 43). Freud did not fully approve of the direction of Gross's work, however, for the latter was developing, in several books and a stream of articles, as well as in his own increasingly deviant practices, a radical creed of sexual liberation. Bourgeois society was, in Gross's view, a patriarchal order which trampled on women's sexuality. The only lasting solution to repression and neurosis was not individual therapy but social and cultural change, beginning with free sexual love and the abolition of the family.

Gross's favourite expression was the exhortation '*Nichts verdrängen!*' – 'repress nothing!' – and this set him in opposition to Freud's insistence on the necessary compromise between libidinal desire and the requirements of civilisation. Gross increasingly saw the psychoanalytic relationship as another form of patriarchal authority, and he defended instead the individual's right to be herself in an oppressive and possessive world. Jung, whose medical treatment of Gross ended when his patient absconded over the wall of the Burghölzli Mental Hospital in 1908, had earlier expressed his reservations about Gross's ideas in a letter to Freud. For Gross, Jung wrote, 'The truly healthy state for the neurotic is sexual immorality.' Jung countered: 'It seems to me, however, that sexual repression is a very important and indispensable civilising factor, even if pathogenic for many inferior people.' In his view, which he knew Freud would endorse, 'Gross is going along too far with the vogue for the sexual short-circuit, which is neither intelligent, nor in good taste, but merely convenient, and therefore anything but a civilising factor' (cited in Turner 1990: 142).

Gross divided his time between Munich's Bohemian district, Schwabing, and the Swiss village of Ascona, where he rented a barn, apparently for group sex and drug taking (Green 1974: 64). Two hundred miles southwest of Munich, sitting neatly on the eastern shore of Lago Maggiore, Ascona had been a regular retreat for political refugees, anarchists and Tolstoyan pacifists since the 1870s. In 1902, a small international group of intellectuals had tried to create a more organised utopian community in the village, and though the plan petered out it did result in the establishment of a vegetarian sanatorium, 'Der Berg der Wahrheit' ('Mountain of Truth'). Within a couple of years there was, living alongside the bemused peasants of Ascona, a semi-permanent population of philosophers, anarchists, feminists, artists, pagan mystics and occultists, political exiles and military deserters, and various back-to-nature enthusiasts (*Naturmenschen*) seeking a healthier and more spontaneous lifestyle. Isadora Duncan, Kropotkin, Bakunin, Fanny zu Reventlow, Erich Mühsam and even Max Weber all spent time there.

In 1906, a former patient of Gross, Lotte Hattemer, killed herself in Ascona with an overdose of drugs that Gross had supplied, seemingly supportive of her suicidal intent. Another patient, Regina Ullmann, became pregnant with his child, and when she approached Otto's family for financial support Hans Gross ordered his son to go abroad to escape responsibility, though not before Otto had left within her reach another fatal dose of drugs (Green 1974: 57). Ullmann was not tempted, but a third patient, Sophie Benz, who had lived with Gross in Ascona in 1910–11, killed herself with his opiates when he was away in Berlin. Scandalised by his behaviour, Gross's father forced him to undergo psychiatric treatment, almost certainly saving him from manslaughter charges in the process. As Otto had been earlier diagnosed as schizophrenic by Jung, Hans Gross used Jung's letter of diagnosis to finally have his son arrested in 1913 as a dangerous psychopath, and have him confined at an asylum in Austria. Professor Gross, whom for Otto was the archetype of the patriarchal tyrant, also disinherited his son from his will, and took legal proceedings against his daughter-in-law, Frieda Gross. In Hans Gross's view, Frieda's own sexual promiscuity, which Otto had actively encouraged, made her unfit to be a mother. He fought for custody of his grandson, but cared nothing for Frieda's daughter, for he knew her to be the illegitimate child of the Swiss anarchist Ernst Frick, who in 1912 had been arrested for exploding a bomb outside a police station in Zurich in 1907.

As Otto had been seized in Berlin by Prussian police under instructions from his father in Austria, his arrest made him something of a martyr in anarchist circles. Released from Troppau asylum in 1914, Gross befriended Max Brod and Franz Kafka in Prague, and moved progressively closer to communist politics, participating in the Vienna Revolution of 1918 and seeking to radicalise as well as liberate those he associated with. He died, probably from complications relating to his drug use, in a Berlin sanatorium in 1920, four days before his 33rd birthday.

The liberation of Frieda Weekley

Otto Gross was one of the most important figures in a counter-culture movement for sexual liberation that came to an end with the First World War. His relevance to Lawrence's understanding of love would be inexplicable were it not the case that Lawrence's wife, Frieda, had also been Gross's lover. Frieda von Richthofen was the middle child of minor Prussian aristocrats who had fallen on hard times. She was born in the French garrison town of Metz, then annexed by the German empire following the Franco-Prussian war. In 1898, when she was 18 and on a family vacation staying with friends in Freiburg, she met and fell in love with Ernest Weekley, a philologist and lecturer in modern languages who had recently been appointed to a Chair at Nottingham University College. Sixteen years her senior and fluent in German and French, Weekley had previously held temporary appointments at the Sorbonne and Freiburg, and had come back to the Black Forest to visit a former colleague and enjoy a rare holiday. Charmed by the professor's English reserve and academic erudition, Frieda accepted Weekley's offer of marriage, which promised, as the author of one biography of Lawrence noted, advantages that were notably missing from her home life: 'respect for women, male devotion, financial security' (Worthen 2005: 109). Frieda soon found bourgeois marital domesticity in a provincial Midlands city a staid and lonely experience, however, and she despaired of her husband's neurotically compartmentalised sexuality and his fetishised view of her as a virginal beauty – 'my white snowflower' is how he liked to address her (Byrne 1995: 61).

Although an affair with a local industrialist, William Dowson, who was a neighbour and godfather to her youngest child, had offered her some distraction from the tedium of domestic suburbia, it was Otto Gross who was the most powerful agent of Frieda's sexual awakening. They met in Munich in 1907, when Frieda was visiting Gross's wife, 'Friedel' (Frieda), whom Frieda and her sister Else had befriended in their youth when they were fellow students at a finishing school in Freiburg. The surviving letters from Gross to Frieda – passionate but intellectually excessive, littered with superlatives and double and triple underlining – suggest that it was Frieda who started the affair, but that in the course of their liaisons Gross brought to light something that she had yet to fully feel and understand about herself. Gross wrote that he believed he had found in Frieda a model of the sexually emancipated woman his work was dedicated to. 'You were born for freedom and only for freedom', Gross declared to her. Frieda was, he wrote in another letter, the tangible confirmation of what had previously only been 'a prophetic dream of the woman of the future, alive only in my imagination' (Gross in Turner 1990: 167, 165).

Frieda spent a week with Gross in Munich, and later a second week with him in Amsterdam, following which he accompanied her on the Channel crossing back to England before saying goodbye. Gross tried to persuade her to join him again in Holland in the autumn of 1907, when he was due to deliver to the First International Congress of Psychiatry and Neurology a paper that seems to have been the fruit of their own bedroom conversations. But Frieda reluctantly declined, and though for a time they continued to write lovingly to each other, the relationship slowly fizzled out. It also came to light – Gross was not a man for keeping sexual secrets – that Otto had been having a relationship with Else, Frieda's older (married) sister. Pregnant with Gross's child, Else ended her relationship with Gross during this same period. With a more cautious and discerning temperament than her sister, she also wrote to warn Frieda against Gross's manic nature and the destructive, irresponsible side of his drug dependency. 'You have to remember the tremendous shadows around the light', she counselled her younger sister. 'As a "lover" he's incomparable, but a person doesn't consist of that alone.' She was sympathetic but concerned over Frieda's enchantment with Gross: 'You are under that tremendous shadow of suggestion which emanates from him and which I myself have felt' (cited in Green 1974: 53).

Else herself had started another affair with a doctor, a relationship which Gross, complaining in a fraught letter to Frieda, condemned as an unconscious reaction to the jealousy Else felt towards her sister and him. This affair was, Gross wrote to Frieda, 'a revenge upon *our* love', a revenge which Else had made more exacting by choosing as a lover a man destined to lead her back to a world – the repressive world of plebeian 'democracy' and 'High Society Asceticism' – from which Gross had worked so hard to release her (Gross in Turner 1990: 175–6). In the spring of 1908, when Frieda returned to Munich, she visited Gross's wife, Friedel, again. But this time, instead of reviving her relationship with Otto, she practised what the prophet of free love had preached, beginning an affair with Friedel's own lover – the anarchist Ernst Frick – apparently with her friend's blessing (Byrne 1995: 84). The relationship continued until 1910, with Frick often visiting Frieda in England. Meanwhile Else had cleanly severed her own connection to Gross, spelling out in a measured and eloquent letter to him her view that, for him, love was something he only felt for, and recognised in, his faithful 'disciples', and that he, thinking himself a 'Prophet', could therefore not tolerate a woman who 'can't completely believe', but who nonetheless 'could perhaps stay with the *man*, giving him her own kind love'. Else defended a more dignified and responsible form of love, and related his sexual promiscuity to his drug-taking. 'We cannot know how much of what seems to us indiscriminateness in your ideas, and an entire lack of nuance, and an incapacity to distinguish one individual from another, finally derives from morphine.' She also noted his lack of interest in their son: 'You never give a thought to your little Peter any longer' (cited in Green 1974: 57). Gross ignored the daughter he had fathered with Regina Ullmann as well, and although the child was given to foster parents before being put in a convent boarding school, Else treated her as part of her extended family, allowing her to stay with the Jaffés during school holidays.

Lawrence in love

When she met D. H. Lawrence for the first time in March 1912, Frieda was a 32-year-old mother of three, comfortably ensconced in a spacious house in the affluent Nottingham suburb of Mapperley, with a motorcar and several domestic servants at her disposal. Taken ill with a serious bout of double pneumonia the previous November, Lawrence had begun to recover his health, but had been warned by his doctor that returning to his Croydon teaching job could put him at risk of tuberculosis. His mother's sister, Ada, had married a German, and now that there were cousins whom he could stay with in the Rhineland, Lawrence had begun to entertain the idea of travelling abroad. With his first published novel – *The White Peacock* (1911) – already behind him, and drafts of his next two nearing completion, he paid a visit to his old French lecturer, Ernest Weekley, hoping for advice on how to obtain a less stressful post teaching English in a German university. Within a matter of weeks, Lawrence and Frieda were socialising and spending time alone together, and although Lawrence baulked at the indecency of having sex in his former professor's marital home, he urged Frieda to go away with him. Lawrence, then 26, had undergone a late and prolonged adolescence, and though love and sexuality had been a constant theme in the stories he had been working on over the last five years, he had not slept with a woman until he was 23 or 24. Of the two or three women he had known intimately, moreover, none had shared his enthusiasm for sex, nor received from Lawrence the genuine respect, if not the love, by which he might have surmounted the degrading separation of appetite and appreciation described by Freud. In Frieda, however, Lawrence had stumbled upon a woman who was more erotic, and more uninhibited, than himself. Frieda was the 'excess', the 'flower', the 'magical spurt of being' which Lawrence had exalted in his study of Hardy; 'a woman uncontrovertible, distinct from everything and from everybody'. She was also very different from the passive and humble women who had previously loved him, such as his pious teenage confidante and loyal muse Jessie Chambers ('Miriam' in *Sons and Lovers*). Frieda was perfectly comfortable arguing with Lawrence; and indeed her initial attitude to the relationship was that it was a fleeting sexual affair which she would not allow to jeopardise her marriage.

Frieda was already planning to return to Germany at the beginning of May for the fiftieth anniversary of the start of her father's military career, and Lawrence seized the opportunity to travel with her, combining the trip with a visit to his German cousins. What was intended, by Frieda at least, as a week's holiday, turned into an elopement that kept them abroad until the summer of the following year. First they were in Metz for the von Richthofen jubilee, though Frieda's insistence on secrecy meant that they saw even less of each other than they had in Nottingham. Then, after he'd stayed a few days, mostly alone, in the town of Trier, Lawrence braved the eleven-hour journey to the remote village of Waldbröl to spend two weeks with his Krenkow relations. Later in the month, the couple met up again in Munich, where Frieda had fled, preferring the company of her sister Else to that of her hectoring parents. This was followed by a 'honeymoon' week in the Bavarian village of Beuerberg, where they were at last able to enjoy each other's uninterrupted company. This was, nonetheless, a turbulent month for the couple, with Frieda first intending to keep the relationship secret from her parents, then prevaricating in the face of their disapproval – which was an expression of realism as well as moralism, for a penniless miner's son with aspirations to be a writer was hardly a sensible choice of lover – then working through the implications of her betrayed husband's grief and fury, not least for the future of her relationship with her children. In Metz, Lawrence had been arrested by an overzealous policeman who had heard them speaking English and suspected Lawrence to be a spy. Frieda had felt it necessary to invoke her father's name to secure Lawrence's release, and after this she could no longer keep the baron in the dark about the relationship. With the military authorities still suspicious of Lawrence's presence, he was told to leave Metz. He agreed to Frieda's suggestion that he take the train to Trier, 80 miles away. But he was growing worried by Frieda's apparent lack of commitment, and was irritated by her refusal to tell her husband that she had left him.

Before she departed for Germany, Frieda had told her husband about her affairs with Gross and Frick, but in this tearful exchange she had not mentioned Lawrence (Worthen 2005: 113).[2] Suspecting that Frieda was returning to Germany to start, or rekindle, another affair, Weekley wrote to her in Metz demanding clarification. On arrival in the town, Lawrence had drafted his own letter to Weekley, asking Frieda to send it, or else write her own version, in order to set the record straight. Apparently believing, incorrectly, that Frieda had finally written to her husband, Lawrence did the same. 'There are three of us,' he wrote to his old professor, 'though I do not compare my sufferings with what yours must be, and I am here as a distant friend, and you can imagine the thousand baffling lies it all entails.' And in words that might have come from (a sober) Otto Gross: 'Mrs. Weekley is afraid of being stunted and not allowed to grow, and so she must live her own life. All women in their nature

---

[2] Frieda was later recorded as saying that 'Lawrence before we went made me tell my husband I would leave him' (Frieda Lawrence 1959: 10). The accuracy of this statement is unclear, especially as in the same recording Frieda misremembers the year they met and how old she was at the time. 'I would leave him', rather than 'I was leaving him', may also indicate that Frieda's statement of intent was not unequivocal. Who, if anyone, she was leaving her husband for also doesn't appear to have been part of that marital conversation.

are like giantesses. They will break through everything and go on with their own lives' (cited in Byrne 1995: 107). Frieda was not impressed by Lawrence's presumptuousness, however. While Lawrence was languishing alone in Trier, she slept with a titled German soldier who had long been her admirer, perhaps trying to demonstrate to herself that her feelings for Lawrence were not serious enough to justify leaving her husband and children.

At the beginning of June the couple were properly reunited in the Bavarian town of Icking on the Isar River, where Else's lover, a professor at Heidelberg University, had agreed they could use the apartment he normally rented during the summer. There Lawrence finalised his latest draft of 'Paul Morel' (the text that would become *Sons and Lovers*) and posted it to William Heinemann. With Else and her husband staying nearby, Lawrence slowly warmed to Frieda's sister, a fondness reflected in his instruction that the original 1915 edition of *The Rainbow* begin with the inscription 'Zu Else' (Lawrence 1932: 234), and in his subsequent endorsement of her as his preferred German translator. Leaving Icking at the start of August, Frieda and Lawrence spent the next month hiking over the Austrian Alps. Lawrence carried in his knapsack the manuscript of 'Paul Morel', which Heinemann had flatly rejected and which he was once again revising, partly because Frieda had helped him achieve more emotional distance from the memories of his mother (Mrs Morel), and partly in response to suggested editing by Edward Garnett, who promised he would recommend its publication to Duckworth. At the foot of the Pfitscherjoch pass they were joined by Edward Garnett's son David, and his friend Harold Hobson, son of the economist J. A. Hobson. While Lawrence and David, a student of botany, went exploring up a mountain one evening, Frieda and Harold had sex in a roadside hay-hut, though it was several days later when Frieda disclosed to Lawrence what had happened. The couple arrived at Lago di Garda by train in early September, finally settling in the Italian lakeside village of Gargnano, where they stayed until the spring.

The dialectic of love

Much of what we know of the first year of Lawrence's love affair with Frieda comes from the many letters he wrote while he was away from England, as well as from the poems of this period that were published in the collection *Look! We Have Come Through!* (1917). The trauma of Frieda's separation from her children, and Lawrence's fear that she would never give herself fully to a life with him, is self-evident in 'She Looks Back', for example, which was penned in Beuerberg.

> Therefore, even in the hour of my deepest, passionate
> malediction
> I try to remember it is also well between us.
> That you are with me in the end.
> That you never look quite back; nine-tenths, ah, more
> You look round over your shoulder;
> But never quite back.

By far the most revealing text, however, is the second half of his posthumously published novel, *Mr Noon*. Written in 1920, Part 1 of the story appeared to have been completed to Lawrence's satisfaction, and he had agreed with his American agent that releasing it in instalments might reduce the likelihood of it being suppressed, as had happened to *The Rainbow* (1915), or of it facing libel actions, as with *Women in Love* (1920). Lawrence seemed to lose interest in the project, however, and Part 1 was only published in 1934, four years after his death, as part of a collected edition of Lawrence's short stories. The manuscript of the lengthier Part 2 only surfaced at auction in 1972, where it was bought by the University of Texas. The two parts were finally published together in a single volume in 1984.

Mr Noon does in fact read like two separate stories. In the first half the protagonist Gilbert Noon appears to be modelled on George Henry Neville, a boyhood friend with whom he subsequently lost contact when he eloped with Frieda to Germany. When Gilbert crosses the Channel to begin the second half of the story, however, there is no doubt that he has metamorphosed into D. H. Lawrence himself. From this point on, the plot shows a strikingly accurate convergence with the events of May–September, from the confrontation with the suspicious sergeant in the military town of Detsch [Metz], to the condescending reaction and disapproval of Johanna's [Frieda's] family, the letters and telegrams exchanged with the angry and grief-stricken Everard [Ernest], the often farcical quarrels, separations and reunions of the couple, and the details of their journey over the Alps into Austria and then Italy. Most important, however, is the light shone by the narrative on Frieda's earlier relationship with Otto Gross, and Lawrence's niggling anxiety that he had fallen in love with a woman whose sexuality would always conjure the shadowy presence of another, more passionate man.

Johanna, Lawrence writes, 'was full-bosomed, and full of life, gleaming with life, like a flower in the sun, and like a cat that looks round in the sunshine and finds it good' (XIV, 156). Her husband, she complains, 'is quite capable of killing me because I'm not a white snowflower. Don't you think it's absurd? When I'm a born dandelion. I was born to get the sun. I love love, and I hate worship' (XIV, 158). Johanna, 'who took her sex as a religion' (XVI, 175), explains that it was a psychologist, Eberhard [Otto], who taught her to 'love love'. 'I had a wonderful lover – a doctor and a philosopher, here in Munich. Oh, I loved him so much – and I waited for his letters', Johanna explains to Gilbert. 'He was Louise's [Else's] lover first. It was he who freed me, really. I was just the conventional wife, simply getting crazy boxed up' (XIV, 159–60). She continues:

> I was only with him two weeks – two separate weeks – here, and in Utrecht. He was a marvellous lover – but I knew it was no good. He never let one sleep. He talked and talked … . He took drugs. And he never slept. He just never slept. And he wouldn't let *you* sleep either. And he talked to you while he was loving you. He was wonderful … . Oh, he was a genius – a genius at love. He understood so much. And then he made one feel so free. He was almost the first psychoanalyst, you know – he was Viennese too, and far, far more brilliant than Freud. They were all friends. But Eberhard was spiritual – he may have been demoniacal, but he was spiritual. (XIV, 160)

Gilbert 'was becoming depressed' with this account. But he invites more explanation:

> He made me believe in love – in the sacredness of love. He made me see that marriage and all those things are based on fear. How can love be wrong? It is the jealousy and grudging that is wrong. Love is so much greater than the individual. Individuals are so poor and mean. – And then there can't be love without sex. Eberhard taught me that. And it is so true. Love *is* sex … . And there is no strong feeling in anybody that doesn't have an element of sex in it – don't you think? (XIV, 161)

Unsurprisingly Gilbert/Lawrence is uncomfortable with his lover's insistence that 'marriage is vile and possessive', as well as her reduction of everything to sex. Johanna/Frieda states that sex is the 'magnetism that holds people together', and that 'sex is always being perverted into something else – all the time'. Gilbert retorts that 'you don't have a sexual connection with everybody', and that 'perhaps something else is always being perverted into sex' (XIV, 161). Johanna also invokes the presence of her other lovers – 'Freyling' [Frick] and 'Berry' [William Dowson]. 'I rather love Freyling and Berry. I do, and so I do. It's no use denying it. And I won't deny it. Why should I deny them any more than Everard

[Weekley]?' (XIV, 163). Gilbert accuses Johanna of having a 'spiritual' concept of love – 'general love', love as 'Panacea' – which is abstract and indiscriminate. 'One should love all men', Johanna tells him; 'all men are loveable, somewhere'. Gilbert is dismissive: 'You can be spiritually in love with everybody at once, and take all men under your skirts in the same instant, like a Watts picture. But that's not physical.' He declares: 'I want exclusive physical love. – There may be aberrations. But the real fact in physical love is the exclusiveness: once the love is really *there*' (XVI, 207–9).

In these exchanges we see Lawrence sparring with the spectre of Otto Gross, and struggling through the 'aberrations' to formulate a doctrine of sexual love that would allow him to take all that Frieda had taught him, while at the same time setting limits to Frieda's passion so as to make mutual fidelity a realistic and meaningful goal. This dialogue, this dialectic, is in a way emblematic of Lawrence's vocation. For Lawrence was never content with the sheer physical pleasure of loving; he was a writer before he was a lover, and indeed his creative imagination became even more important as his health deteriorated and his physical vitality waned. Desperate to prove he could earn a living from writing, but also keen to put his new experience of love into words, in the first eight months of his relationship with Frieda he finished *Sons and Lovers* (1913), wrote two plays, started several new novels (which he then abandoned), composed poems and short stories, wrote notes and sketches that he would draw on for his first travel book, and penned lengthy letters almost every day. As a writer and a thinker, Lawrence was wrapped in a constant conversation about erotic love, in which the universal and the particular, the said and the unsayable, the mental idea and the body's reality of feeling and touch were dynamic and conflictual companions.

While Lawrence carried with him over the Alps the manuscript of his next novel, Frieda carried her own treasured bundle of Gross's love letters. When she felt the need to explain her elopement to Weekley, it was these letters from Gross that she sent him (Byrne 1995: 122). On another occasion, she posted him a copy of Anna Karenina, believing Anna's predicament would clarify to her husband why she felt trapped by marriage and needed to escape. It was a sad and farcical irony that Frieda had overlooked a note she had left in the pages of the book, which had come from her previous lover in Nottingham, William Dowson. 'If you wanted to run away with someone', Dowson had written to Frieda, 'why didn't you run away with me?' Weekley promptly dispatched the note to Lawrence for him to see what he had gotten himself into (Worthen 2005: 127).

It is significant, too, that *Lady Chatterley* ends not with the lovers united but with a piece of text. Reflecting back on what he has just written in his letter to Connie, Mellors adds: 'Well, so many words, because I can't touch you. If I could sleep with my arms round you, the ink could stay in the bottle'(XIX, 370).[3] Having married Frieda in 1914, it wasn't physical distance that compelled Lawrence to keep writing of erotic love. From then on they were together, but their quarrels were often bitter, and by the time he wrote *Lady Chatterley* his wife was beginning to feel oppressed by his deteriorating health and was spending more and more time with her lover Angelo Ravagli (whom she would marry after Lawrence's death). There is no doubt that Lawrence found refuge from this situation in his writing. But *Lady Chatterley's Lover*, Lawrence's most romantic book, was also clearly the reenergising of a connection, with every new page delivered like a daily love letter for Frieda's enjoyment. As John Worthen, Lawrence's most recent biographer, remarks:

> If on the one hand its sexuality was an astonishing tribute to Frieda, and to how Lawrence felt about her feelings and her experience, it was above all a final tribute to the life of the body, male and female, which now occupied him more in the imagination and recreation than it could in actuality or in desire. It is not too much to say the second and third versions of *Lady Chatterley's Lover* were verbal acts of love to Frieda, written in the words she would have read or heard each time he came back from writing, towards the end of a partnership which started out as violent sexual attraction … . Lady Chatterley was, then, a way of insisting that he was not too withdrawn, ill or fragile to imagine making intense love to Frieda, as he always had done; and to experience (and make his reader feel) what she felt. (2005: 353)

By writing about love, Lawrence could show his closeness to Frieda while also embracing the distance between them. Frieda knew, and Lawrence knew that she knew, that in the battle between love and the idea of love Lawrence's allegiance was necessarily divided. 'Sometimes she thought he was a big fountain pen which was always sucking at her blood for ink' (I, 106), Lawrence writes of Paula, whose strained marriage to Peter is the subject of the short story, 'New Eve and Old Adam', written by Lawrence during those first months together in Italy. But we should not let the conflict between Frieda's wilful sensuality and Lawrence's

---

[3] That Karl Marx wrote something similar in a love letter to his wife in 1856 suggests that the interplay of love, loss and language is a common experience, particularly for writers. 'You will smile, my sweet heart, and ask, how did I come to all this rhetoric? If I could press your sweet, white heart to my heart, I would keep silent and not say a word. Since I cannot kiss with my lips, I must kiss with language and make words' (cited in Gane 1993: 102–3).

writerly vocation hide a more profound truth. For there is, as Polhemus observes, a vital note of realism in Lawrence's mysticism: 'people are almost never, if ever, "truly together"; therefore the ink, which signifies separation, must flow to sanctify touch'. This was Lawrence's vocation: 'to shepherd with words as well as touch' (Polhemus 1990: 298).

'My great religion', Lawrence (1932: 96) wrote to Ernest Collings from Italy in January 1913, 'is a belief in the blood, the flesh, as being wiser than the intellect'. The body is a flame, Lawrence continued with majestic Nietzschean imagery, and consciousness is but the light that the body shines on the things around it. But to sustain this belief in the brilliant light of the flesh, Lawrence had to keep fashioning a language capable of shaping, inspiring and refining the mind. Lovers must draw apart, not simply because they are separate beings, nor because separation is necessary for the rekindling of desire, but because, if there is to be love, then there must be room for lovers to talk about love – because space must be made for words to fall between them.

7

The classical sociology of love

Even Marxists fall in love

When one thinks of modern theorists of love, the founders of the sociological canon rarely spring to mind. For the classical sociologists of the nineteenth and early twentieth centuries, the domain of sexual intimacy was overshadowed by the dramatic structural and economic changes associated with the development of industrial capitalism. The early sociological thinkers were, nonetheless, not indifferent to the impact these changes were having on domestic life. Friedrich Engels, for instance, was keen to show how the bourgeois institution of marriage was a mechanism for the protection and reproduction of men's property. 'Monogamy arose from the concentration of considerable wealth in the hands of a single individual – a man – and from the need to bequeath this wealth to the children of that man and of no other' (Engels 1942: 67). In *The Condition of the Working Class in England* (1845), Engels had observed how women's employment in the expanding textile industry had in some working-class households made women the principal breadwinners, an 'unnatural' role reversal which in turn showed that 'the former rule of the husband over the wife must also have been unnatural' (Engels 1958: 164). No doubt drawing on the experiences of his own lover, the illiterate Irish millworker Mary Burns, Engels later argued, in *The Origin of the Family, Private Property, and the State* (1884), that a new generation of independent proletarian women was coming into being – 'women who have never known what it is to give themselves to a man from any other considerations than real love, or to refuse to give themselves to their lover from fear of economic consequences'. These women were the revolutionary protagonists of an egalitarian 'sex-love' relationship which 'becomes, and can only become, the real rule among the oppressed classes' (Engels 1942: 73, 63).

In an earlier, more philosophical mood, Marx and Engels had mocked their intellectual rivals for being so horrified of carnal love. We should not be surprised, the young dialectical materialists argued in *The Holy Family* (1845), that the conservative Hegelians should repudiate something so unintellectual, so unspeculative, so passionate and sensuous as love, for it is the defining error of idealism to reject the primacy of the physical senses and, along with those senses, the force and the reality of material things.

> *Object!* Horrid! There is nothing more damnable, more profane, more massy than an *object* – down with the object! How could absolute subjectivity, the *actus purus*, 'pure' Criticism, not see in love its *bête noire*, that Satan incarnate, in love, which first really teaches man to believe in the objective world outside himself, which not only makes man an object, but the object a man! (Marx and Engels 1956: 32)

Ortega y Gasset (1933: 529) had similarly described how love, unlike the self-centredness of desire, lifts us out of ourselves: 'When we love we abandon all inner peace and security and virtually desert ourselves and enter the object.' But the exclusiveness of love's attraction to the object is also what Arendt identified as its unworldliness, for by drawing lovers closer to each other love obliterates the communal world of objective things, or at least makes the lovers blissfully indifferent to its existence (Arendt 1958: 242). From his own personal experience, Marx knew full well that love was closer to mysticism, erotic enchantment closer to a subjective state of grace, than his criticism of the Hegelian idealists might suggest. Not long after his secret engagement to Jenny von Westphalen in 1836, the letter he wrote to his father from the University of Berlin shows how empty and insubstantial the object world appears to the soulful, subjective world of the lover:

> Dear Father,
>
> When I left you, a new world had come into existence for me, that of love, which in fact at the beginning was a passionately yearning and hopeless love. Even the journey to Berlin, which otherwise would have delighted me in the highest degree ... left me cold. Indeed, it put me strikingly out of humour, for the rocks which I saw were not more rugged, more indomitable, than the emotions of my soul, the big towns not more lively than my blood, the inn meals not more extravagant, more indigestible, than the store of fantasies I carried with me, and, finally, no work of art was as beautiful as Jenny. (Cited in Gabriel 2011: 25)

A later letter from Jenny to Marx also described, from her side, the exclusiveness and magnetism of their original mutual attraction: 'Oh, my darling, how you looked at me the first time like that and then quickly looked away, and then looked at me again, and I did the same, until at last we looked at each other for quite a long time and very deeply, and could no longer look away' (cited in Gabriel 2011: 24).

The desacralisation of marriage

Marx's burning ambition in his youth was to become not a political revolutionary but a romantic dramatist and poet. Though it was seven years before they were finally wed, Marx's love for a beautiful aristocratic woman well above his own social station probably elevated the moral status of marriage to him. It is perhaps unsurprising, therefore, that he and Engels parted company on the issue of marriage, with Jenny Marx converting this difference of opinion into a thinly veiled hostility towards Engels' proletarian lover (Gane 1993: 144–5). Marx himself opposed those Prussian radicals who were calling for the legal right to freely terminate a marriage, warning that 'indulgence of the wishes of individuals would turn into harshness towards the essence of the individuals, towards their moral reason, which is embodied in moral relationships' (cited in Gane 1993: 100). This idea that marriage is a moral bond, superior to the immediate wishes of those who comprise it, was defended more systematically by Emile Durkheim, a more conservative sociologist with a keen interest in the nature of social order. Durkheim's writings on the family are rarely given much attention today, partly due to their association with the now unfashionable field of American structural-functionalism, and especially with Talcott Parsons's account of how the 'romantic love complex' evolved to ensure that the modern family continued to fulfil its societal functions despite the decline in the normative pressures of kinship (Parsons 1943). Alongside this structuralist interpretation of Durkheim, it is also generally assumed that Durkheim was too much of a traditionalist to have written openly about sexual love, and that his understanding of heterosexual intimacy was inevitably impaired by a view of women that was 'reactionary and arch-conservative' (Gane 1993: 21–58; Cristi 2012: 433).

For Durkheim, social order ultimately rests on a reverence for the sacred. The sacred is not, as religions imagine it to be, a thing touched by the hand of divinity, but is instead those collective entities – roles and obligations, laws and values, shared patterns of judgement, behaviour and feeling – which possess moral authority by virtue of the fact that they transcend, and typically outlast, the particular instances in which specific individuals enact, embody or are cognisant of them. Romantic love, we have seen, has for centuries been understood as an irresistible enchantment warranting the surrender of rational self-interest. For Durkheim, marriage was the institutional social representation of this moral idealism, protecting the unity and solidarity of lovers by stamping their relationship with the insignia of an even greater collective authority. Marriage was not just a private bond, but also a public act, consecrated by law and ritual, symbolising the existence of a social good attractive and powerful enough to rouse individuals to serve something other than their solitary selves. In the absence of an attachment to a collective entity such as matrimony, the individual was at risk, Durkheim argued, of sinking into introspective egoism, or else the condition of angry frustration that he associated with 'anomie'.

Durkheim's treatment of matrimony as a dimension of the 'sacred' had two clear consequences for his thinking. One was that it made him reluctant to support calls to liberalise divorce laws and allow spouses to dissolve a marriage by mutual consent. The other was that it led him into conflict with the sexual revolutionaries who believed the rules of erotic love should go no further than those of medical hygiene and anatomical pleasure. In his 1906 essay, 'Divorce by Mutual Consent', Durkheim acknowledged that no social institution was beyond criticism or dispute, making clear his approval of divorce as an indispensable right. He argued, however, that allowing spouses to divorce without legal authorisation by a judge would desacralise marriage as an institution, and impair marital relations in their 'normal functioning'.

Referring back to his 1897 study of suicide, Durkheim noted the positive statistical correlation between the number of male suicide rates in a country and the number of divorces. The fact that the greatest increase in suicide in communities where divorce is more frequent is among *married* men proved to Durkheim that the spread of divorce enfeebles the moral authority of matrimony. As marriage as an institution loses collective reverence and respect, the meaning and value of fidelity to another person is weakened, and increased numbers of married men find themselves in a state of anomic disillusionment that leads some to self-destruction. Marriage, Durkheim argues,

> by subjecting the passions to regulation, gives the man a moral posture which increases his forces of resistance. By assigning a definite, determinate, and, in principle, invariable object to his desires, it prevents them from wearing themselves out in the pursuit of ends which are always new and always changing, which grow boring as soon as they are achieved and which leave only exhaustion and disenchantment in their wake .... But it only produces these effects because

it implies a respected form of regulation which creates social bonds among individuals.

On the other hand, to the extent that these bonds are fragile, that they can be broken at will, marriage ceases to be itself and, consequently, can no longer have the same virtue. Regulation from which one can withdraw whenever one has a notion is no longer regulation. A restraint from which one can so easily liberate oneself is no longer a restraint which can moderate desires and, in moderating them, appease them. (1978b: 247–8)

As we shall see in a moment, Durkheim was not the only classical sociologist to associate the pursuit of ever-changing ends with 'disenchantment', but he was more distinctive in his belief that anomic disquiet could be remedied by institutional restraint. That said, Durkheim never gave an entirely convincing explanation for why women are not morbidly afflicted by the weakening of marriage in the same way men are, nor why marriage is more likely to be experienced by women not as a healthy regulation of desire but as a 'heavy, profitless yoke' (Durkheim 1951: 272–6). Despite acknowledging that marriage does not favour men and women equally – 'their interests are contrary; one needs restraint and the other liberty' – the ethical primacy of restraint over liberty in Durkheim's sociological thinking meant that women's stake in the liberalisation of divorce laws barely registered in his discussion of the issue. In a respectful and sometimes approving review of Marianne Weber's book on the legal history of women as wives and mothers, *Ehefrau und Mutter in der Rechtsentwicklung* (1907), Durkheim did write more candidly about the patriarchal subordination of women. Agreeing that reforms were needed to improve the legal status of women, he nonetheless argued that the modern nuclear family, by intensifying the emotional content of domestic life, had brought with it a moral elevation of women's role, and that the devaluation of marriage as a social institution would threaten 'this source of feminine grandeur'.

> The respect shown her, a respect that has increased over historical time, has its origin mainly in the religious respect which the hearth inspires. If the family were henceforth considered only as a precarious union of two beings who could at any moment separate if they wished to, and who, as long as the association lasted, each had his or her own circle of interests and preoccupations, it would be difficult for this religion to subsist. And women would thereby be diminished. (Durkheim 1978c: 144)

Durkheim's liberalism was progressive for his time, but his thinking was still fettered by the constraints of seemingly unquestionable gender roles, as well as his tendency to legitimise those roles on the grounds that, although undoubtedly historical products of the division of labour, they were the internalisation of social laws that had effectively shaped, if not perfected, the biological constitution of the sexes (1951: 215; 1964: 56–62, 264). His understanding of the relationship between individual and society, though nuanced, was also contradictory. His default position was the quasi-Freudian view that civilisation – the 'collective conscience' – was needed to externally restrain the naturally egocentric impulses of the individual. But he also understood that civilisation shaped and defined 'the individual', constructing and legitimising both selfish and moral forms of individualism. 'As soon as men are inoculated with the precept that their duty is to progress,' Durkheim observed, 'it is harder to make them accept resignation; so the number of the malcontent and disquieted is bound to increase' (1951: 364). In speaking in the same passage about the 'morality of progress and perfection' and its tendency to increase anomie, Durkheim was recognising that moral discourses and ideals can construct and magnify desires as well as control and moderate them. He needed to take this further in order to address the ideological legitimisation of greed and ambition, however. Indeed, he also needed to acknowledge the way political, moral and romantic visions may justly arouse the unhappiness of the downtrodden, and not just the decadent appetites of the rich. In categorising married women's suicides as 'fatalistic' – 'deriving from excessive regulation' (1951: 276), as he put it – Durkheim ignored, for instance, the impact which the culture of romantic love may have had in making oppressive marriages even more intolerable for some women by raising rather than restraining their hopes. (Durkheim drew on French literature to illustrate egoistic and anomic suicide, but his examples were all male characters, and he made no mention of Emma Bovary and Anna Karenina – two characters who would have almost certainly been instances of 'anomic' suicide in his formulation.)

In a way that sometimes feels antiquated and anti-liberal today, Durkheim wanted to use sociological thinking to show how legal and political reform cannot be driven solely by the needs and desires of individuals. Society, for Durkheim, is neither the sum nor the division of self-interests, and he believed that to change social institutions purely on the basis of what particular individuals want at a particular point in time is to miss something crucial about the social existence of human beings. At the same time, Durkheim's classic study of suicide was also repeatedly used by him to demonstrate the personal stakes involved in the preservation of collective health. Rising rates of suicide were the clearest possible evidence that social dysfunctions are symptomatic at the level of humans' organic existence. The proof that social institutions matter, Durkheim kept arguing, is that when they become weak or unstable, the individual is at risk of extreme morbidity, tending to question the very purpose of life.

An individual estranged from collective life, Durkheim wrote, only 'becomes a mystery to himself, unable to escape the exasperating and agonising question: to what purpose?' (Durkheim 1951: 212). There is nothing inherent in the individual as a living organism that justifies treating human existence as something precious, valuable or worthwhile. 'You are a randomly united lump of something', Tolstoy (1987: 40) sagely reminded his readers. 'This lump decomposes and the fermentation is called life.' Durkheim's answer to Tolstoy's existential question – how can one find meaning in a life that will be destroyed by death? – is partly Tolstoyan in flavour, with both thinkers acknowledging the role of 'faith' in the cherishing of the community as a transcendent object, and both recognising the role of collective action in creating and energising that faith:

> a faith is above all warmth, life, enthusiasm, the exaltation of all mental activity, the transport of the individual beyond himself. Now, without leaving the self, how could he add to the energies he has? How could he surpass himself with his forces alone? The only source of heat where we might warm ourselves morally is that formed by the society of our peers; the only moral forces with which we might sustain and increase our own are those we attribute to others. (Durkheim 2001: 320)[1]

One might also ask of Durkheim why the desacralisation of marriage would engender such frustration and disappointment among married men. Why would loosening the restraints of matrimony lead to disillusionment rather than hope, optimism or release? Durkheim's answer to this echoes Freud's concept of the 'reality principle'. We do not live in paradise, and whether it is food, sex, love, friendship or esteem, *Ananke* – scarcity – is the inescapable condition of human existence. To live well under this condition is, and must be, to live

---

[1] Tolstoy's own spiritual conversion, as documented in *A Confession* (1879), located the meaning of life not in the specific doctrines of the Church but in the religious-inspired 'union of all people, united through love' (Tolstoy 1987: 68–9). In 'The Death of Ivan Ilyich' (1886), the dying court judge, finally acknowledging the truth of his own mortality, suddenly realises 'that he had spent his life not as he ought' (XI, 127), attaching himself to superficial proprieties and trivial vanities rather than to anything of lasting meaning. The only figure in Tolstoy's story who is not in denial of either his own or Ivan Ilyich's death, is the peasant youth Gerasim, who nurses Ilyich with ingenuous good humour and attentiveness. Gerasim seems to understand that death is the great equaliser that makes wealth and status irrelevant. He takes the trouble to care for 'a dying man, and he hoped that for him too someone would be willing to take the same trouble when his time came' (VII, 116). Gerasim feels attached to a more lasting stream of ethical practice; in his *Gemeinschaft* world, death doesn't destroy the meaning of life but rather makes care for one's fellows a self-evidently meaningful endeavour.

with missing out. Faith in the exclusiveness and longevity of marriage, in other words, protects the (male) spouse from wanting something that, for most, is not practically attainable. Thus Durkheim describes those 'gentle' but 'mediocre marriages' which he believes would be irreparably damaged by the possibility of no-fault divorce. There are, he says,

> marriages for which the spouses do not have for one another all the sympathy which might be hoped for, yet in which, nonetheless, each has sufficient feeling for his duty usefully to fulfil his function, while this attachment to the common task brings them together in mutual tolerance … . Where will they draw the moral force necessary to bear with courage an existence whose joys can be no more than rather austere if public authority solemnly proclaims that they have the right to free themselves of it whenever they please? Thus, divorce by mutual consent can only take the resiliency out of domestic life and disorganise a greater number of families without, however, resulting in an increase of happiness or a diminution of unhappiness for the average spouses. (1978b: 250)

The beloved's right to secrecy

The sober realism of Durkheim's analysis here must be read alongside his appreciation of how social bonds, when they rise above the crude exchange or combination of self-interests, create and sustain a sense of the sacred. The sexual bond is no exception to this, and although Durkheim was conservative in his desire to protect the institution of marriage, he saw this institution as the symbolic adornment and ennoblement of erotic love as much as a functional joint in the structural fabric of society. In the published transcript of a conversation with a medical doctor and advocate of sex education, Jacques-Amédée Doléris, who believed the most sensible lesson against extramarital affairs was one that emphasised the risk of sexually transmitted diseases, Durkheim noted the tendency for scientists like Doléris to treat the mysterious character of the sexual act as an outdated relic of religious thinking. What needs explaining, Durkheim argues, is why a mystical conception of sexual relations is apparent even in the most primitive of societies. 'The dark, mysterious and awe-inspiring nature of the sexual act' is recognised throughout history, Durkheim points out, and this suggests something more than a religious slogan or aberrant superstition, indicating a primordial sentiment that people have always felt (Durkheim 1979: 144).

One source of the mystery that surrounds the sexual relation, Durkheim argues, is the fact that it is experienced as something exceptional, beyond the profane world of material interests, practical calculations and mundane things. But sex is not only a quasi-religious surpassing of the everyday world, for in its strange passion and its inherent immodesty it also violates our sense of virtue. Sex is not only a transcendence of the profane but also, paradoxically, a profanation of the sacred. The moral anxiety that we today feel about sex is, Durkheim suggests, partly a reflection of the importance we attach to the integrity of the person: the individual has been allotted a sacredness which we normally respect by concealing our bodies, fleeing intimacy and keeping our distance. From the ethical perspective of moral individualism, it is 'a kind of desecration to fail to respect the boundaries separating men'. In sex, however, where 'each of the two personalities in contact is engulfed by the other', this profanation is almost unprecedented (Durkheim 1979: 146).

Yet while it seems that in the sexual act there is neither reason nor morality, Durkheim also highlights the paradox that alongside the anomic nature of erotic passion there is also something in the sexual relation which is 'profoundly moral', precisely because it stands above the practical, the rational and the mundane. For Octavio Paz (1995) the moral component of the sexual relation comes from love: love is pious because it addresses itself to something more than a physical body; the soul of a person is a heavenly mystery which invites loving reverence because it cannot be grasped, mastered or used. Georg Simmel, a German contemporary of Durkheim, wrote perceptively about the role of modesty and discretion in erotic life in similar terms, suggesting that mutual attentiveness and understanding in intimate relationships are put at risk by the greedy demands of reason. Erotic love, Simmel says, has to exercise a kind of intellectual restraint, dwelling in 'the interstitial realm, in which faith replaces knowledge'.

> The mere fact of absolute knowledge, of a psychological having-exhausted, sobers us up, even without prior drunkenness; it paralyses the vitality of relations and lets their continuation really appear pointless. This is the danger of complete and (in more than an external sense) shameless abandon, to which the unlimited possibilities of intimate relations tempt us .... It is highly probable that many marriages founder on this lack of reciprocal discretion – discretion both in taking and in giving. They lapse into a trivial habituation without charm, into a matter-of-factness which has no longer any room for surprises. The fertile depth of relations ... is only the reward for that tenderness and self-discipline which, even in the most intimate relation that comprises the total individual,

respects his inner private property, and allows the right to question to be limited by the right to secrecy. (Simmel 1950a: 329)

The mystery of love's object, which for Plato was the sublime metaphysical Forms that became visible through the vessel of the beloved's beauty, is transposed in the modern world to the hidden depths of the individual and her unique interiority. For what is loved is always more than the sum of its parts, and those parts can deteriorate or be lost without that love diminishing. Love, as we understand it today, attaches itself to the unity and totality of a person that lies behind her contingent empirical gestures and appearances. But the individual whom it addresses is also opaque to perfect reasoning and representation, being an 'unanalysable unity, which is not to be derived from anything else, not subsumable under any higher concept, set within a world otherwise infinitely analysable, calculable, and governed by general laws' (Simmel 1971: 244). If love touches the hidden soul of the other, this contact must therefore be something more than sensory pleasure or rational agreement. 'What has been inherited from Plato', Simmel observes, 'is the feeling that in love there lives something mysterious, beyond the contingent individual existence and meeting, beyond the momentary sensual desire, and beyond the mere relations between personalities'. Love reaches past earthly, profane existence to something timeless and immeasurable, as the mutual pledging of souls seems to articulate. 'In the sacrament of marriage, this metaphysicalising has just grasped a historical-social form' (1971: 242).

Simmel notes how the sublimation of love into wider social structures and concerns – children, neighbourhood, the nation, the planet, the future of humankind – is a modern echo of the Platonic dissipation of love into the universal. The 'species life', Simmel writes in terms that Tolstoy would have endorsed, 'leads the individual out of himself, makes him participant in an unending process of development in which the impulses of love join one link of its chain with the other' (1971: 243). And yet, just as a universalist morality cannot fully penetrate the sphere of the modern individual conscience, so Simmel argues that, contrary to Tolstoy's denunciation of the egoism of sexual passion, we must also recognise 'something like an Individual Law of erotic life'.

> In the incomparable relationship of incomparable individuals there lies a meaning which is wholly limited to that relationship and yet extends beyond its surface manifestation, not dominated or justified by a universal idea of Beauty, or Value, or of Amiability, but just by the idea of these individual existences

and their perfection. And if we say that this would be somewhere beyond their fleeting individual existence, the Beyond is but an inadequate designation of the form of its presence within the individual exclusiveness of this love. (1971: 243–4)

The sacrament of sex

This, I think, is how best to understand Durkheim's defence of marriage as a symbolic form capable of honouring and protecting both the strangeness of lovers to each other and the strangeness of the lovers' bond to society at large. The sexual relation stood out for him in this respect because he believed there was 'no act which creates such strong bonds between human beings' (Durkheim 1979: 142). Sex engenders a decentred sense of unity, a blending of bodies and personalities that is both mutual loss and mutual gain, a sacrifice of self to something greater than the self. For Durkheim, this transcendence of self-interest was the hallmark of all morality.

In moral terms, however, sexual love is contradictory. Sexual intimacy, Durkheim writes, 'has an associative, and consequently moral power without compare'. Yet because sex does not respect that 'ideal sphere' described by Simmel, 'whose trespassing by another person insults one's honour' (Simmel 1950a: 321), it is also morally subversive. The common moral conscience, Durkheim observes, therefore 'cannot advocate such an act, nor condemn it, nor can it praise, stigmatise or above all declare it unimportant' (Durkheim 1979: 142). Instead sexual desire and its satisfaction must be 'veiled in darkness and mystery', protected with discretion and reserve, the ritual patterns and formal and informal observances of marital life providing the symbolic resources to mark out the boundaries between the sacred and the profane. Marriage as a symbolic form thus provides a public representation of union that both elaborates the lovers' necessary respect for the mystery of each other, and gives moral meaning to the transgression of personal boundaries that is a necessary element of sex. By contrast, treating sex 'as no more than the manifestation of a biological function' that is shared with non-human animals – this is how Durkheim depicts the medical-health model of sex education – 'denatures' and denies what Durkheim calls the *sui generis* reality of the sexual bond, the love relation being a sacred community (a 'communion') greater than the two who comprise it. The sexual relationship, he argues, contains within it the wherewithal to eradicate and redeem its constitutional immorality. For in fact this desecration also produces a communion, and a communion of the most intimate kind possible between two conscious beings. Through this communion, the two persons united become one; the limits which originally circumscribed each of them are first displaced and later transferred. A new personality is born, enveloping and embracing the other two. Should this fusion become critical and the new unity thus constituted become lasting, then from that moment onwards the desecration ceases to exist, since there are no longer two distinct, separate people, but one. (Durkheim 1979: 147)

It is, of course, the intoxicating promise of all new lovers to create a new world, a new community to replace the lovers' communities of birth. But the idea that marriage entails a loss of individual identity sits awkwardly with the keener sense of personal autonomy that we have today. Indeed it is hard not to be seduced by the idea that it is precisely the freedom of lovers – their permanent entitlement to 'exit' the relationship – which is what really makes their union so pure. Divorce is in this sense the 'central axis' of marriage in the modern world, as Pascal Bruckner puts it. 'The commitment is all the more authentic because it can be challenged' (Bruckner 2013: 15). Our more individualist sensibilities have also made us more aware than Durkheim probably was of the repressions, confusions and estrangements caused by the way the demands of moral discretion and censorship encroached into the sexual lives of Victorian men and women, and which even today make it difficult for many lovers to talk openly about sexual desire. But Durkheim's insistence on not 'giving in to bourgeois prudery' (1979: 143) suggests he had a more enlightened view of sexual relations than is often assumed – perhaps, in fact, a *too enlightened* view, given how confident he was in lovers' ability to open themselves to one another through the act of sex. Durkheim thus criticised Kant for regarding the immorality of using another person as a means of pleasure as correctable by a reciprocal act of sacrifice, the idea that a 'barter of personalities' could remedy the transgression being 'pathetic' in Durkheim's view (1979: 148n4). But no doubt he was most ignorant here of the repressed needs and desires of women, for it is much easier for a man to imagine sex as an elevated communion of souls when he has never had to take his wife's sexual pleasure into consideration.

Durkheim's faith in marriage as a *sui generis* union does echo, nonetheless, the experiences of those who have enjoyed – and perhaps even some of those who have endured – long-lasting relationships. 'I do not feel anything when I brush against the legs of my wife,' Paz (1995: 265) reports the Spanish poet and novelist Unamuno saying in his old age, 'but mine ache if hers do.' The congruence of bodies that have grown together over a lifetime may diminish the queer spell of the erotic, but this comes with the greater certainty that both one's pleasures and one's sufferings are shared. Durkheim's warnings about the liberalisation of divorce laws may remind us, too, of the origin of the embarrassment that is often felt when former lovers must meet in the role of acquaintances, 'whereas, in fact, neither holds any mystery for the other' (Durkheim 1979: 147). What was previously redeemed by the sacredness of a mutual commitment is now profaned. Even the most beautiful and sincere love, when the partners concede defeat and it comes to an end, is likely to suffer a kind of retroactive defilement. And if a former love retains anything of its original mystery and extremism, it can only do so by passing into the domain of the unreal, robbing people of a part of their past whose meaning must now become unfathomable.

Love, as Alain Badiou puts it, is a 'minimal communism', for 'the real subject of love is the becoming of the couple and not the mere satisfaction of the individuals that are its component parts' (Badiou 2012: 90). In an article ostensibly inspired by Durkheim's *The Elementary Forms of Religious Life* (1912), but in practice owing more to Erving Goffman, Sasha Weitman (1999) has catalogued, in a way that was probably impossible in Durkheim's era, the reciprocal expectations and rules that govern the practices of modern sexual intimacy. Noting that variations of these same interactional principles and ideals – such as playfulness, aestheticism, freedom and solidarity – are also part of the participatory rules of non-intimate social occasions, Weitman suggests that both belong to a broader domain that he calls the 'socioerotic', one important function of which is to provide 'psychosocial moratoria' from the violence, indignities and alienations of profane social life. One might argue that Weitman's analysis exaggerates the continuity between the intimate and non-intimate domains of sociality, and that he underemphasises the intensity of transgression and vulnerability in the practices of sexual intimacy, as well as the challenge which transcendent love between two people poses to the wider order of sociality. But perhaps what symbolism we have lost, since Durkheim's time, through the decline in the conventions of marriage, we have gained through more artful and sophisticated rituals of sexual contact. In any case, Weitman's persuasive argument is that we need to appreciate how the ritualised patterns and rules of erotic and social activity 'serve as matrices, as microfoundaries, for the production and reproduction of the bonds that attach us to others', and how in producing and reproducing these bonds we 'keep alive our hopes and dreams for a different social world' (1999: 101).

The asceticism of Max Weber

The work of the German sociologist Max Weber – and indeed the life of the man himself – is renowned for its focus on rationalism, and in many respects this makes Weber an unlikely source of insight into the 'irrational' sphere of erotic love. Weber's story is more complex and contradictory than appears at first glance, however, and there are subtleties and shifts in his thinking that are inseparable from the historical context of his life. This context includes his knowledge of, and personal relations with, the sexual revolutionaries of Schwabing, among them Frieda Lawrence's older sister, Else Jaffé.

Weber's father was a worldly magistrate whose hedonistic impulses and authoritarian rule of the family household had regularly set him at odds with his Huguenot wife's religious puritanism. As a child, Weber had, like D. H. Lawrence, sympathised and identified with the more principled, if morally demanding, character of his mother. As a young man, Weber grew to hate his father's bullying chauvinism, repudiating in the process all paternally marked signs of complacency, indolence and greed (Mitzman 1970). When he became a student of Law in Heidelberg, and subsequently embarked on a year of military service in Strasbourg, he apparently had plentiful opportunities to enjoy a more indulgent lifestyle. According to his wife, however, he faithfully deployed the asceticism he had inherited from his mother as a defence against desire.

> Certainly, as a student he had abandoned himself to the vulgar high spirits of fraternity life. He had done a lot of drinking, spent far more money than was necessary and than his parents expected him to spend, and had had companions in Strasbourg who gratified all their sensual appetites in a coarse, irresponsible, and mindless manner. But his mother has reason to be thankful. Without using words … she had implanted in him indestructible inhibitions against a surrender to his drives. He withstood the example of the others and thought it better to struggle more and more painfully against the demonic temptations of the spirit by a robust corporeality than to give nature its due. (Marianne Weber 1975: 91–2)

Weber's attraction to women was apparently not devoid of eroticism, but sensuality for Weber needed to be sublimated into something more profound and edifying. His wife wrote of how Weber was capable of a 'sensitive enjoyment of the pure magic of feminine grace, a grace in which sexuality is dormant or has been completely transformed into spiritual energy' (Marianne Weber 1975: 92). As for the attractiveness of 'erotic women', as he referred to those who had been touched by the philosophy of Otto Gross, Weber said that for them he could not feel 'an inner attachment on which a friendship could develop', explaining in one letter to his wife that 'I could never rely upon the permanence and certainty of such a strongly subjective perceived sense of camaraderie of such women … for whom in truth only the erotic man would have value' (Weber 1999: 64). Weber's letter of proposal to Marianne, written at the beginning of 1893, conveyed the same sense of restrained and displaced passion, paving the way for a companionate marriage that was loving and respectful but, by all accounts, sexually unconsummated, with Weber's libidinal energy channelled instead into his intellectual vocation.

> The tidal wave of passion runs high, and it is dark around us – come with me, my high-minded comrade, out of the quiet harbour of resignation, out onto the high seas, where men grow in the struggle of souls and the transitory is sloughed off. But *bear in mind*: in the head and heart of the mariner there must be clarity when all is surging underneath him. We must not tolerate any fanciful surrender to unclear and mystical moods in our souls. For when feeling rises high, you must control it to be able to steer yourself with sobriety. (Cited in Marianne Weber 1975: 179)

Weber carried a deep sense of love and gratitude towards his own mother alongside a nagging sense of guilt for having failed to defend her against her domineering husband. He finally stood up to his father in 1897, refusing to host him when he insisted on accompanying his long-suffering wife on a visit to the new Heidelberg home of their son and daughter-in-law. As Weber's father died seven weeks later, that was, however, the last time he saw him alive. Feeling that he had wronged both his mother and now his father in different ways, Weber was left with 'a guilt never to be expiated' (Marianne Weber 1975: 389). After this tragedy, nervous breakdowns and bouts of depression and insomnia became an almost constant accompaniment to the punishing work schedule of Weber's life.

The parcelling-out of the soul

Weber was a towering intellectual figure in the Heidelberg scene of the early twentieth century, a man whose depth of character was sometimes nourished, and sometimes overwhelmed, by inner torment and the ghosts of his past. As a sociologist of modernity, Weber is commonly thought of today as a pessimistic thinker who understood the development of Western industrial societies as a linear process of scientific growth and increasingly utilitarian thinking. In this tragic reading of Weber's work, the advance of modernity is calibrated in terms of a progressive repression and disfigurement of the human personality, being trampled beneath the juggernaut of economic calculation, scientific measurement and value-neutral instrumental reasoning. Even when Weber flirted with the possibility of resistance to the alienating world of rational capitalism, his thinking was still impeded by what feminists have argued is a strong patriarchal bias. Devaluing the role of love and compassion in fostering human solidarity, Weber seemed to believe that only the heroic manliness of the charismatic individual could oppose the relentless march of bureaucratic petrification (Bologh 1990).

The sources inspiring the more gloomy interpretations of Weber's work are well-known. There is, for example, the famous image, from *The Protestant Ethic and the Spirit of Capitalism* (1905), of a 'steel-hard' (*stahlhartes*) and 'factually unalterable' (*faktisch unabänderliches*) 'casing' (*Gehäuse*), terms which Weber used to depict the 'pulsating mechanism' of 'the modern economic order' once rational action had lifted itself free of its religious and ethical foundations. This steel-hard casing – or 'iron cage' in Parson's original, if now discredited, translation – transforms people into 'economic functionaries', Weber argued, who are compelled to specialise, calculate and compete, and to abandon the 'Faustian multi-dimensionality of the human species' and the Goethe-inspired ideal of a 'full and beautiful humanity' (2002: 18–19, 123–4).

The triumph of scientific specialisation over cultural depth and personality, of the '*Fachmensch*' over the '*Kulturmensch*', was also predicted by Weber in his mammoth treatise on economic sociology, *Economy and Society* (1922). There he associated secular modernity with the 'irresistible advance of bureaucratisation', describing bureaucratic discipline as an 'indestructible' phenomenon that, 'as the satisfaction of political and economic needs is increasingly rationalised', becomes 'universal'. Priding itself on the principles of objectivity, efficiency and precision – which 'primarily means a discharge of business according to calculable rules and "without regard for persons"' – the bureaucracy, Weber observed, 'develops the more perfectly, the more it is "dehumanised"', and the more it 'restricts the importance of charisma and of individually differentiated conduct'. For Weber, the spread of bureaucratic organisation was the inevitable consequence of humans' logical efforts to master their surroundings through empirical knowledge and scientific planning. The bureaucracy, a machine-like system of regimented human actions, was the 'animated' compliment to the 'inanimate machine' of factory technology. Together these separate manifestations of 'coagulated spirit' or 'objectified mind' [*geronnener Geist*] were, Weber wrote, 'busy fabricating the shell of bondage which men will perhaps be forced to inhabit some day, as powerless as the fellahs of ancient Egypt' (1978: 975, 1402–3, 1156). Not unlike Kafka, who had studied sociology under Weber's brother Alfred in Prague, Weber was alarmed by

> the idea that the world should be filled with nothing but those cogs who cling to a little post and strive for a somewhat greater one – a condition which, as in the papyri, you rediscover increasingly in the spirit of contemporary officialdom and above all of its next generation, our present students. This passion for bureaucratisation ... is enough to drive one to despair. It is ... as though we knowingly and willingly were *supposed* to become men who need 'order' and nothing but order, who become nervous and cowardly if this order shakes for a moment and helpless when they are torn from their exclusive adaptation to this order. That the world knows nothing more than such men of order – we are in any case caught up in this development, and the central question is not how we further and accelerate it but what we have to *set against* this machinery, in order to preserve a remnant of humanity from this parcelling-out of the soul, from this exclusive rule of bureaucratic life ideals. (Weber, cited and translated by Mitzman 1970: 178)

A final source of reference for the tragic reading of Weber is the process of scientific disenchantment described in 'Science as a Vocation'. Weber had been invited to give a talk at Munich University in 1917 as part of a lecture series organised by the Munich Free Students on '*geistige Arbeit als Beruf* – intellectual labour as a vocation. A certain thawing of Weber's own punitive asceticism in the years leading up to this event, combined with a desire to return to teaching after a 15-year medically necessitated sabbatical, seemed to have encouraged some admirers of Weber to believe that he now had the energy to support, and perhaps lead, a moral and political cause. Students engaged in Tolstoyan pacifist, socialist and other radical youth movements hoped that Weber might use his intellectual charisma and public authority to press for a utopian alternative to a society on the brink of military defeat and class war.

Having previously believed in the potential marriage of social science and nationalism, Weber must have had some private sympathy for the apocalyptic enthusiasm of Germany's youth. But his public stance was unforgiving. Speaking on '*Wissenschaft als Beruf* – '*Wissenschaft*' having a broader meaning in German than 'science' does in English, including history, anthropology, sociology and the wider disciplines of the humanities – Weber mocked the 'naïve optimism' of those 'big children' who believed that science, which he now conceded was nothing more than a means of mastering the world by calculation, could somehow lay a path towards meaning or happiness, and he rebuffed those students 'who come to our lectures and demand from us the qualities of leadership' (Weber 1970a: 143, 150). In early 1919, against the backdrop of revolutionary and counter-revolutionary violence, Weber came back to Munich to talk about 'Politics as a Vocation', and this time he opened by explicitly warning his audience that what he was going to say 'will necessarily disappoint you in a number of ways' (Weber 1970b: 77). One reason for this was that, in his view, the political vocation required a sober acknowledgement of facts and a reckoning of consequences that ruled out the uncompromising fervour of ethical absolutism which he believed was characteristic of both revolutionary socialism and Tolstoyan pacifism. Measuring up to the practical realities of political life, Weber argued, requires an 'ethic of responsibility' which necessarily 'endangers the "salvation of the soul"' (1970b: 126). Here, again, Weber's repudiation of the emotions seemed implacable.

In his '*Wissenschaft*' lecture Weber had noted that for something to be ethically meaningful it must be held to be 'worthwhile', but because science only deals with the practical and technical (with the 'means'), its logic demands the suspension of passionate value commitments – of the holding and cherishing of a worthwhile 'end'. Science proves its efficacy through the technical manipulation of things, and in doing so demonstrates the need for cool-headed rigour and value-freedom (*Wertfreiheit*). But whether this technical manipulation of the empirical world of people and things is good or just is not a question that science, for all its practical value, and indeed social prestige, can answer. Facts and values are now divorced, with no possibility of reunion: 'it is one thing to state facts, to determine mathematical or logical relations or the internal structure of cultural values, while it is another thing to answer questions of the *value* of culture and its individual contents and the question of how one should act in the cultural community and in political associations' (1970a: 146). The judgements, cares and concerns of different people are ultimately matters of personal or political faith, and neither reason nor evidence can supply the proof that might adjudicate between conflicts of values, for 'the ultimate possible attitudes toward life are irreconcilable, and hence their struggle can never be brought to an end' (1970a: 152). In this disenchanted world the social and cultural sciences can only present us with a lonely existential choice between 'warring gods'. The inescapable nature of this choice, and the impossibility of knowing with certainty which god is the right one, means that it cannot 'be proved that the existence of the world which these sciences describe is worth while, that it has any "meaning", or that it makes sense to live in such a world' (1970a: 144).

Even if one ignores the arbitrariness of values and focuses instead on the unambiguous practical and intellectual achievements of science, there is still the dispiriting certainty, Weber points out, that every form of insight or knowledge is destined to be surpassed. Here we can see the endemic condition of 'anomie' that Durkheim, in contrast to Weber, thought was a pathological failure of social regulation that could still be remedied through rational institutional reform. Since science, Weber observes, is always an unfinished project, chained to the course of infinite progress – 'each of us knows that what he has accomplished will be antiquated in ten, twenty, fifty years' (1970a: 138) – the scientifically rationalised world is one where it is impossible to live (and die) a completed existence. The price to be paid for material and intellectual progress is thus an inescapable sense of inner emptiness. The technical mastery of material life can offer no satisfactory answer to Tolstoy's question: 'What shall we do and how shall we live?' (1970a: 143). More accurately, we can calculate and define the 'how' – we can establish and control the means – but answers to the question 'why' can be mustered only in the shadowy domain of the irrational and incommunicable.[2]

Between passion and cognition

This, then, is the conventional intellectual portrait of Weber: an austere workaholic, a sociological pessimist and the advocate of an emotionally desiccated, value-free science. This latter 'advocacy', however, should immediately strike a discordant note, for it indicates that Weber's life and work was not the model of cool-headed, Platonic intellectualism it is often imagined to have been. We must not overlook the fact that Weber was a strident defender of the scientific enterprise – he was, according to his colleague Robert Michels, a man who 'loved science as passionately as a young bride' (cited in Scaff 1987: 739). Indeed

---

[2] A similar picture of senseless growth and expansion was painted by Marx, but for him this was a direct product of capitalist relations of production. 'Accumulation for the sake of accumulation, production for the sake of production: this was the formula in which classical economics expressed the historical mission of the bourgeoisie in the period of its domination' (Marx 1976: 742). The parallel between this description and Weber's account, in *The Protestant Ethic*, of how 'irrational' the striving for wealth as an end in itself looks from the standpoint of human happiness is noteworthy (Weber 2002: 17, 31). Marx believed, unlike Weber, that this historically specific 'law of value' would eventually collapse under its own contradictions, to be replaced by an economic system subordinated to collectively agreed definitions of justice and need.

Weber explicitly argued that only those who felt a deep moral calling for the scientific vocation – only those who lived 'for' rather than 'off' science, those for whom science was a 'strange intoxication' pursued with a 'passionate devotion' that was 'ridiculed by every outsider' (1970a: 135) – would be able to defy the disenchanting effects of the very enterprise of science and through this achieve something meaningful. Although Weber has been criticised for neglecting and devaluing the role of feelings and values in both social and intellectual life, it is clear that he believed that sustained engagement in scientific work presupposes the strong emotional conviction that such engagement is worthwhile. In this we can see an echo of his oblique recognition that the seventeenth-century Puritan's repressive attitude towards emotions, which was the cultural–psychological origin of the spirit of rational capitalism, was itself rooted in an emotional complex of 'angry hatred' and 'contempt' for both one's own and others' sins (Weber 2002: 113, 74; see Barbalet 2000: 345–6).

Weber's predilection for treating values as warring gods impervious to persuasion by factual evidence, dialogue and the consensus-forming force of reason was also a position he didn't maintain with a great deal of consistency. Though Weber spoke as if the conviction that science is a meaningful enterprise was his own personal, idiosyncratic faith, the logic of this faith – that social science performs a 'moral' service by helping people understand their values, their value-choices and the likely consequences of their value-oriented actions, thus 'bringing about self-clarification and a sense of responsibility' (1970a: 152) – would hardly be disputed by the community of social scientists today. In some respects Weber is closer to Durkheim than is often imagined here, Durkheim being far more convinced about the moral presuppositions of social science, as well as its morally beneficial effects, than his avowed 'positivism' would suggest.

That Weber (1970a: 147) said it was a 'moral achievement' of science to acquaint people with 'inconvenient facts' – 'facts that are inconvenient for their party opinions' – further demonstrates that Weber was, at the very least, inconsistent in claiming an unbridgeable divide between facts and values. For all Weber's tendency to treat values as the products of heroic but essentially arbitrary existential choices, 'Science as a Vocation' presents the teacher and researcher as a catalyst for reasoning about values, suggesting that logic and evidence, by encouraging people to enter into an informed dialogue with their beliefs, feelings and commitments, can disturb dogmatic opinions, disqualify transient whims, and promote self-understanding and rational accountability.

The same message is conveyed in 'Politics as a Vocation', where Weber applauded that 'ethic of responsibility' which political protagonists display when they reckon realistically with the empirically probable consequences of their decisions, and choose actions that may compromise the purity of their values. 'Mature' political actors, Weber says, bear up to the factual evidence, but at same time resist the lure of unprincipled opportunism, the significance of their values being sharpened and intensified though dialogue with the facticity of things. Just as students bring their values to be tested by the 'inconvenient facts' of science, so too science takes its facts to the politician, who is then 'aware of a responsibility for the consequences of his conduct and really *feels* such responsibility *with heart and soul*' (1970b: 127, my emphasis).

But where does love, erotic love, sit in this exchange between passion and cognition? The key text here is Weber's 'Intermediate Reflection' essay, which appeared in English under its original subtitle, 'Religious Rejections of the World and Their Directions'. The text was originally written in 1915 as a linking chapter between Weber's study of Confucianism and Taoism and his discussion of Hinduism in the *Sociology of Religion* (1920), and was revised by Weber shortly before his death in 1920. Here the theme of disenchantment remains prominent, but Weber links it as much to the disunity and incompleteness of a life lived within different and essentially irreconcilable value spheres, as to the dominance of science, bureaucracy and the instrumental rationality of economic life. Weber identifies 'the erotic' as one of those value spheres, but to do justice to his reflections on sexual love we need to read them in the narrative context of the essay, as well as place that essay in the biographical context of Weber's life. This I shall do in the next chapter.

8

Religion, rationality and eroticism in Max Weber

Religious rejections and the acosmism of love

Weber's phrase, 'religious rejections of the world', refers to the way religions of salvation sought redemption from a fragmented and contradictory world by abnegating that world and ethically devaluing it. The origin of that existential disquiet which led, first, to a religious belief in the salvation of the soul, and later, to a more inward search for meaning, is described by Simmel as the failure of the human spirit to assimilate and unify the disparate forms and changing practices of a social environment which, as early as the Greco-Roman era, had become too complex, and too extended in its linkages of motives, actions and consequences, to yield a clear and singular meaning:

> in the practical life of our mature cultures our pursuits take on the character of chains, the coils of which cannot be grasped in a single vision … . Thus people are eventually surrounded everywhere by a criss-crossing jungle of enterprises and institutions in which the final and definitely valuable goals are missing altogether. Only in this state of culture does the need for a final goal and meaning for life appear. Life, as long as it consists of short means-ends relations, each of which is sufficient and comforting in itself, knows nothing of the restless questioning which is a product of reflection about a being that is captured in a network of means, detours, and improvisations … . Beyond individual means, which now become transparent as being not the end but only a stage, the problem looms of forming a truly perfect union in which the soul is redeemed from the confusion of peremptory existence and in which unfulfilled desires ripen and are stilled. (Simmel 1991: 4)

For Weber, the sharpest tension between the soul's search for redemptive unity and the technical practices and concerns of material life arose when the ancient norms of neighbourliness, which had previously regulated family and clan relations, were appropriated, rationalised and sublimated into an organised 'religion of brotherliness'. In its most pure and consistent form, this religious outlook, versions of which occur in all the major world religions, was in Weber's words 'an objectless acosmism of love' which saw selfless sacrifice and indiscriminate *agapē* as the key to human solidarity and the eradication of sin. From the absolute standpoint of this acosmic ethic – which is an example of that fundamentalist ethic of conviction (*Gesinnungsethik*) that Weber contrasted with the 'ethic of responsibility' in 'Politics as a Vocation' – the world of temporal and material interests was irredeemably wicked, unreliable, divisive and unjust. Weber therefore describes a general process of 'ever-increasing devaluation of the world' by religion, exacerbated in part by the evermore rigorous attempts – always doomed to fall short of success – to eliminate arbitrary suffering and solve the unequal distribution of happiness and misery by rational, secular means. The anti-political salvation doctrines of late Hellenic and Roman times, as well as the pacifist religions of Buddhism and Jainism in India, were some of the earliest movements which repudiated a world in which violence produced violence, and where conflict was resolved not by justice but by power, manipulation or cleverness. These religious movements were typically led by educated people who had lost influence in politics or become disgusted with it, and whose intellectual constitution demanded from the world a totalising intelligibility.

> The intellectual seeks in various ways, the casuistry of which extends into infinity, to endow his life with a pervasive meaning, and thus to find unity with himself, with his fellow men, and with the cosmos. It is the intellectual who transforms the concept of the world into the problem of meaning. As intellectualism suppresses belief in magic, the world's processes become disenchanted, lose their magical significance, and henceforth simply 'are' and 'happen' but no longer signify anything. As a consequence, there is a growing demand that the world and the total pattern of life be subject to an order that is significant and meaningful ... . The distinctive world-fleeing character of intellectualist religion also has one of its roots here. (Weber 1965: 125)

One notably irony is that the more consistent and systematic the renunciation of practical–instrumental considerations, the more these rational religious movements were drawn towards an irrational 'illumination' mysticism, in which the intellect overflows itself, finding revelation in contemplative ecstasy, unconditional reliance on divine providence, and an acosmic ethic of humility and love. 'At some point in its development, every genuinely devout religious faith brings about, directly or indirectly, that "sacrifice of the intellect" in the interests of a trans-intellectual, distinctive religious quality of absolute surrender and utter trust which is expressed in the formula *credo non quod sed quia absurdum est* [I believe because it is absurd]'. In Weber's view, 'every pure intellectualism bears within itself the possibility of such a mystical development' (Weber 1965: 196, 226).

Weber therefore offers a classic account of a historical process of reciprocal differentiation, in which the disentanglement of religious ethics from the base operations of the world accelerated both the purifying perfection of ethical ideals and the freeing of practical action from regulation by ethical norms that are increasingly abstract and impractical. The historical development of empirical science, purposive–rational action, and the political apparatus of force all contribute, over time, to a world which progressively 'pushes religion from the rational into the irrational realm'. At the same time, however, the very process of rationalisation exposes the purposelessness of life, and this, combined with the failure of scientific reason to eradicate unjust suffering, allows religion to strengthen its claim to special authority over the true 'meaning' of the world, and with it salvation from the world's ethical irrationality, 'not by means of the intellect but by virtue of the charisma of illumination' (Weber 1970c: 351–3).

The search for meaning

We should note here that the disenchantment of the world described by Weber in his 'Religious Rejections' essay is understood to be not simply a result of the growth of science, for all forms of culture are subject to the same ongoing processes of rational refinement, sublimation and specialisation, in which diffuse and unthinking sentiments are replaced by self-conscious value judgements and ideals that form clear objects of conviction. In Simmel's account, which undoubtedly influenced Weber's thinking, the maturation of culture is inseparable from its growing complexity, and from this complexity arises the need for 'a definitive goal beyond the meaninglessness of an individuated and fragmented life'. When the moral authority of religious doctrine began to decline, Simmel observes how the soul's search for absolute value and unity of experience was increasingly driven back towards its own heroic capacity to create meaning – and thus, ultimately, towards that Nietzschean standpoint from which only 'life can become the goal of life' (Simmel 1991: 6). With the constant tendency towards rational differentiation, advancement and distillation of values and practices, Weber argued that this inward turn in modern culture, this intensification of human vitality, could never be self-gratifying. The highest achievements of the existentially aware person – the one 'who strives for self-perfection, in the sense of acquiring or creating "cultural values"' – will never be enough to overcome the senselessness of what is now an infinitely perfectible life. Nor can those specialised accomplishments, Weber cautioned, reveal to the individual 'either culture as a whole or what in any sense is "essential" in culture' (1970c: 356). As for the specifically *religious* rejection of this culturally sophisticated world, this rejection is animated not just by the world's growing meaninglessness but also by its ethical irrationality, for excellence in cultural and intellectual pursuits is measured independently of the moral qualities of the individual, and the striving for cultural as much as economic enrichment inevitably produces an 'unbrotherly aristocracy' that is incompatible with Christian *caritas*.

Though primitive forms of magical and mystical beliefs were originally integrated with economic practices and interests, as the religious ethics of salvation became more absolute and more internally consistent, and economic life became more rational and impersonal, Weber notes how the conflict between the Christian ethic of brotherliness and the economic sphere in particular grew sharper, leaving all forms of economic activity 'entangled in the same guilt'. 'The routinized economic cosmos, and thus the rationally highest form of the provision of material goods which is indispensable for all worldly culture, has been a structure to which the absence of love is attached from the very root' (1970c: 355). A similar tension emerged in relation to politics, as the rational development of the bureaucratic state apparatus made growing elements of political and legal decision making as depersonalised as economic actions: 'In this, the political man acts just like the economic man, in a matter-of-fact manner "without regard to the person", *sine ira et studio*, without hate and therefore without love' (1970c: 333–4).

Notwithstanding its responsibility for public welfare, the state is primarily concerned with the internal and external distribution of power, and its 'monopoly of the legitimate use of violence' always places it in conflict with the ethical principle of brotherly love. 'The more matter-of-fact and calculating politics is, and the freer of passionate feelings, or wrath, and of love it becomes, the more it must appear to an ethic of brotherliness to be estranged from brotherliness' (1970c: 334–5). During war, this mutual estrangement of religious ethics and politics may turn into something more rivalrous, as military conflict between nations typically engenders patriotic feelings of compassion and kinship that are akin to the ethic of brotherliness. Weber also argues that war provides the rare opportunity for an individual to defy the meaningless of death that is our common fate in a world of everlasting cultural and intellectual advancement.

> Since death is a fate that comes to everyone, nobody can ever say why it comes precisely to him and why it comes just when it does. As the values of culture increasingly unfold and are sublimated to immeasurable heights, such ordinary death marks an end where only a beginning seems to make sense. Death on the field of battle differs from this merely unavoidable dying in that in war, and in this massiveness *only* in war, the individual can *believe* that he knows he is dying 'for' something ... . Only those who perish 'in their callings' are in the same situation as the soldier who faces death on the battlefield. (1970c: 335)

According to Weber, Western Puritanism and Slavic mysticism were two different attempts to escape the tension between the religious pursuit of ethical meaning and the depersonalised and disenchanted worlds of science, economy and state. The inner-worldly asceticism of the Puritans, with their belief that the elect were predestined for eternal life and their dedication to work in a profitable calling, was effectively a repudiation of the universalism of love and of a genuine religion of salvation. Ethical barbarism and the depraved world of political and economic interests were, for the early Protestants, creations of an omnipotent God whose motives were ultimately incomprehensible. For this reason the Puritans did not have to concern themselves with the ultimate meaning of their conduct, since this was hidden from them by an inscrutable and unchallengeable power. But engagement with the fallen world of enterprise, money and violence remained, for that 'redemptive aristocracy' who believed in their divinely ordained vocation, a valued means of testing and demonstrating their election (1970c: 332–3, 336). The particularism of grace meant, as Habermas puts it, 'an elitist separation between the religiosity of the virtuosos and that of the masses', and this in turn allowed for the 'strategic objectification of interpersonal relations' based on an 'an understanding of one's neighbour as an other who is neutralised in strategic contexts of action' (Habermas 1984: 225).

While inner-worldly asceticism adapted itself to the unbrotherly world of instrumental interests, in the ancient mysticism of Greek and Russian orthodoxy, by contrast, all forms of material activity were regarded as unholy compromises with a diabolic world, and it was contemplative illumination and the renunciation of self that opened the gateway to the divine. In opposition to economic self-interest, the mystic – who must of course rely for survival on the alms and charity of others who are more willing to struggle with the demands of material existence – preaches 'objectless devotion to anybody' (1970c: 333). In opposition to the violence of politics, mysticism seeks redemption through pacifism and an attitude of 'acosmic benevolence' (1970c: 336). Tolstoy's fundamentalist gospel of brotherly altruism was the secularised version of this religious ethic. It would later be revived in the moral sociology of Pitirim Sorokin (1950).

Aestheticism and eroticism

Any form of rational action in the world, Weber emphasises, must accept and assimilate, whether 'as means or as ends', conditions which 'are remote from brotherliness'. But it is not only 'purposive-rational conduct' which stands in tension with the religious ethic of brotherliness, for there are also 'non-rational or basically anti-rational' domains of value that are in conflict with religious ethics. These are the spheres of aesthetics and eroticism.

Weber notes that religion and art have historically had a dynamic interrelationship, with music, dance, iconography and aesthetic symbolism and imagery all serving at one time or another as conduits and catalysts for magical and religious zeal. As art developed its own independent standards of appreciation and expertise, however, a tension emerged in relation to salvation religions, as the latter regarded attentiveness to the contingent and creaturely *form* of art as a distraction from the sacred meaning of things. This conflict was again magnified by competition, as art began to offer a more readily available, and more privately amenable, 'this-worldly' escape from the profane demands of rational calculation, bureaucratic routine and utilitarian self-interest. From the ethical perspective of the religious community, art 'is a realm of irresponsible indulgence and secret lovelessness', which substitutes for the true religious experience an '*ersatz*' form of salvation, a blasphemous 'deceptive bedazzlement' which borders on idolatry. From the viewpoint of artists and their initiates, on the other hand, the ethical norms of religion 'appear as a coercion of their genuine creativeness and innermost selves'. The influence of art as a competing sphere of value is already apparent in what Weber describes as a 'shift from the moral to the aesthetic evaluation of conduct', and our tendency 'to transform judgements of moral intent into judgements of taste ("in poor taste" instead of "reprehensible")' (1970c: 342).

In its most sublime and enchanting forms, art retains the power to arouse sentiments of pathos, joy and generosity that rival religiously inspired sentiments of compassion and brotherly love. When we turn from aesthetics to the sphere of sexual love – which Weber calls 'the greatest irrational force of life' – the rivalry with religion is more obvious. Here the conflict between the two grows, Weber argues, as sexual pleasure is consciously cultivated and the shameless naturalism of sex is sublimated into a more disciplined and self-knowing eroticism (1970c: 343–4). In its primitive, more impulsive historical forms, sexual ecstasy was a fruitful partner to religious and magical rites. Weber highlights the way the orgy expressed 'the communal religious behaviour of the laity at a primitive level' (1965: 236), but he also emphasises the perceived link between ecstasy and charisma, and how sexual possession and divine revelation were experienced as kindred psychological states. As ethically rationalised religions, fearing the anomic irrationality and unpredictability of sexual desire, assigned it to the separate sphere of marriage and procreation, Weber observes a gradual historical trend towards the treatment of erotic relationships as an independent source of value. 'The extraordinary quality of eroticism,' Weber argues, 'has consisted precisely in a gradual turning away from the naïve naturalism of sex' (1970c: 344). But this 'turning away' was also a self-knowing return, in which *eros* was constructed and experienced as the ultimate life force. The intellect 'reaffirms the natural quality of the sexual sphere, but it does so consciously, as an embodied creative power' (1970c: 347). The Nietzschean idea of life becoming the purpose of life is self-evident here. So is Otto Gross's *Lebensphilosophie*.

Noting in passing the Greeks' love of boys, and the words of Pericles and Demosthenes, Weber then highlights the troubadour narrative of courtly love as the point at which eroticism appears to develop a distinct and more autonomous form, with sexual desire sublimated into 'abstentious love nights and a casuistic code of duties', and the vassal's courtship of a Lady self-consciously overturning patriarchal power relations and the earlier conventions of Hellenic masculinity (1970c: 346). The rise of salon culture in the seventeenth and eighteenth centuries also gave a new accent to what Weber calls the 'agonistic probation of the cavalier', with women's love letters and the growth of the epistolary novel providing intellectual and literary material to articulate and intellectualise the drama and tragedy of sexual relations. Extramarital eroticism, in particular, assumed increasing prominence as 'the only tie which still linked man with the natural fountain of all life' (1970c: 348).

Being antithetical to the rational, routinised world of practical interests, erotic passion was a natural rival to the salvation religion of brotherly love, and Weber's attentiveness to this rivalry reveals a kinship that is often overlooked by sociologists who emphasise the world-building spirit of *agapē* over the world-denying passion of *eros*. Religions of salvation rejected the animalism of the flesh in favour of the holy spirit, but as sexual desire was sublimated into romantic love and erotic communion, a certain 'psychological affinity' – in Weber's words they are 'psychologically substitutive' – emerged between the selfless devotion of the lover and the altruistic piety and compassion of the mystic. In the rejection of sexual monogamy by libertarians and anarchists such as Otto Gross and his wife's lover, Ernst Frick, Weber indeed saw an attempt to transform this close affinity into what he believed was an impossible marriage – 'to realise "goodness" and "brotherly love" through the acosmicism of the erotic' (Weber 1999: 54).

From the perspective of the religious ethic of brotherhood, Weber notes, the 'euphoria of the happy lover' is not the genuine goodness it claims to be, but rather is, as Socrates depicted it in his first speech in the *Phaedrus*, pathological obsession, undignified loss of control, jealousy, possessiveness, exclusion of others and, Weber writes, 'the most intimate coercion of the soul of the less brutal partner' who becomes a vehicle for the other's enjoyment. This was, indeed, how sex was depicted by Tolstoy, in 'The Kreutzer Sonata' (1889), following his own spiritual conversion. This description has also attracted the attention of feminist critics of sexual love, who have found in Weber's words a frank acknowledgement of the true power asymmetry in erotic heterosexual relations, which masquerade as romantic unions to the widespread detriment of women (Bologh 1990: 199–200). But we should not overlook, as Langford (1999: 17–18) does, the fact that the 'coercive' and unethical nature of love is how it appears, Weber argues, '[f]rom the point of view of any religious ethic of brotherhood'. From the perspective of the erotic relation *itself*, love is experienced, by contrast, as a selfless communion compelled by 'fate', and which, though mysterious, always feels 'legitimised', albeit 'in an entirely amoral sense' (1970c: 348).

> Under these conditions, the erotic relation seems to offer the unsurpassable peak of the fulfilment of the request for love in the direct fusion of the souls of one to the other. This boundless giving of oneself is as radical as possible in its opposition to all functionality, rationality, and generality. It is displayed here as the unique meaning which one creature in his irrationality has for another, and only for this specific other. However, from the point of view of eroticism, this meaning, and with it the value-content of the relation itself, rests upon the possibility of a communion which is felt as a complete unification, as a fading of the 'thou'. It is so overpowering that it is interpreted 'symbolically': as a sacrament. The lover realises himself to be rooted in the kernel of the truly living, which is eternally inaccessible to any rational endeavour. He knows himself to be freed

from the cold skeletal hands of rational orders, just as completely as from the banality of everyday routine … . The experience is by no means communicable and in this respect it is equivalent to the 'having' of the mystic. (1970c: 347)

Weber's depiction of eroticism as an independent sphere of value is significant for a number of reasons. It is one piece in a larger picture of the differentiated and heterogeneous nature of social life, which corrects the simplistic conception that Weber theorised rationalisation as a monolithic process of progressive depersonalisation and mechanical discipline. The modern world is splintered into different life orders; the good, the true and the beautiful are no longer identical (Weber 1970a: 147–8), and social existence now comprises a pluralism of experience and a polytheism of values. The approach taken here is also rigorously interpretivist in its analysis, with Weber assessing the meaning of each value sphere from the perspective of its own inner practices, and from the perspective of other value spheres and other practices, but never from a spurious Archimedean point that claims to be independent of all practical presuppositions and values. Weber has been criticised for refusing to countenance a form of brotherly love that might mediate the extremes of indiscriminate benevolence characteristic of Slavic mysticism on the one hand, and the antisocial solipsism of sexual relationships on the other (he does not consider the possibility of an ethical community founded on what Bologh (1990) argues is a human desire for 'erotic sociability'). But it is also clear that Weber now contests the totalising power of rational capitalism as much as he repudiates the Tolstoyan utopia of love, and the inserts to the essay that Weber added in the year before his death also suggest that the icy hand of ascetic discipline had loosened its grip on his own thoughts and feelings. All the references to love as 'fate', the 'fusion of souls' and the 'amoral' self-legitimacy of the erotic relation were added for the revised 1920 publication of the text. The explanation for this, we now know, was a revolution in Weber's personal life.

Weber falls in love

In her biography of her husband, Marianne Weber describes how, around 1907–8, the Heidelberg intellectual scene was stimulated by a current of new thinking carried by younger people arriving from Munich. 'New types of persons, related to the Romantics in their intellectual impulses, once again called in question bourgeois systems of thinking and living.' These new types rejected 'law' and 'duty' and wanted 'to let only *feeling* influence the flow of life'. Their doctrine 'was particularly concerned with the liberalisation of sexual morality'.

> What was the value of norms that so often stifled the magnificence of vibrant life, repressed natural drives, and, above all, denied fulfilment to so many women? Law, duty, asceticism – were not all these ideas derived from the demonization of sex by an outgrown Christianity? To shape one's future entirely on the basis of one's own nature, to let the currents of life flow through one and then to bear the consequences, was better than to sneak along on the sterile paths of caution hemmed in by morality. (Marianne Weber 1975: 370–1)

The Webers were pragmatically, and somewhat condescendingly, sympathetic to the concerns of this new generation of thinkers, some of whom were their friends. Marianne Weber's instinct was to praise those 'courageous women' who rightly attacked the state's sanctioning of prostitution and the effect of the 'double standard of morality' on women, but to oppose those who 'caricatured chastity as the morality of monks, and marriage as the state's compulsory institution for the protection of private property', and who 'demanded the right to "free love" and illegitimate children' (1975: 372–3). Simmel expressed similar sentiments about this 'new morality' when he argued that the 'self-assured life' which 'wishes to liberate itself from the yoke of form' must be mature enough to recognise that absolute rejection of objective culture is impossible, for 'erotic life, as soon as it is expressed in cultural contexts, necessarily requires some form' (1968: 22). For the Webers, Marianne reports, the radical ethos of the sexual revolutionaries seemed like a 'delusion'. Even so, 'they could not turn away in indignation, since they felt deep concern for the noble and lovable human beings involved and wanted to help them as much as they could. They wanted, too, to learn to understand this strange, unbourgeois world of adventurism and to carry on an intellectual dialogue with it' (1975: 380).

The chief figure in the movement for sexual liberation was of course Otto Gross, whom Marianne Weber refers to as having 'the magic of a brilliant mind and heart', but whose influence on their personal acquaintances left the Webers 'torn by horror and revulsion at the theory and by a profound sympathy for the unhappy lives that prepared the ground for such misleading teachings' (1975: 374). The Webers first encountered Gross's philosophy second hand, through one of his early converts. Else von Richthofen, the elder sibling of Frieda Lawrence, was the most intellectually cultured of the three sisters. Having got to know Marianne Weber, from whom she had gained advice on how to obtain a university education, she progressed to doctoral study, initially under Max

Weber's supervision in Heidelberg. Publishing her thesis on labour legislation in 1901 – and in doing so becoming one of the first women in Germany to obtain a PhD – she began work as a factory inspector in Baden, inspired in part by Marianne Weber's own political profile. A year later, however, Else abandoned her job and married Edgar Jaffé, a dull but wealthy protégé of Weber who, in 1904, bought from Heinrich Braun the prestigious social science journal, *Archiv für Sozialwissenschaft und Sozialpolitik*, and effectively gave it to Weber (to be co-edited with Jaffé and Werner Sombart).

Else probably became erotically involved with Gross when she visited his wife, Frieda ('Friedel'), in Munich in 1906. A year later Gross stayed with the Jaffés in Heidelberg, and converted Edgar to his faith (Fanny zu Reventlow became Edgar's lover for a time). Else bore Gross's child in 1907, and in the midst of all this sexual experimentation Max Weber felt sufficiently concerned about the complicated lives of his friends to begin studying Freud. He very soon received a submission to the *Archiv* from Gross himself, apparently prompted by Else, who also seemed keen to arrange a meeting between Gross and Weber. Weber declined the invitation and rejected the article, addressing his long letter of explanation to Edgar Jaffé, but posting it to Else, in what Martin Green (1974: 55–6) describes as 'an obvious but covert repudiation of Gross as a whole and a pleading with her to reject him also'. Green also wonders whether Else's intention was to use Gross's psychoanalytic insights to liberate her former mentor and 'release Weber from his crippling neurosis'.

The version of the rejection letter that appears in Marianne Weber's biography accuses Gross of transgressing beyond the specialist 'scientific' field of psychiatry to indulge in *Weltanschauung*, moralism and 'metaphysical speculations', and of doing precisely what Weber argued social scientists could not do, which is use scholarly insights or technical discoveries to justify an ethics (to derive an 'ought' from an 'is'). 'His entire essay fairly bursts with value judgements,' Max Weber writes to Edgar Jaffé in his letter of 13 September 1907, 'and I have simply no respect whatever for allegedly scientific achievements that do not meet the demands of sobriety and objectivity and are not "*value-free*"' (cited in Marianne Weber 1975: 380). Weber's criticism of Gross also mirrored Durkheim's attack on the sexual hygienists. Gross's philosophy is that of a 'medical philistine', Weber argues, who confuses the 'hygienic' function of sexual liberation with an ethics, and who fails to see that values can only be contested from the standpoint of other values – 'otherwise one gets into the area of the shabbiest "calculation of costs"' (1975: 379). Gross reduces the nobility of human beings to a bundle of emotional and sensory desires, and then tries to derive from this a 'nerve ethics' which would logically justify such behaviour, Weber scornfully writes, as that of a deserter who flees combat in order not to have to repress his feelings of anxiety. What seems like radical ethical idealism is really nothing of the sort, for it makes no demands of individuals other than that they follow their basic instincts. From this perspective, Weber writes, every moral ideal must be measured against the sacrifice of instinct that it demands: 'I am believed capable of being shabby enough to ask, "How much does it cost?" before I act the way I think I owe it to my human dignity to act' (1975: 378).

By the spring of the following year, however, the shockingly unconventional behaviour of his cultured friends had started to affect Weber's viewpoint. Marianne Weber records that he began to take an interest in the way a 'norm-free eroticism' could lead in some cases to a certain greatness or at least depth of character, where the fulfilment of sexual desires was treated not as an ethical 'right', but rather 'as a "fate" with which one must cope and often *cannot* cope, because one is only human' (Weber, cited in Marianne Weber 1975: 388–9). A year or so later,[1] on a trip to Italy with the Jaffés, Max Weber and Else Jaffé became close, their intimacy made possible by Marianne's early return to Germany and Edgar's later morning sleeping habits (Mitzman 1970: 286–7). Whether this was, at this stage, simply an emotionally close friendship or something more, as Whimster (1995: 456) suggests, is not entirely clear. Mitzman believes the events in Venice were a watershed, if not a 'revolution', in Weber's emotional and interpersonal life. Martin Green (1974: 129) states that Weber had declared his love to Else, but that she had refused him out of loyalty to Marianne. In 1911 it appears that he began a romantic–sexual relationship with an unnamed woman – the informed speculation is that this was the Swiss pianist Mina Tobler – and whatever intimacies had passed during this period between Weber and Else they were apparently sufficient to make Weber feel that awkwardness towards a former lover that Durkheim had highlighted as the inevitable by-product of divorce. In his letters to his wife from Ascona in the spring of 1914, the master of self-discipline and emotional restraint tells how he has been hiding like a frightened child in order to avoid crossing paths with Else, who was visiting Frieda Gross in the village. 'I am blockaded in my room today, because yesterday Frieda installed Else in the room directly opposite. On my instructions she has explained that I am away and there is no way she can see me' (Weber 1999: 56).

---

[1] Mitzman (1970: 286) dates this trip to 1910. Whimster (1995: 456) says it occurred in 1909, which fits more accurately with the surrounding events.

Allusions in the letters to Weber's brother, Alfred, combined with the fact that Weber was relaxed enough about the moral context of the scenario to tell his wife about his behaviour perhaps counsels against a too hasty reading of this averted encounter with Else. Alfred, who had escaped the shadow of his mother's repressive puritanism and was much more sympathetic than his brother to the ideas of *Lebensphilosophie*, had moved from Prague to Heidelberg in 1907. He was not part of his brother's intellectual circle, however, and the feelings the two siblings had for each other ranged from rivalry to unfriendliness. In late 1909, not long after the Webers' trip to Italy, Alfred began what was to be a long-lasting sexual partnership with Else. It was this relationship that enabled Else to secure the use of Alfred's apartment in Icking for her sister and D. H. Lawrence in the summer of 1912.

Weber certainly disapproved of this affair, which Edgar Jaffé was particularly unhappy about. But it seems likely that Weber was also disturbed on a more personal level. In January 1910 Weber and Else met to discuss her relationship with his brother, and how she was going to manage the separation from Edgar, who had decided to move to Munich. Weber and Else subsequently exchanged letters, and the copies of Else's correspondence that have survived suggest that during their encounter Weber had expressed a gracious, non-possessive love for Else, which she then praised in a letter to Alfred: 'he has a truer love for me than you!' (Weber 1994: 367). According to Else, Weber had recognised her need for freedom and her 'secret lightness of being', demonstrating this by reading to her Rilke's 'Requiem für eine Freundin' (1908). The poem is a haunting lament to Paula Modersohn-Becker, the German painter whom Rilke had almost certainly, if secretly, loved, and who tragically died at the age of 31 following a postpartum embolism. As well as reading the poem to Else, Weber had marked on the pages of the book the passage he found most significant (Weber 1994: 367). Here Rilke wrote of the need to avoid the 'tangled suffering' of a 'counterfeit love' which 'feeds on injustice', and which wrongly seeks to possess that which lives so lightly that it 'does not hold its self'.

Wir haben, wo wir lieben, ja nur dies:
einander lassen; denn daß wir uns halten,
das fällt uns leicht und ist nicht erst zu lernen.

[We have, when we love, only this:
to let each other go; for holding on to each other
is easy and doesn't need to be learned.]

In letting Else go, Weber appeared to be expressing the quintessential sentiment not of *eros* but of *agapē*. '*Agape*', as Luc Ferry defines it, 'is the intelligence of love, the wisdom of love that consists in leaving room for the other, letting the other be, leaving the other free' (Ferry 2013: 40). Weber had sublimated his erotic passion into a benevolent expression of restraint, converting his feelings not only into something morally decent but also into a literary recital that was fit for the formal elegance and intellectual theatre of the salon. But even a beautiful love, a beautiful separation, becomes sterile and meaningless if it is not fed by its contrary – a desire for closeness, intimacy, mutual possession. This desire was not extinguished by the events of that winter. Weber was the godfather of Else and Otto's child, Peter, who died in 1915 at the age of 8. A rapport between Weber and Else began in 1917, with their shared memories of the child serving as an initial occasion for rapprochement. The suicide of Weber's sister in 1919 deepened their mutual sympathies, though Green states that they had already become lovers by then. This was not the conventional aristocratic segregation of carnal pleasure from marital companionship. A letter from Weber to Else written in 1919 suggests that Weber had discovered the passionate communion of souls, with its self-legitimising moral compulsion, that gave eroticism the power of a rival religion. 'Above all, I can live toward only one person in truth', he wrote to Else, 'and that I can and must do that is the last and decisive necessity in my life, loftier and stronger than any god' (cited by Green 1974: 164). Marianne also wrote to Else, signalling her acceptance of the situation. When Weber fell ill with pneumonia in 1920, Marianne and Else took turns nursing him. He died in the presence of both women, who would remain loyal friends until Marianne's death in 1954.

Rationalisation revisited

There is, as noted earlier, a tension in Weber's theory of rationalisation which, together with the fragmented and incomplete nature of his writings, has contributed to different readings of his work that are not simple to reconcile. Keith Tribe (1988: 6–8) credits Talcott Parsons with promoting the popular view that Weber's sociology presents a panoramic vision of Occidental rationalism, conceived as a universal, teleological process leading to the disenchantment of the world and the disappearance of authentic value commitments. This fashionable reading, however, clashes with Weber's depiction of the way religious beliefs, as they were rationalised, became more rigorous and binding, creating systematic value orientations capable of driving social action in different directions and towards different outcomes. Even in *The Protestant Ethic*, for example, Weber had been at pains to emphasise that 'one can in fact "rationalise" life from a vast variety of ultimate vantage points. Moreover, one can do so in very different directions. "Rationalism" is a historical concept that contains within itself a world of contradictions' (Weber 2002: 37). This early qualifying statement, plus the later essay on 'Religious Rejections', has led more contemporary scholars to argue that Weber saw modernity as a polytheistic cosmos characterised by ever sharper distinctions between conflicting spheres of value – including the erotic, the artistic, the political and the economic – whose separate rationalisation leads each to become an increasingly autonomous domain of thought, feeling and action.

Jürgen Habermas has perhaps made the most constructive effort to integrate these two dimensions of Weber's thought, arguing that what Weber was studying was a 'selective pattern of rationalisation' whose 'imbalanced' form to some extent prefigures the difficulties we face today ensuring that different forms of rationality and value are recognised and expressed. Although different value orientations carry the *potential* to be equally institutionalised and anchored in distinctive social practices and relationships, with the development of Western modernity what actually took place, Habermas argues, was that the cognitive–instrumental rationality of science and economic calculation, initially rooted in and energised by the inner-worldly asceticism of the Protestant work ethic, raced ahead of other value-rational complexes, eventually detaching itself from value motivations altogether: 'the foundation of the vocational orientation in an ethic of conviction is washed away in favour of an instrumental attitude toward work interpreted in utilitarian terms' (Habermas 1984: 241).

Instrumental rationality, by appealing to people's utilitarian self-interest, offers a superior means of coordinating the actions of society's members precisely because it bypasses those conflicts over values which grow as modernity becomes more diverse and differentiated, thus relieving social actors of the increasingly time-consuming task of achieving mutual understanding and agreement. But the price to be paid for the growth of instrumental rationality is the relegation of values, and reasoning over values, to the margins of social and political life. Thus 'the capitalist economy and modern administration expand at the expense of other domains of life that are structurally disposed to moral-practical and expressive forms of rationality and squeeze them into forms of economic or administrative rationality' (Habermas 1984: 183).

Weber's iconic image of the 'iron cage' reflected the fact that he was, as Habermas puts it, 'troubled by the fact that subsystems of purposive-rational action are breaking loose from their value-rational foundations and becoming independent, following their own dynamics' (1984: 233). Yet the final shape of the 'Religious Rejections' essay suggests that Weber, in his later years, recovered his conviction that modernity entails a pluralism of irreconcilable value spheres whose intensity and distinctiveness increase rather than decline with the process of rationalisation. We can only speculate on the influence which the changes in Weber's personal life may have had on these observations, and we cannot say for certain how much ethical or spiritual significance Weber believed could be attributed to relations of sexual intimacy. Habermas (1987: 323), for his part, takes the famous passage in *The Protestant Ethic*, where Weber says the modern individual is torn between two ethically barren alternatives – 'specialists without spirit, sensualists without heart'[2] – as evidence that Weber saw the growing prominence of the erotic sphere as nothing more than a compensatory hedonism reacting against, but also mirroring, the ethical emptiness of instrumental reason. But it is equally legitimate to suggest that Weber came to understand loving intimacy in more transcendent terms, albeit terms which had to take their place, and take their turn, in a world of competing logics, pressures and values.

Disputing what he regards as Weber's undue pessimism, Habermas claims that Weber's stark choice between 'specialists' and 'sensualists' overlooked the democratic ethical potential unleashed by what he calls the 'rationalisation of the lifeworld', that is, the advancements made in our ability to reason clearly with one another and reach consensus over values and goals by means of uncoerced debate or 'communicative rationality'. It was the rationalisation of the lifeworld, Habermas argues, and particularly the cognitive understanding of facts, norms and experiences as separate ontological categories with their own distinctive modes of investigation and validation, that originally made possible the independent development of social systems governed by the instrumental production and manipulation of material things. For Habermas, however, it

---

[2] This is how Parsons originally translated the passage, which appears as an unattributed quote – possibly from Nietzsche – at the end of Weber's text. Kahlberg's more recent translation is less elegant: 'narrow specialists without mind, pleasure-seekers without heart' (Weber 2002: 124). Simmel also made a similar distinction, observing how typical responses to the interchangeability of values brought about by the market economy and the processes of commodification include both 'cynicism' and the 'blasé attitude', and both produce a thirst for their antithesis – the antidote of mindless sensuality: 'Out of this there emerges the craving today for excitement, for extreme impressions, for the greatest speed in its change ... . The satisfaction of such cravings may bring about a temporary relief, but soon the former condition will be re-established, though now made worse by the increased quantity of its elements' (Simmel 2004: 257).

is not the existence of autonomous economic and administrative subsystems that creates pathological problems in contemporary societies, so much as their extension into areas of life where communication and mutual understanding are crucial. The issue is not the 'separation of system and lifeworld', as Habermas puts it, but rather the 'colonisation' of the lifeworld by the uncontrolled spread of functional reason. 'The rationalisation of the lifeworld makes possible the emergence and growth of subsystems whose independent imperatives turn back destructively upon the lifeworld itself' (Habermas 1987: 186).

Since Weber's death, and most strikingly over the last 60 years, we have seen an extraordinary growth in the power and reach of market forces in most countries across the world, and a corresponding commodification of more and more aspects of public and private life, including the domain of love. The commercial sexualisation of public culture, and the use of romantic ideals and imagery as vehicles for a rampant consumer individualism, would indicate to some that economic rationality has now colonised the most intimate aspects of our physical and emotional lifeworlds. At the same time, however, sexual life has advanced in the West towards a much greater openness, the rigid constraints of gender and heteronormativity have been progressively demystified, and some sociologists now argue that couples today are able to talk about love – indeed *must* talk about love if their relationships are to be mutually satisfying – with a well-reasoned honesty that previous generations would have balked at. Is love, today, colonised by utilitarianism, or does the stability and vitality of modern intimate relationships, as Berger and Kellner (1964) argued over 50 years ago, now depend as much on the 'talking through' of a shared reality as on the cultural and religious legitimation of marriage? Are we seeing a communicative democratisation of personal life, as theorists such as Anthony Giddens have argued, or has the realm of intimacy been restructured by new rational imperatives that are impoverishing our ability to form deep and lasting emotional bonds? In the final chapter I will try to answer these questions by looking at contemporary sociological treatments of sexual love.

9

Love in late modernity

The sexual revolution of the early twentieth century could never have withstood the wretchedness and ruin of a world war. Although the flame of erotic emancipation flickered hopefully in Bohemian circles in the 1920s and 1930s, it was not until the economic, political and technological advances of the 1960s that sexual liberation became a meaningful aspiration for millions of people in the West. The idea that emotional intimacy and sexual satisfaction should be the combined aim of, and reason for, marriage had already become dominant among the Western middle classes by the 1950s. In England, as the cultural historian Claire Langhamer (2013) documents, an 'emotional revolution' had occurred during the interwar years, and although the prejudices of class, race and heteronormativity continued to shape people's beliefs about what kind of pairings were viable, mutual passion and desire were now widely considered to be an indispensable test of love's authenticity, and romantic attraction the most important precondition for a happy and meaningful marriage. In the United States, too, the spiritual understanding of love that characterised Victorian marriages had slowly given way to a moral and psychological appreciation of the importance of sexual fulfilment, as erotic satisfaction became 'a new standard of successful love marriage' (Seidman 1991: 117). The double ring marriage ceremonies that became mainstream in the United States in the 1950s signalled the appearance of a new suburban culture that now valorised masculine domesticity and marital togetherness (Howard 2003). Even though the actual experience of a great many couples continued to fall short of the egalitarian ideals of companionate marriage (Finch and Summerfield 1991), personal relationships had clearly undergone a psychological softening over the course of the century. Romantic love was now commonly believed to be compatible with wedlock, and although rising divorce rates suggested a more complex story, the second half of the century saw the emergence of a new discourse of psychological and emotional intimacy which promised to solve the crisis of marriage with a more sensible model of conjugal happiness based on a therapeutic model of selfhood and on the controlled communication of feelings (Shumway 2003; Illouz 2007).

The transformed political landscape of Western societies in the 1960s also affected the domain of the erotic. The energy and optimism of the new social movements, including second-wave feminism, anti-racism and gay rights, were changing people's perceptions and understandings of their personal lives, raising the appetites and expectations of young people in particular. Christian advice on sex and marriage gamely sought to adjust itself to these changes, as the deductive morality of traditional ethics began to be replaced with a more inductive model of personal growth and responsibility. This concession to individual autonomy was not a licence for moral permissiveness, however, and as the counterculture revolution unfolded it became apparent, as Jane Lewis (2001: 89) notes, that the new Christian moralists 'expected too much of their fellow human beings in hoping for such a high standard of other-regarding personal morality'. Moral restraints were being further loosened by changes in law, technology and commerce. Abortion and homosexuality were decriminalised, divorce was made easier and the contraceptive pill enabled women to separate heterosexual pleasure from reproduction. As the taboos on the use of sexual language and imagery were progressively relaxed, the marketing and beauty industries, ever conscious of the close affinity between erotic desire and consumer hedonism, provided a respectable face for the growing sexualisation of public culture. If the first half of the century saw a shift in Euro-American societies from the spiritualisation of love to its sexualisation, the 1960s and 1970s were marked by the growth of a more independent culture of eroticism which valued sensory pleasure, self-expression and communication, and which relied less and less on the ideals of romantic love to legitimise it (Seidman 1991).

Looking back from the vantage point of a new millennium, the French philosopher Luc Ferry argues, more positively, that love remained at the core of this cultural transformation, and that it was in the second half of the twentieth century that the values of affective individualism finally became universal in the West. Only then did the 'revolution of love' that began in the nineteenth century fulfil its promise, making love 'the sole legitimate basis for couples and families', and allowing personal feelings to finally triumph over the rigid constraints of community, class and sexual biology (Ferry 2013: 8). Today many social scientists and anthropologists argue that Euro-American ideals of romantic intimacy have been effectively globalised, with young women and men in a diversity of cultures now asserting their right to choose their own partners and to prioritise physical attraction and emotional fulfilment ahead of the requirements of social and biological reproduction. These 'Western' ideals have of course been appropriated, refracted and sometimes repudiated, in culturally specific ways, often in societies with their own endogenous traditions of romantic love that sometimes resemble, and sometimes depart from, core Western values and beliefs.

It is curious to note, for example, that the spread of companionate marriage in Hong Kong and Singapore has shifted the locus of patriarchal power from the extended family to the husband (Chan 2006), while the change in marital ideals from *respeto* to *confianza* (intimacy or trust) among younger Mexicans has ironically made it morally more difficult for the wives of seasonal migrant workers to the United States to protect themselves against migration-related heterosexual transmission of HIV (Hirsch et al. 2006). In Papua New Guinea, young Huli women appeal to Christian notions of conjugal love in order to resist forced marriages and stake an effective claim to 'modern' romantic individualism (Wardlow 2006). Among the Igbo-speaking people of Southeastern Nigeria, egalitarian ideals of romantic love are deployed by most young women and many young men in mate selection and premarital courtship practices, but postnuptial relationships swiftly revert to more traditional patriarchal gender dynamics (Smith 2006). The young Magars of Nepal increasingly associate romantic passion in courtship and marriage with being modern, successful and independent (Ahearn 2001), while young unmarried mothers in urban Mali were found to share romantic ideals of love that were partly informed by the characters and storylines of an imported Venezuelan TV soap opera (Sølbeck 2010). Latin American *feuilletons* are also widely consumed by impoverished young people in Niger, who acquire from these imported teledramas romantic role models and images of emotional intimacy with which they can position themselves against the traditional practices of arranged marriage, polygyny and the customary spatial separation of the lives of husband and wife (Masquelier 2009). Similar egalitarian ideals of marital companionship and emotional and sexual fulfilment have grown in influence in Kenya since the deregulation of the media industry in the early 1990s, and are now essential ingredients of what young professionals in Nairobi believe is necessary for a progressive and cosmopolitan identity (Spronk 2009).

Examples like these allow us to set modern conceptions of romantic love and emotional intimacy in a more inclusive global content. Yet it is important to note that, even in the West, scepticism over the progress made through the cultural changes of the post-war years was widespread from the start. Conservatives were naturally dismayed – making sexual fulfilment the foundation of relationships was always going to render the 'mediocre marriage' commended by Durkheim unsustainable, and if falling in love was a licence to get married, falling out of love, or falling in love with someone else, was also a licence to get divorced. In 1940 Rougemont had already warned that 'passion wrecks the very notion of marriage at a time when there is being attempted the feat of trying to ground marriage in values elaborated by the morals of passion' (1983: 286). And even earlier, American sociologists in the 1920s were reflecting on the way romantic ideals were inflating marital expectations, with destabilising effects on the modern family (Burgess 1926; Mower 1927).

Repressive desublimation

Perhaps more surprisingly, social theorists on the left also began to express unease about the implications of the sexual revolution. Synthesising the insights of Marx and Freud, Herbert Marcuse was an early advocate of sexual liberation who had initially written with optimism about the harmonising power of love and the ascendance of the pleasure principle over the divisive effects of alienated labour and the competitive 'performance principle'. The repression of desire may have been functionally necessary at earlier stages of economic development, Marcuse observed in *Eros and Civilisation* (1955), but the rapid post-war expansion of production heralded the possibility of a more joyful and spontaneous mode of social existence. Capitalism had advanced the forces of production well beyond what Marx had believed was possible within the structural constraints of such an exploitative class system; but capitalism's success also meant that the transitional phase of socialism could be dispensed with, with Marcuse suggesting that there was now a realistic prospect of moving directly to a communist society, in which the realm of necessity was reduced to its inescapable minimum and the realm of freedom became the prevailing reality for everyone.

Marcuse had disputed Freud's ahistorical claim that the advance of civilisation necessitates the deflection, sublimation and desexualisation of desire. The progressive conquering of scarcity, Marcuse argued, should instead permit the restoration of a more primordial structure of libido, in which 'the primacy of the genital function is broken', the human 'organism in its entirety becomes the substratum of sexuality' and all social relations are infused with affection, sensuality and love (Marcuse 1972: 146–8). By the time he wrote *One-Dimensional Man* (1964), however, the political contours of the affluent society had assumed a clearer shape, and Marcuse was now aware that the libertarian ethos of the nascent counterculture could easily satisfy the strategic interests of what would later be called 'neo-liberal' capitalism. Sexual freedoms were readily convertible into consumer demand, individual liberties could be extended without upsetting the structures of power, and commerce was showing an uncanny ability to manage what Daniel Bell (1976) called the 'cultural contradiction' between the work ethic and consumer hedonism. Freedom, pleasure and fulfilment were being trivialised by their reduction to instant gratification and consumer choice, as if one could be genuinely happy with meaningless work and mindless consumption, happy to live in a world of radical inequality, happy with pizza and pornography while hunger, homelessness, environmental destruction and neo-imperialist wars continued unabated. 'Under the rule of a repressive whole, liberty can be made into a powerful instrument of domination' (Marcuse 1991: 7).

Marcuse coined the term 'repressive desublimation', or 'repressive tolerance', to describe the controlled release and co-opting of hedonistic individualism by consumer capitalism. From this later, more pessimistic, perspective, Marcuse now looked back with nostalgia towards the older cultural sublimation and 'artistic alienation' of sexual desire. In *Eros and Civilisation* he had repudiated the process of sublimation, arguing that it was unnecessarily 'repressive'; but now he praised the way aesthetic sublimation had shielded the subversive power of *eros* from economic exploitation and functional reasoning. The classical literature of earlier centuries had rightly testified to the world-rejecting nature of erotic passion, but now representations of sexuality were becoming ubiquitous, daring and uninhibited, 'and, precisely because of that, perfectly harmless. Freed from the sublimated form which was the very token of its irreconcilable dreams – a form which is the style, the language in which the story is told – sexuality turns into a vehicle for the bestsellers of oppression' (1991: 77–8).

> Artistic alienation is sublimation. It creates the images of conditions which are irreconcilable with the established Reality Principle but which, as cultural images, become tolerable, even edifying and useful. Now this imagery is invalidated. Its incorporation into the kitchen, the office, the shop; its commercial release for business and fun is, in a sense, desublimation – replacing mediated by immediate gratification. But it is desublimation practised from a 'position of strength' on the part of society, which can afford to grant more than before because its interests have become the innermost drives of its citizens, and because the joys which it grants promote social cohesion and contentment.

> The Pleasure Principle absorbs the Reality Principle; sexuality is liberated (or rather liberalised) in socially constructive forms. This notion implies that there are repressive modes of desublimation, compared with which the sublimated drives and objectives contain more deviation, more freedom, and more refusal to heed the social taboos. (Marcuse 1991: 72)

The deployment of sexuality

Michel Foucault had little time for what he saw as the essentialism in Marcuse's earlier Freudian analysis, which from his own social constructionist perspective was the relic of an obsolete humanism. For Foucault, 'para-Marxist' thinkers like Marcuse and Wilhelm Reich were not sexual revolutionaries so much as unwitting accomplices to the 'deployment of sexuality'. Their thinking conspired with a power which does not, as critical humanists contend, prohibit, censor or repress some pre-existing yearning for freedom, but which instead fashions and defines that freedom by giving it the form of a primordial impulse called 'sex'. What the critics of sexual repression fail to realise, Foucault argued, is that 'power would be a fragile thing if its only function were to repress, if it worked only through the mode of censorship, exclusion, blockage and repression, in the manner of a great Superego, exercising itself only in a negative way'. The efficacy of power, on the contrary, is its creativity: 'it produces effects at the level of desire' (Foucault 1980: 59).

Power is the force which creates 'the imaginary element that is "sex"', which compels us to define ourselves, in the most intimate and primary structure of our being, as beings of sex, thus making irresistible the injunction to search out and disclose that sex, 'to have it, to have access to it, to discover it, to liberate it, to articulate it in discourse, to formulate it in truth'. Foucault believed that in the future people would smile when recollecting how foolish their enthusiasm was for the work of someone like D. H. Lawrence, who was 'pretending to rouse from its slumber a sexuality which everything – our discourses, our customs, our institutions, our regulations, our knowledges – was busy producing in the light of day and broadcasting to noisy accompaniment' (Foucault 1990: 156, 158). Of course the parallels here with Marcuse's later critique of repressive tolerance are obvious, and Foucault even referred approvingly at one point to 'what has been called a hyper-repressive desublimation' (1990: 114). 'We must not think that by saying yes to sex, one says no to power', Foucault (1990: 157) emphasised, using words that Marcuse himself would not have been uncomfortable with.

The fact that so many things were able to change in the sexual behaviour of Western societies without any of the promises or political conditions predicted by Reich being realised is sufficient proof that this whole sexual 'revolution', this whole 'anti-repressive' struggle, represented nothing more, but nothing less – and its importance is undeniable – than a tactical shift and reversal in the great deployment sexuality. (Foucault 1990: 131)

Foucault revolutionised cultural and sociological understandings of power, but his radical rejection of the so-called repressive hypothesis was compromised by lyrical exaggeration and philosophical polemic, and it conveyed to some a complacent attitude to the oppressive miseries suffered by sexual minorities, black people and women. His argument that the nineteenth century saw a veritable explosion in medical, scientific and demographic discourses of sex ignored the way this literature was censored or kept out of reach of the majority of even the educated population of Europe and North America. Summarising the findings of two pioneering sex surveys conducted with middle-class Victorian women, D'Emilio and Freedman (1997: 176) noted how 'Ignorance about sex stands out in bold relief as a prominent cause of the ambivalence many women felt about sexual passion.' As well as its censorship, women's sexuality was subject to oppressive policing, as Anthony Giddens points out: 'Anyone who believes that the "repressive hypothesis" contains no truth should ponder the fact that, only some seventy-five years ago, in Britain, unmarried girls who became pregnant were sent in their thousands to reformatories and mental hospitals' (Giddens 1992: 77).

The history of anti-miscegenation statutes in the United States – laws prohibiting interracial marriage, some dating back to the seventeenth century, were finally ruled unconstitutional only in 1967 – as well as the forced sterilisation of tens of thousands of black, Native American and Hispanic women from the 1930s to the 1970s, is testimony to the state's destructive interference in the sexual bodies and practices of minority groups in the United States, a repression which continued for much of the twentieth century (Davis 2003). Racist stereotypes inherited from the colonial consciousness often depicted African people as dangerously sexually prolific but incapable of finer loving feelings, and internalised elements of these stereotypes lingered long in black self-identities and practices, even in the midst of militant struggles for black self-determination (hooks 2001). Laws prohibiting sex between white women and native males were also passed in British colonies – such as the 1903 Immorality Suppression Ordinance in Southern Rhodesia, which was extended in 1916 to criminalise any form of solicitation of black men by white women (Bland 2005: 31). By the

1940s and 1950s, one cultural historian reports, violent miscegenation discourses were firmly rooted in the white English consciousness: 'Every autobiographical account of black migrants to Britain in this period which I have come across testifies to the fact that all pretence of English civility collapsed at the point when black men were seen to be with white women. It was in this moment, precisely, that sanctions would be unleashed and abuse and beating begin' (Schwarz 1996: 197).

Foucault's theory of the construction of sexuality has perhaps been applied with more success in the field of gay and lesbian studies. Foucault had described how the nineteenth-century 'technologies of sex' transformed homosexuality from a deviant practice to an organic 'species', constructing the homosexual as an 'interior androgyny', a 'hermaphrodism of the soul' (Foucault 1981: 43). More contemporary Foucauldians have argued that the same conflation of heterogeneous practices with categorical identities can today be seen in the liberal humanist normalisation of homosexuality, whose moral legitimacy now rests on the assertion that same-sex relationships are as virtuous and loving as heterosexual ones ('love is love is love'). This of course de-stigmatises not *all* private consensual sex, as Ruskola (2005: 241) points out, 'but only certain kinds of intimacies' – the kinds that most resemble the conventional heterosexual norm of a stable monogamous partnership. When homosexual sex was presumptively criminal, 'there was little need to draw distinctions between kinds of homosexual sex – it was all bad'. The landmark 2003 Supreme Court ruling, *Lawrence v Texas*, may have made homosexual sex legal in every US state and territory, but it came with the implicit normative condition that queerness be repudiated and 'that our sex lives be respectable' (Ruskola 2005: 239). Similar reservations are expressed by queer theorists in regard to the petitioning for state recognition of non-heterosexual unions. The campaign to allow the rights, benefits and symbolic entitlements of marriage to be enjoyed by same-sex couples is here seen to give false legitimacy to a heterocentric and patrilineal institution that is otherwise crumbling, while at the same time delegitimising – rendering illegible or untenable – sexual practices and relationships that fall outside the heteronormative construction of desire, love, family and kinship (Warner 1999; Phelan 2001). We need to ask, Judith Butler writes, 'what happens to sexuality when it runs through this particular circuit of fantasy':

> is it alleviated of its guilt, its deviance, its discontinuity, its asociality, its spectrality? And if it is alleviated of all that, where precisely do these negativities go? Do they not tend to be projected on to those who have not or will not enter

this hallowed domain? And does the projection [not] take the form of judging others morally, of enacting a social abjection and hence becoming the occasion to institute a new hierarchy of legitimate and illegitimate sexual arrangement? ... . For as surely as rights to marriage and to adoption and, indeed, to reproductive technology ought to be secured for individuals and alliances outside the marriage frame, it would constitute a drastic curtailment of progressive sexual politics to allow marriage and family, or even kinship, to mark the exclusive parameters within which sexual life is thought. (Butler 2002: 23, 40)

The chalice of legal rights may be a poisoned one, but these Foucauldian insights should not distract attention from the history of violence and discrimination against gay and lesbian people, the length of time it took to repeal sodomy laws in many US states, and the continued criminalisation of homosexuality in dozens of countries across the world today. In most Western societies, these laws may have been rarely or sporadically enforced, but their existence certainly provided the legitimacy for a range of collateral repressions and paralegal punishments, ranging from anti-gay violence and harassment by police to discrimination by employers, immigration officers, and the providers of health and social services. 'In short, gay citizens are treated and punished as criminals, but without any of the procedural safeguards afforded criminal defendants' (Leslie 2000: 116). An analogy with the Jim Crow laws and the sanction they provided for lynching is not entirely specious here.

It is worth remembering, too, that it was only in 1987 that homosexuality was completely removed from the American Psychiatric Association's official classification of mental disorders, while it took another five years before The World Health Organization finally took homosexuality off its statistical classification of 'diseases'. Foucault's argument that the medicalisation of sexuality allowed for the managed 'deployment' of desire rather than its repression underplays the way physicians and psychiatrists sought to 'cure' non-conforming sexualities, as well as simply grading, surveying and stabilising them through the biopolitical management of bodies.

Reflexive rationalisation and the pure relationship

Against Foucault's theory that modernity constructs the self as a known and manageable entity, Anthony Giddens has argued that the advancement of modernity is characterised by the problematising of the self and the increasing openness of identities to self-interrogation and self-definition. For Giddens,

Foucault's account of power-knowledge and the way discourse determines social reality is too linear and undialectical, neglecting the reflexivity of social actors who adopt dominant discourses as frames of reference rather than definitive identities or behavioural scripts. Giddens sees 'a certain beauty' in Reich and Marcuse's 'respective visions of a non-repressive order', and he emphasises the way sexuality today is 'a medium of emancipation' as well as an object of surveillance and control (1992: 181).

Giddens highlights the way the post-war medico-scientific investigation of sexuality led to more reliable methods of family planning, and later to IVF, which progressively differentiated sexual pleasure from the exigencies of reproduction, and thereby also from heterosexuality. In Giddens' view, the ultimate outcome of these developments was the realisation of a 'plastic', 'decentred' sexuality which has, in turn, finally made possible the democratisation of intimate life and the emergence of what he calls the 'pure relationship'.

Giddens defines the pure relationship as one which 'is entered into for its own sake, for what can be derived by each person from a sustained association with one another; and which is continued only in so far as it is thought by both parties to deliver enough satisfactions for each individual to stay within it' (1992: 57). For Giddens the roots of the pure relationship actually go back to eighteenth- and nineteenth-century ideals of romantic love, which sublimated the passionate eroticism that earlier societies had assigned to the realm of the irrational, and made from it a socially constructive force of psychological security, a narrative of self-identity and a culturally sanctioned 'gamble against the future'. Romantic love expressed the belief 'that a durable emotional tie can be established with the other on the basis of qualities intrinsic to that tie itself' (1992: 2). Although in this sense romantic love was the 'harbinger of the pure relationship', it was also 'essentially feminised love', Giddens points out, for men lagged well behind women in the domain of emotional intimacy, typically dissociating – as Freud recorded – marital love from eroticism, and often treating romantic love with thinly veiled cynicism.

Only today, as women's sexual emancipation and autonomy have exposed the fictions and failures of romantic love, are men finding 'masculinity' to be a cultural construction that is increasingly dysfunctional to personal life, impeding the intimacy and openness on which egalitarian love depends. Whereas romantic love assumed sexual contentment to be a natural by-product of spiritual union and marital companionship, today's pure relationships are founded on 'confluent love', Giddens argues, in which the reciprocal giving and receiving of pleasure is the primary goal. 'Confluent love', Giddens says, is 'active, contingent love' which 'jars with the "for-ever", and "one-and-only" qualities of the romantic love complex' (1992: 62). In confluent love it is 'the relationship', not the singularity of the beloved, that counts, Giddens argues, and this relationship can only be sustained if trust is actively communicated and returned. This in turn requires emotional literacy, self-understanding, and the ability and willingness to open oneself up to the other – traits that have made women the pioneers of the transformation of intimate life and the 'emotional revolutionaries of modernity'.

The concept of the pure relationship is one component of Giddens' wider theory of 'reflexive rationalisation'. Giddens wants to highlight the dynamism of late modernity, and, like Habermas, to draw attention to the empowering and democratising effects of the rationalisation process, as opposed to the more sombre account of growing alienation, bureaucratisation and meaninglessness associated with Weberian sociology and with Foucault's concept of disciplinary power. Social life is more uncertain, but by the same token more open, more self-directed and potentially more egalitarian. The domain of intimacy is no exception to this. In the pure relationship, which Giddens suggests, as Weeks (1999, 2007) also argues, is most typical of same-sex couples for whom the asymmetrical expectations of hetero-normative gender roles are obsolete, there is a 'transactional negotiation of personal ties by equals' (Giddens 1992: 3). This negotiation is underpinned by 'an implicit "rolling contract" to which appeal may be made by either partner when situations arise felt to be unfair or oppressive' (1992: 192). Confluent love is contingent, revocable love which is given 'until further notice'. The pure relationship 'can be terminated, more or less at will, by either partner at any particular point' (1992: 137). Although this does not necessarily require a continual auditing of costs and benefits, Giddens states, it does mean that all actions which affect the happiness of the other must be premised on testable reasons. Confluent love is rational, reflexive and carefully measured, and is clearly opposed to the passionate self-abandonment of romantic love. For Giddens, in fact, the 'giving up of self' that is idealised in the romantic tradition is actually a 'pathology of self-discipline', a form of 'reverse reflexivity' that is typical of all forms of addiction (and which in personal relationships gives rise to what is known as 'co-dependency').

Giddens does not deny the insecurity, uncertainty and potential for hurt that arises with the pure relationship, and for good reason. Most Western countries saw a doubling or even tripling of the divorce rate in the period from the late 1960s to the early 1990s, while marriage rates themselves have fallen so dramatically that today they are around a third of what they were in the early 1970s. It is true the likelihood of a marriage ending in divorce has actually been declining over the last 25 years – longer periods of premarital cohabitation, an increase in age at first marriage, and the long-term decline in the number of marriages, indicate that wedlock is today approached with much more caution and foresight than in previous decades. But it remains more or less accurate to say that half of all marriages will end in separation.[1]

The fatal heroism of love

Perhaps one can interpret Giddens' account of a sober, rational, self-disciplined love in the light of these statistics, both as an explanation of and a response to the greater fragility of intimate life. Romantic pledges lose their lustre once wedding vows have already been broken, and it is hardly surprising that divorcees, or their disillusioned offspring, enter new relationships with more restraint and prudence than the discourse of romantic love would recommend. Love affairs in later life, when the weight of the past is more dense and compelling than the openness of the future, cannot be the reciprocal creation of virgin selfhood that marks the exuberant optimism of young lovers. Nor can love that must be shared, compromised and hybridised in reconstituted families be the absolute and undivided love dramatised in literary fiction. Greater individualism, increased social and cultural complexity, the questioning of rigid gender roles and the assertion of the individual's right to define her or his own desires and to pursue their satisfaction, together make romantic ideals of mutual love and belonging seem more and more utopian, if not delusory.

It is perhaps surprising, then, that a number of other sociological commentators have traced the instability of personal relationships in contemporary societies not to the 'reflexivity' that Giddens claims is characteristic of confluent love, but instead to the pervasive influence of the older romantic utopia of love which, since it has been transformed into an object of mass consumption, has become a profound threat to the decency and longevity of intimate partnerships. In Wendy Langford's psychoanalytically informed study of women's experiences of love, for example, belief in the emergence of an egalitarian model of coupledom – 'confluent love', in Giddens' analysis – is merely the latest version of a romantic

---

[1] In England and Wales, 42 per cent of marriages are estimated to end in divorce, with half these divorces occurring in the first 10 years of marriage (ONS 2018). In the United States, the comparative figure is 43–46 per cent. When the number of marriages that end in *de facto* separation but not legal divorce is included, 'the common belief that about half of all marriages are voluntary disrupted is a reasonable approximation' (Amato 2010: 651).

ideology which conceals the forms of power, hostility, domination and control that materialise in all heterosexual relationships founded on passion. Submission and self-objectification are the true fate of women who fall in love, Langford argues, the initial unity of lovers being an illusory bond based on self-denial and the projection of unconscious fantasies rooted in the psychic dramas of the past. When lovers finally wake from their euphoric stupor, they discover only mutual disillusionment, anger and conflict, with men typically resorting to emotional withdrawal and women descending into desperate spirals of self-abasement. In Langford's account, 'the strength of love's revolution is matched by that of counter-revolution which destroys intimacy and brings the lovers to a state of mutual alienation, characterised by gendered dynamics of control and submission'. If lasting intimacy or equality between partners is to be achieved, then it is not because but rather 'in spite of falling love' (Langford 1999: 115). The way romantic love, by mobilising ideas of complementary togetherness and the unity of opposites, constructs and perpetuates heteronormative gender roles has also been scrutinised from the standpoint of queer theory. As Paul Johnson (2005: 101) argues, 'love is a carrier of heterosexuality, a vehicle for gender production, and a mechanism for transferring heteronormative social relations into enduring subjectivities and identifications'.

For Mary Evans, on the other hand, the problem with romanticism is not the unconscious reproduction of destructive gender relations, but rather the destabilising of marriage and families. While marriage, as late as the nineteenth century, was largely a pragmatic economic affair indifferent to, or exclusive of, erotic satisfactions, Evans argues that affective individualism and the fantasy of 'marriage for love' have since moved from being an ideological prop for the bourgeois-patriarchal family, to a macerator of male intransigence, and finally to an egocentric, if not infantile, force which has progressively corroded the conjugal bond from within. Such is the power of the popular ideology of romantic love that erstwhile loving couples are today easily convinced that dwindling desire, the exhaustion of curiosity, and the irresistible demands of work, domestic labour and dependent children are proof that a relationship has failed, and that love must be rekindled elsewhere instead. Hence the sobering title of Evans' book, *Love: An Unromantic Discussion* (2003).

In the past the most likely dampener on a sexual fling would have been unwanted pregnancy, and the most likely consequence, Evans points out, would have been a 'shot-gun' wedding, with marriage arranged, and in most cases sustained, out of a concern for moral decency rather than love. This was, however, a starkly gendered morality: male gallantry saved the woman from the ignominy of unfeminine lustfulness, while female modesty civilised and constrained the supposedly natural insatiability of masculine desire. Today, however, women's own sexuality is no longer denied or tabooed, the risk, as well as the stigma, of out-of-wedlock pregnancy is greatly diminished, and the sobering up of sexual partners – typically through sexual routinisation rather than sexual accident – is more likely to result in separation than in a faithful, if unromantic, commitment to one another based on honour, realism and mutual tolerance. Adultery and desertion are now readily justified by the irresistible passion of 'true love', Evans argues, and the shame that led Emma Bovary and Anna Karenina to take their own lives makes little moral sense to the modern reader of romantic fiction. In our apparent failure to recognise the limitations and delusions of romantic love, 'the very idea which humanised marriage and emancipated women from patriarchal control becomes the idea which destroys marriage. Romantic love modernised marriage, yet it also subverts it' (Evans 2003: 119). Romantic love is for Evans an infantilising invocation of the unrepeatable intimacy of the infant–mother bond, a fantasy that seems sustainable in the heady period of mutual infatuation, but which, when reality sets in, ultimately 'distorts and limits the possibilities of human relationships', even making misunderstanding, aggression and violence more likely (Evans 1999: 273).

Evans associates romanticism with a commercialised, consumerist view of love, and argues instead for something more Platonic, something more akin to Jane Austen's model of dispassionate affection: 'Rather than regarding the rational as the cold and uncaring enemy of love,' she concludes, 'we might well regard it as its only true defender in a social world awash with deadly cocktails of romance, hedonism and personal entitlement' (Evans 2003: 143). The idea that romanticism is mixed with 'hedonism and personal entitlement' suggests, however, that contemporary consumerist romance may be closer to rational utilitarian individualism than Evans indicates. It is certainly far from the elaborate arts and rituals of courtesy, modesty and symbolic appreciation that have been enshrined in the Western tradition of erotic love since the twelfth century. Arguably there is less and less in our culture today that points towards the sacredness of the sexual bond, the dominant ideology of intimate relationships being one which promotes neither emotional sensitivity nor passionate self-sacrifice, but rather the rational self-limiting of love and its replacement with something more avaricious and therefore more prone to repletion and ennui. What remain of the irrational and mysterious elements of love appear today in the crude form of sexual and emotional curiosity, expressing the kind of erotic voyeurism and thirst for novelty and spectacle that St Augustine, in the *Confessions*, would have called the 'lust of the eyes' (X.xxxv.54–5). This is not a love that is deepened and enriched by romantic literacy and the imaginative idealisation of feeling. It is not love as giving, cherishing, suffering and transcending. It suggests a love that has been casualised and reduced to a form of entertainment, not elevated and intensified in a search for deeper meaning.

The French philosopher Pascal Bruckner would not complain about this. He shares Evans' view that love is in crisis not because we treat it too lightly but because we take it too seriously. 'Our couples are not dying of selfishness and materialism,' he argues, 'they're dying of a fatal heroism, an excessively great conception of themselves' (2013: 30). Bruckner's outlook recalls Rougemont's warnings regarding the narcissism of courtly love. Not unlike Evans, his suggestion is that we remain in the grip of an older, irrational model of *amour passion* that has been set loose by the slackening of normative rules and institutional regulations, but which has not yet adjusted itself, in the way Giddens implies it has, to the realities of reflexive rationalisation. The repressive constraints of marriage may, in the past, have 'killed love', but today the hunger for love has triumphed not only over marriage but also over the possibility of love itself. In our naked freedom we are now 'channelling by assent the impetuous torrent of emotions that our ancestors held back by prohibitions'. Because of the uncompromising veneration of love, 'the possibility of two people living a life in common has been put in question again' (2013: 7, 24). The secular religion of love is destroying relationships from the inside, overloading them with unrealistic desires and expectations.

> A terrible absurdity: living as a couple has become more difficult to endure since of all its roles it has retained only that of being a model of fulfilment. Because it wants to succeed at any cost, it is consumed with anxiety, fears the law of entropy, the aridity of slack periods. The slightest decrease in tension is experienced as a fiasco, a rejection … . The domestic sphere has become the stake in a titanic battle between the sublimity sought and the trivial felt … . Passionate love is the love of passion, that is, of torment; it is war, constant demand, the reign of the highest bidder, a face-to-face encounter forever … . In order to live together, there is no need to adore each other in the canonical sense of the term; it suffices to like each other, to share the same tastes, to seek all the happiness possible in the framework of a harmonious coexistence. If we want it to last, let's stop subjecting life in common to the despotic law of exuberance. (Bruckner 2013: 32–3)

Bruckner favours the slogan 'love me less but love me longer', and playfully imagines a scenario in which the age at which marriage is permissible is raised to 40, giving would-be spouses more time for reflection, and transforming marriage from a mark of conformism to 'a symbol of the elite, an adventure for a minority, a very exclusive club reserved for the happy few' (2013: 76, 80–1). With average life expectancy in the West increasing at a rate of two and half years per decade, Bruckner's pragmatism resonates with Jeanette Winterson's suggestion that marriage would be more attractive if it were not treated as a life-long commitment:

> We are all living longer, and not all of us can stay with that same one person for ever. Marriage has always been a contract, so why not discuss fixed-term contracts? I want to stay with Susie, and I hope I can, but I would have preferred to sign up for 10 years because 'for ever' makes me panic. (Winterson 2017)

The casualisation of love

French sociologist Jean-Claude Kaufmann shares his compatriot's scepticism towards the utopian absolutism of romantic *eros*, arguing that relationships wither not for want of passion but through lack of *agapē* (Kaufmann 2011: 131–2). But Kaufmann is more attentive than Bruckner or Winterson to the corrosive effects of rational individualism on personal relationships, which founder not just because of the irrational deification of love but also because of the reduction of love to the calculated pursuit of pleasure. Kaufmann notes how the need for love has escalated in the contemporary world, as people are deprived of security and recognition in increasingly competitive social and economic environments. But the frustration of that need is in turn exacerbated when lovers adopt in their private lives models of evaluation and exchange that belong to the traditionally masculine world of economic calculation and cognitive self-interest (Kaufmann 2011: 50, 107–12).

This indeed seemed to be one of the findings of Arlie Hochschild's (2003) study of women's advice books published between 1970 and 1990. Over time the emotional thematic of these books changed, becoming less patriarchal but also less sentimental. Hochschild noted an increasing tendency to 'recycle male rules of love' as the model for women readers, with the prevailing message being 'that love should play an altogether less central role than it has had in the lives of women'. Hochschild's observations clearly dissent from Giddens' account of the feminisation of love, as well as from the claim that lovers today are deluded by deadly ideologies of heart-busting romance: 'We've moved from living according to two emotional codes – one for men and another for women – to a unisex code based on the old code for men. We've also moved from a warmer code to a cooler one, aspects of which both fit with and exacerbate a move to lighter family bonds' (Hochschild 2003: 27).

Being 'cool' is an apt expression for the disposable relations of convenience which Zygmunt Bauman argued are characteristic of 'top-pocket relationships' in the modern era of 'liquid love'. For Bauman, the heat of passion is always an emotional step towards personal involvement in the life of another, and if lovers are turning the temperature down this is as much a desire to keep their options open as it is an expression of sensible realism: 'whatever other features human acts and interactions might have, interaction should not be allowed to warm up and particularly stay warm; it is OK as long as it stays cool, and being cool means being OK' (Bauman 2003: 90). In the dampening down of passion and desire there are echoes here of the 'blunting of discrimination' that Simmel (1950b) argued was typical of the 'blasé attitude' that he believed was the common defensive response to the sensory and symbolic overload faced by inhabitants of the modern metropolis, and which Meštrović (1996) later theorised as 'post-emotionalism'.[2] A corollary 'Taylorisation' of sexual life has also been documented by feminist critics of the patriarchal rationalisation of love (Jackson and Scott 1997).

Research conducted by sociologist Eva Illouz paints a similar picture to that of Hochschild, Bauman and others of an ironic, demystified, de-intensified love. 'In the equanimity with which they recount falling in and out of love, the respondents' autobiographical accounts bear a decisively untragic "lightness", Illouz (1999: 177) reports of her interviews with 50 men and women exploring their romantic lives. 'Nowhere could I find the poignancy and existential gravity of the Romantic idea of the "great love". Illouz's findings belie the claim that clichéd fantasies of romantic love have indoctrinated Western consumers with unrealistic ideals. What she found, on the contrary, was a disenchanted, over-knowing realism which treated 'love at first sight' with suspicion if not disdain. The miracle of a new beginning is of course no measure of the long-term viability of a love affair, but it is notable that the memory, mystery and mythology of a

---

[2] A 'post-emotional society' is not, as one might assume, a society without emotions (as a quick glance at a reality TV programme would readily demonstrate). The term refers, instead, to a society where emotions are too fleeting, too superficial and too self-aware, to motivate and sustain resolute forms of *action*.

relationship's origins are often what feed the faith of couples who are able to see subsequent conflict and disharmony as something that can and must be surmounted. For why shouldn't we treat the intoxication of love as a fleeting glimpse of an exemplary truth, and every subsequent disillusionment a false but irresistible perversion? Most of Illouz's interviewees, by contrast, dismissed the passionate experience of spontaneous emotional and physical recognition that we call 'falling in love', downgrading it to a fleeting phase of animalistic lust or infatuation divorced from any grander meaning, sustainable romantic narrative or revelatory experience of self.

Giddens' own description of the pure relationship seems to embrace more positively this model of a lighter, cooler love, and one can see why some critics have dismissed Giddens' theory as a crass defence of the 'commodification or consumerisation of human partnerships' (Bauman 2000: 89). Citing Mallarmé's definition of poetry as 'chance defeated word by word', Alain Badiou reminds us that love, when it is declared, is always poetic in essence: 'locking chance into the framework of eternity' (Badiou 2012: 45, 47). In bidding farewell to the aestheticism of romantic love, the danger is that we are also dispensing with the emotional power of symbolism and ritual, and with it the narrative resources that enable couples to transform the magical contingency of a new relationship into something they believe will endure.

It is also possible to see how the transactional conception of the pure relationship, when it is adopted by couples themselves, may generate a degrading dynamic of conflict and competition rather than intimacy. Some feminist sociologists have criticised Giddens for reducing sexual partnerships to purely emotional exchanges, an idealisation that conveniently ignores both the way domestic relationships are structured by the gendered distribution and non-intimate negotiation of material resources, and the way intimacy is often experienced by couples as a by-product of practical caring and sharing rather than as the deliberate outcome of self-knowing emotional disclosure (Jamieson 1998, 1999). The 'gender division of emotion work' in heterosexual relationships has also been extensively documented by sociologists who report men consistently failing to reciprocate the efforts that women typically make in their pursuit of emotional and physical intimacy (Duncombe and Marsden 1993, 1995, 1996).

It is nonetheless true that, just as personal relationships bear the imprint of impersonal structures and constraints, so too are the practical and worldly aspects of domestic life always experienced and understood by couples through the passions and prejudices of personal feeling. 'Fairness' in a personal relationship, in other words, is not simply a question of what one does, since the value of what one does, in a relationship that is premised on affect, cannot be determined independently of how it makes both oneself and the other *feel*. Moreover, if the goal of a relationship is happiness, then this must be happiness in giving as well as receiving. This is why love is such a dangerous ideal, both to societal standards of reason, equity and justice, and indeed to lovers themselves, who must expose themselves, by their 'irrational' generosity, to the risk of exploitation and harm.

The risk of harm is also magnified by the fact that 'equality' in the domain of feelings presupposes a psychological transparency that is rarely attainable. It is precisely the opacity of the emotions which makes them a latent source of distrust in personal relationships, and it is the same opacity which also creates the opportunity, when trust is low, to bargain higher through deception. If two separate people enter into or continue with a relationship in order to take from that relationship an equal share of personal pleasure, and if the source of each person's pleasure is believed to be what the other person puts in, then it makes rational sense, so long as symmetry is formally recognised by both parties as a normative ideal, to deny or disguise the extent of one's pleasure. The relationship, in other words, will naturally default under stress not to 'the reign of the highest bidder' (Bruckner), but to a Dutch auction, in which expressions of happiness or contentment weaken one's bargaining position, permitting the other to reduce her or his effort or to demand that one gives more in return. Being – or at least appearing to be – unhappy, on the other hand, means one can demand more and offer less.

The obvious point that needs to be made here is that if we really want to conceptualise love as labour – to make a relationship a success, the rational–therapeutic discourse now advises us, you have to 'work' on it – then leisurely love is clearly a lesser love, and it is better to find loving hard than to find it free and easy. The artistry of love is also an inevitable casualty of this approach, for the genius of the virtuoso lies precisely in making things look effortless.

Trust is clearly one missing ingredient in this depiction of sexual relationships. The weighing of costs and benefits implies a superficialisation of love; and yet the calculable 'weight' of pleasure and dissatisfaction in this transaction also exposes the fatal gravity of emotional lives when they are not leavened by grace. For Giddens (1991: 96–7) it is self-understanding and the gamble of self-disclosure which generates the trust that is so preciously needed when the autonomy of lovers reaches the heights of reflexive agency. But Giddens' exchange model of intimacy misses Durkheim's well-known observation that contractual relations are only sustainable if they are underpinned by a non-contractual consensus: 'a contract is not sufficient unto itself, but is possible only thanks to a regulation of the contract that is originally social' (Durkheim 1964: 215). Stjepan Meštrović argues that in ignoring Durkheim's insight – which in the domain of intimate life implies a shared, 'romantic' belief in the sacredness of a couple's union – Giddens actually ends up with a jaundiced theory of human agency, in which authentic forms of engagement are barely conceivable. Meštrović draws attention to the primary role of 'faith' in making possible the establishment of trust: 'a certain amount of "letting go" – a deliberate decision to suspend agency – is a prerequisite for genuine, non-cynical faith in relationships and commitments' (Meštrović 1998: 85). In Giddens' theory of the pure relationship, by contrast, the choice of exit is a constant companion to the reflexive individual's actions and deliberations: 'the possibility of dissolution … forms part of the very horizon of commitment' (Giddens 1991: 187).

> The human agent who enters a relationship with such a calculating, cautious, and gaming attitude toward trust is paradoxically not an agent in the fullest sense of the term, because he or she is holding back in commitment. If one is weighing the capability of the bond to withstand future traumas as an index of how much to invest in the relationship, one is not really committed to the relationship. No amount of rhetorical skills by Giddens can obfuscate this straightforward truth. (Meštrović 1998: 85)

Existential love

Giddens is certainly aware of the internal tensions that trouble the pure relationship, but his perspective is generally regarded as overly optimistic, narrowly selective and blind to the way entrenched gender roles and expectations remain an impediment to loving intimacy – as continues to be apparent, for example, in young women's accounts of their first sexual encounters with men (Thompson 1995: 17–46; Jamieson 1998: 124–6). Nonetheless, few would seriously dispute the claim that there has been a 'transformation of intimacy' in the West over the last 60 years, and that the needs, hopes and demands of lovers in their personal lives are today more complex and more reflexive than what we know of them in the past. If we take the theory of reflexive modernity as valid, we may at least gain a more balanced analysis of the challenges to personal life posed by the turbulence of late modernity from Ulrich Beck and Elisabeth Beck-Gernsheim's popular book, *The Normal Chaos of Love* (1995). Beck had for some time argued that the process of 'individualisation' is the most radical aspect of late modernity, and the book repeatedly emphasises the need to understand individualisation not simply as a cultural norm or a personal yearning, but as a structural imperative inseparable from the rise of a market system that demands loose personal attachments, social and geographical flexibility, competitive self-interest and an ever-growing readiness to take personal risks and shoulder oneself the consequences of change.

'Individualism' was of course the watchword of the nineteenth-century bourgeoisie, but it was also an ideological motif that does not tell the true story of what Beck (1999) calls the period of 'first modernity'. The concept of the individual was modelled on and monopolised by an unsustainable masculinity, it was bounded and contained by class formation and the power of the nation state, and it was mediated by an array of hidden normative assumptions concerning the linear role of science and technology and the imagined destiny of human beings as lords and masters of the earth. In the 'second modernity', Beck and his collaborators argue, the structures, prejudices and essentialisms which fabricated and fixed the supposedly liberated bourgeois individual in a socially sanctioned project of self-assertion have come unstuck, and individuals now really do face their freedom naked, vulnerable, uncertain and alone (Beck, Bonss and Lau 2003).

The reality of individualisation, and the burden of freedom and responsibility it has engendered, has, Beck and Beck-Gernsheim argue in *The Normal Chaos of Love*, broken the legitimacy of marriage as a moral and legal institution independent of the will of the spouses. And in now demanding individualism from women as much as men, it has also broken the patriarchal, semi-feudal compact of Fordist capitalism, which could reproduce itself only so long as women were willing and able to accept rigid gender roles and devote themselves to servicing the damage that economic individualism did to their male partners. The 'one-and-a-half-person jobs' of capitalist productivism could be managed when a second person was available to perform auxiliary household labour and related emotional services, but the large-scale absorption of women into the labour market over the last 50 years has destabilised this arrangement and left both men and women feeling overworked and underappreciated. The result is an increasingly 'nomadic' society that makes a calm and settled family a difficult and unlikely achievement. The move towards equalising men and women's involvement in the market economy 'does not lead to a happy world of co-operative equals but to separateness and diverging interests'. 'If equality is pursued in the sense that everyone is a mobile member of the labour force, then this implies a society of singles' (1995: 145, 144).

The global growth in single-person households, and the trend towards what Irene Levin (2004) called 'living apart together', lend support to this analysis, though as Jamieson and Simpson (2013) point out in their own empirical study, we must be careful not to assume that structural processes of individualisation are always accompanied by individualism as a cultural value system. People who live alone are not necessarily disconnected from social and civic life, are not necessarily single and are not necessarily subverting or repudiating the ideal of a companionate relationship. Jane Lewis's study of British couples found that the growing desire for personal autonomy and self-fulfilment is not expressed at the cost of obligation and commitment in intimate relationships, and that cohabiting couples who have rejected the public morality of marriage still tend to dedicate themselves to privately negotiated norms of fidelity and fairness (Lewis 2001). In Beck and Beck-Gernsheim's view, the desire for emotional commitment and lasting companionship has in fact never been keener, not least because a loving alliance between increasingly distinct and autonomous individuals becomes increasingly attractive as social life becomes more impersonal, more unpredictable and more uncertain. The more individual we become, the greater is our need to bond with another person, and to gain from that bond the conviction that our singular existence really matters to somebody. When we are loved, our individuality and difference is verified; yet when we love we also cherish the otherness of the beloved, wilfully decentring ourselves and our own sovereign perspective on the world.

Relationships inevitably come under enormous strain because of this existential enterprise, with conflicts magnified by the need to constantly question and decide one's own biographical course in ways which respect and accommodate the choices of an equally autonomous and uncertain lover, and all this in the context of a market system that treats compromise and commitment to anything other than economic productivity as an abnegation of ambition. The staging and pacing of a relationship and decisions over jobs, careers, houses, contraception, marriage, children, diet, schooling, parenting strategies, health and much, much more have to be negotiated and renegotiated by partners and family members on a day-to-day basis. Every consensus that is reached in these 'do-it-yourself relationships' and 'post-familial families' may, moreover, be subsequently cancelled and undone, for its very achievement always testifies to the partners' ongoing freedom (Beck and Beck-Gernsheim 1995: 52–6).

Meanwhile, the loosening of the prejudices that previously separated people from different classes and ethnic backgrounds, combined with the greater opportunities for bi-cultural relationships that arise with labour migration, refugee displacements, as well as growing tourism and travel for business and education, is also increasing the scope for cultural incongruity and value conflict in intimate partnerships. 'The question, "Who am I, what do I want?" is posed anew in the course of a bi-national marriage. And it leads on to further questions that call for a crucial decision: "What do I want to keep?", "What can I give up?", "What is important to me?"' (Beck-Gernsheim 1999: 63). Relationships are no longer underwritten by a community of common traditions, and the upshot of the individualisation process is that they must be constantly worked on, and worked out, by partners themselves. Lovers must become 'the legislators of their own way of life, the judges of their own transgressions, the priests who absolve their own sins and the therapists who loosen the bonds of their own past' (1995: 5). This, too, is why love can lead to dreadful suffering and unremedied pain, for there can be no 'justice' or 'injustice' in love once partners have pledged to build a common life by loving one another's radical subjectivity and freedom. 'In creating their own laws, lovers open the door to a form of lawlessness as soon as the magic of being in love has flown away and their own interests take centre stage' (1995: 195).

Beck and Beck-Gernsheim are convinced that love is becoming 'one main source of satisfaction and meaning in life'. Love, they argue, 'is religion after religion, the ultimate belief after the end of all faith'. Love promises truth, meaning and authenticity of feeling 'in a world which otherwise runs on pragmatic solutions and convenient lies'. A form of 'communism within capitalism', love is a 'secular religion' without churches and priests, 'a non-traditional, post-traditional religion which we are hardly aware of because we ourselves are its temples and our wishes are its prayers' (1995: 169, 12, 175–7). But exactly what counts as love – how it is expressed, what it feels like, what entitlements it permits and prohibitions it respects – remain matters of exploration, and contestation, in every partnership. As life expectancy increases and birth rates fall, there may be greater opportunity for couples to settle these questions by building lasting bonds of companionship in the later years of their lives. But if happiness and fulfilment in love is to be part of that programme of 'positive welfare' recommended by Giddens (1998) as the only feasible alternative to neo-liberalism in a society of reflexive individualism – if we are, that is, to imagine the possibility of 'a world in which emotional fulfilment replaced the maximising of economic growth' (Giddens 1992: 3) – then policies are needed to restrain the force of economic rationality and allow couples the breathing space to establish mutual understandings of love and sexuality and to produce stable, as well as diverse and imaginative, forms of intimate life. The decoupling of income from working time, and a legal requirement that employers, or regional consortia of employers, provide employment opportunities for their employees' partners, are policies suggested by Beck and Beck-Gernsheim that push in this direction (1995: 162–5).

Beck and Beck-Gernsheim capture well the challenges faced by lovers in the contemporary Western world. In contrast to those, like Evans and Bruckner, who regard the idealism of romantic love as part of the problem, *The Normal Chaos of Love* also makes a strong defence of love as the only secular religion likely to survive the process of radical individualisation, and the one form of faith that is succoured as much as depleted by the anguished struggles and failures of intimate life. That said, there is a sombre tone to much of Beck and Beck-Gernsheim's analysis, and it is notable that their book ends somewhat dispiritingly, with the authors emphasising the seemingly inexorable paradoxes of love between free individuals, and the temptation to escape these paradoxes by consigning love to the domain of irrational childishness. Thus they cite from the tortured description of eternally dissatisfied lovers in *Being and Nothingness* – where Sartre (1956: 367) writes of how 'the lover wants to be loved by a freedom but demands that this freedom as freedom should no longer be free' – but they curiously ignore Beauvoir's more harmonious vision:

> Genuine love ought to be founded on the mutual recognition of two liberties; the lovers would then experience themselves both as self and as other: neither would give up transcendence, neither would be mutilated; together they would manifest values and aims in the world. For the one and the other, love would be revelation of self by the gift of self and enrichment of the world. (Beauvoir 1972: 677)

It was not long after the 1949 publication of *Le Deuxième Sexe* that Beauvoir fell madly in love with Sartre's young assistant, Claude Lanzmann. 'I adore you with all my body and soul', she wrote in one of many passionate letters to the only man she ever lived with, published for the first time in January 2018 in *Le Monde*. 'You are my destiny, my eternity, my life.' Perhaps this was a relationship of mutual transcendence and a shared recognition of each other's freedom; but even if it wasn't, the experience certainly caught one of France's premier intellectuals by surprise. 'My darling child, you are my first absolute love, the one that only happens once (in life) or maybe never.' The 'revelation of self by the gift of self' is here undeniable: 'I thought I would never say the words that now come naturally to me when I see you – I adore you.'[3]

---

[3] Cited in *The Guardian*, 22 January 2018.

Emotional capitalism

If Beauvoir's letters, donated to Yale University by Lanzmann, are a little shocking to our ears, this may be because Sartre and Beauvoir's dogged rationalism is difficult to reconcile with the irrational self-sacrifice and emotional compulsiveness of erotic love. Eva Illouz is one sociologist who has explored how wider processes of cultural rationalisation have articulated with and shaped the domain of intimate relationships, and how these processes may undermine our ability to experience the ecstasy and abandonment of love. Her analysis is also particularly valuable for the light it shines on the hierarchies and inequalities of love in contemporary capitalism. Illouz's approach offers, in my view, the most sophisticated sociological treatment of the tension between romance and rationality in intimate life, and for these reasons her work is deserving of sustained attention.

The argument that the image of the family as a 'relationship' rather than an 'institution' was part of a twentieth-century ideological discourse promoted by professionals with an occupational interest in serving the needs of 'the individual' is not a new one (Morgan 1991). Illouz develops this insight further, however, focusing on the development of a therapeutic culture of emotional self-awareness in the United States during the twentieth century. The cultural transformation she traces originated with Freud's theory of the self and his emphasis on the family as the crucible of psycho-sexual self-development. Illouz contests what she sees as the tendency for post-Freudian sociologists to uncritically accept, and naively de-historicise, Freud's analysis of the bourgeoisie as emotionally repressed, since in her view this obscures the way twentieth-century capitalism began to mobilise and construct emotional literacy as an economically and socially valued competency of the middle classes (Illouz 1997: 33–4).

Perhaps surprisingly, the first major opportunity for the disciples of psychology to utilise and disseminate their new understandings of the self arose in the sphere of industry, where the first few decades of the century saw a major increase in the numbers of managerial and administrative staff, and where there was a growing receptiveness to psychological advice on how to manage workers' attitudes and behaviour via their emotions. It was Elton Mayo – a trained Jungian who believed that workplace conflicts had less to do with pay and working conditions than with, in Illouz's words, 'tangled emotions, personality factors, and unresolved psychological conflicts' – whose famous Hawthorne studies in the 1920s first introduced the psychoanalytic paradigm to the workplace.

Mayo's researchers were explicitly instructed to listen rather than advise, to acknowledge and respect workers' feelings and opinions, and to interview their respondents in much the same way that a psychologist would conduct a therapeutic consultation. In doing so, the researchers unintentionally elicited Mayo's most important finding, which was that workers' productivity increases when proper attentiveness is shown to their feelings (Illouz 2007: 12–14). Illouz does not overlook the dissonant note sounded here with regard to the feminist critique of masculine truth claims, noting with irony that Mayo's research was heavily gendered, with all his subjects at Western Electric being women.

As corporations and their managers, falling in line with the recommendations of the new 'human relations' school of industrial sociology, began to see the wisdom of adopting a softer, more feminine emotional style and more open practices of communication, so workers themselves were drawn favourably to a system of authority that seemed more democratic, Illouz argues, because it appeared to be based not on inherited class privileges but on semiotic skills, 'positive' energy, and that 'controlled de-control' of the emotions that came to be regarded as one of the hallmarks of 'professionalism'. What followed was the emergence of a new economic culture of the emotions – what Illouz calls 'emotional capitalism' – which was premised on an increasingly androgynous synthesis of rational utilitarianism and sympathetic feeling.

> The economic sphere, far from being devoid of emotions, has been on the contrary saturated with affect, a kind of affect committed to and commanded by the imperative of cooperation and a mode of settling conflicts based on 'recognition'. Because capitalism demands and creates networks of interdependence, and has affect within the very heart of its transactions, it has also brought about a destructuring of the very gender identities it helped establish in the first place. By commanding that we exert our mental and emotional skills to identify with others' point of view, the 'communicative ethos' orients the manager's self to the model of traditional female selfhood. More exactly, the ethos of communication *blurs gender divisions* by inviting men and women to control their negative emotions, be friendly, view themselves through others' eyes, and empathise with others … . Emotional capitalism realigned emotional cultures, making the economic self emotional and emotions more closely harnessed to instrumental action. (Illouz 2007: 23)

Of course the feminine art of sympathy, which in its classical form may well tend towards self-effacement, is not completely adopted here, since, like the 'deadly cocktail of romance, hedonism and personal entitlement' observed by

Mary Evans, the emotional self that is described by Illouz is one that is married with reflexive self-awareness, the voice of self-interest and a Goffmanesque disposition to manage and manipulate social bonds through communicative interaction. 'By an ironic twist of cultural history, the self-interested *homo economicus* of Adam Smith has been recast by psychologists as a *homo communicans* who reflexively monitors his words and emotions, controls his self-image and pays tribute to the other's point of view' (Illouz 1997: 45). As Rose points out, a novel reconciliation of autonomy and subservience is also being crafted here: 'the new experts of the psyche promise that modes of life that appear philosophically opposed – business success and personal growth, image management and authenticity – can be brought into alignment and achieve translatability through the ethics of the autonomous, choosing, psychological self' (1998: 157).

After the 1946 National Mental Health Act was passed in the United States, Illouz notes how the therapeutic model of selfhood spread into the domestic sphere, with psychological services made available to the 'normally neurotic' members of the middle class, and psychological self-scrutiny and emotional self-development soon becoming an intrinsic part of American popular culture. As early as the 1930s, clinical psychologists had been offering public advice on love and marriage, and by the 1950s they had, among the middle classes at least, usurped the authority of moralists and religious figures. Though the latter's concerns over rising divorce rates and the 'crisis' of marriage may have been reactionary, heterosexual relationships were certainly facing new challenges which psychologists were keen to help people address. Important here, according to Illouz, was the fact that female social networks had significantly contracted since the nineteenth century, with heterosexual women now increasingly asking their husbands to provide the kind of emotional support and affection that previous generations had gained from intense friendships with other women. Illouz argues that in the nineteenth century, although 'a certain emotional fervour could be found in middle-class matrimony', the values of affective individualism were not especially prevalent in heavily gendered domestic relationships, and 'by and large, intimacy as a self-referential project was nowhere to be found in Victorian marriages' (1997: 45). Like Ferry, Illouz believes it was only in the twentieth century that emotional intimacy in heterosexual partnerships became a clearly articulated ideal.

As post-war feminist politics began to find traction with the humanistic discourse of emotional self-actualisation and personal authenticity, the goals of sexual expression and fulfilment in intimate life were catalysed and inflected by women's unique experience of being at the juncture between a traditional female culture of emotions and the sphere of economic utilitarianism. When the therapeutic ethos was transferred to people's home lives, the psychological discourse succeeded in redefining intimacy so as to make a unique appeal to liberal middle-class women, combining not just the language of care and the language of autonomous selfhood, but also that of equality, rights and the political ideal of democratic communication. Illouz argues that this represented a dramatic departure from the more sentimental female culture of the nineteenth century, for although feelings themselves remained at the heart of the psychological revolution, instead of a romantic fusing of selves through self-sacrifice and gift-giving, the ideal of personal intimacy was now thought of as a reciprocal relationship of psychological bargaining based on 'emotional disclosure and rational control between two people with equal status, knowledgeable about their respective needs and interests and able to communicate them verbally' (1997: 49).

This was a process of rationalisation that appeared to pull in the opposite direction to the emotional transformation of work relations. Given the different starting points in the traditional division between work and home, however, it actually meant a convergence of sorts – the instrumental deployment of affect to raise productivity in the economy, and the instrumental use of economic models of exchange to achieve gratifying affect in the home. 'In the same way that the therapeutic ethos had introduced a vocabulary of emotions and a norm of communication inside the corporation, it ushered in a rational and quasi-economic approach to emotions in the domestic sphere' (1997: 48). The result was a blurring of the boundaries between work and intimate life and 'the cultivation of a common reflexive and communicative selfhood which in turn tends to blur distinctions of gender roles and identities' (1997: 51).

Love's hurtful reason

One obvious reason why the psychotherapeutic redefinition of love has caused human suffering is that it has popularised the view that anything short of a completely fulfilled life is a sign of morbidity. Illouz rejects Foucault's suggestion that the deployment of sexuality functions by means of a kind of multiplication of named and unnamed pleasures, arguing instead that psychology 'ironically creates much of the suffering it is supposed to alleviate', with a disparate range of cultural, political and economic institutions conspiring to reinforce the idea that emotions are something to be inspected, quantified, exchanged and evaluated. 'In this process of inventing and deploying a wide battery and range of texts and classifications to manage and change the self, they have also contributed to creating a suffering self, that is, an identity organised and defined by its psychic lacks and deficiencies, which is incorporated back into the market through incessant injunctions to self-change and self-realisation' (Illouz 2007: 62, 109).

A second reason that the rationalisation of intimacy may lead to frustration and unhappiness concerns the embodied nature of the emotions, and thus the embodied nature of emotional relationships. Illouz highlights the problematic implications of an 'emotional ontology' which is predicated on the idea that, as our emotional literacy improves, we can detach our emotions from the stream of lived experience and 'objectify' them in the form of fixed, knowable and controllable entities. It is this premise that allows intimate life to be captured in quantitative statements and subject to techniques of calculation, albeit 'for the sake of a broader moral project: to create equality and fair exchange by engaging in a relentless verbal communication about one's needs, emotions, and goals' (2007: 34). This 'disembedding' of the emotions through their communication is paradoxical, however, since it requires 'the suspension of one's emotional entanglements in a social relationship'. Relationships may be weakened rather than strengthened by this intellectualisation of intimacy: 'communicating means to suspend or bracket the emotional glue that binds us to others' (2007: 38). This statement must obviously be qualified, since most troubled couples know that it is nigh on impossible to talk about the differences in a relationship without reproducing those differences – and with them the sticky-repellent 'glue' of emotional conflict – in the mode and manner of one's talk. But for Illouz those differences are often magnified rather than resolved by the process of communicative rationalisation: partners are 'transformed into cognitive objects that can be compared with each other and are susceptible to cost-benefit analysis', a process of 'commensuration' that 'makes intimate relationships more likely to be fungibles, that is, objects which can be traded and exchanged' (2007: 36). This is another factor contributing to the lighter, cooler, casualised love mentioned earlier.

The cognitive rationalisation of love is nowhere more apparent than in the sphere of internet dating, as Illouz's study of the users of dating websites bears out. Because of the extraordinary volume of potential online interactions available to internet daters, her respondents reported economising on the overload of information and choices by using repetitive scripts which were increasingly deployed with weary irony. While traditional romantic love was fashioned in an environment of scarcity, online dating creates 'an economy of abundance' which naturally promotes a consumerist mentality 'where the self must choose and maximise its options and is forced to use techniques of cost-benefit and efficiency' (2007: 85). If nineteenth-century romanticism legitimised an act of idealisation that necessarily 'over-evaluated' the beloved and made her or him unique, Illouz notes how in the economy of abundance people are more likely to under-value the people they meet, judging them against a bewitching array of known, partially known and still-to-be-discovered alternatives. Desire is, in this context, increasingly experienced through the prism of an economic model that assigns greatest value to what is deemed to be scarce. As the pool of potential partners appears essentially limitless, everyone suspects a better deal is obtainable and is therefore loath to take themselves off the market. 'Satisficing' – which seeks the contentment that comes from something that is 'good enough' – is replaced by 'maximising', in which commitment is endlessly postponed in pursuit of the best possible bargain.

Nineteenth-century moral norms which previously defined as romantically appealing such traits as constancy, reliability and the keeping of promises are in this new environment repudiated in favour of a consumerist logic of entitlement which regards dedication to another person as an intolerable infringement of one's freedom to choose. Moreover, while early bourgeois society saw the ability to love passionately, absolutely and inexplicably as a mark of great character, today we are more likely to feel fear and suspicion in the face of enchanted love. The cultural rationalisation of love has encouraged us to measure relationship using 'a utilitarian model of mental health and well-being', and the result is that we approach love in a more ironic and self-conscious way, deliberately protecting the self from the kind of emotional 'over-involvement' that was previously associated with sublime togetherness and the transcendence of self-interest (Illouz 2012: 159–67). Passionate love, in its unpredictability and momentousness, may have threatened the foundations of matrimonial loyalty, but it was also defiance of a utilitarian society and a refusal to submit to the reifying logic of exchange. By contrast, the economic rationalisation of intimate life, as Max Horkheimer remarked almost half a century before the arrival of internet dating, normalises the commercialisation of human bonds by turning lovers into business partners.

> In marriage the relations between the partners must, above all, be rich in results, like those of teams in industry and sport. If a marriage proves burdensome it can be dissolved, and a person may perhaps be more successful with a new partner.

Each partner is evaluated in terms of function, and this affects even the relations of the sexes before marriage, so that these relations become more uniform, more practical, less charged with momentous significance. Our mechanized world, which at present is assimilating man to itself, as well as the invasion of private existence by the machine and the acquisitive spirit, are stripping the romantic love tragedy of its historical relevance, although the tragedies themselves have not become rarer in this age of hasty decisions. (Horkheimer 1985: 17)

If the nineteenth-century romantic sensibility embraced the irrational spontaneity and mysterious epiphany of 'love at first sight', what is promoted by the rational logic of modern partner selection, Illouz argues, is the perception of interchangeability. To facilitate comparison, competition and selection in this boundless marketplace, there is an inevitable standardisation of profiled tastes, feelings, desires and identities. This in turn exacerbates the online concealment of those nuances of character and personhood which are precisely the things which make (or break) an interpersonal bond, and which are only discernible – albeit to others more than to ourselves – in the physical presence, gestures, vocal tone and bodily movements of our practical existence. When we fall in love, the beloved appears to us as an immeasurable whole rather than the sum of its measurable parts. But this 'epiphanic mode of knowledge', as Illouz describes it, is an embodied appreciation of an embodied person, not a cognitive evaluation that matches pre-formulated preferences with pre-categorised traits. The corporeal, non-conscious, intuitively directed self 'constitutes the set of automatic responses to the world which we have little knowledge of and over which we can exert little control. This in turn means that people do not and probably cannot know themselves well, and that they do not really know which kind of persons will make them feel what' (2007: 98).

Illouz thus highlights the way internet dating creates challenges and frustrations because it brackets out the body in which our emotions are grounded, energised and authenticated. Not only does the displacement of the body in virtual dating practices lead to false starts and harsh disillusionments, but the quasi-economic logic of comparison, competition and choice also inhibits the more intuitive processes by which bonds between people are formed. Psychological research shows that our emotional appreciation of things is diminished by our rational evaluation of them, yet our modern ideals of individual autonomy and self-realisation have converged with the growth of dating markets to produce courtship practices that are spoiled by rational deliberation and the self-conscious freedom to choose.

Decisions based on intuition are made faster, require emotions to be mobilised and use tacit knowledge unconsciously accumulated over time, and involve a willingness to take a risk. Weighing and comparing options, by contrast, involves decomposing an object, person, or a situation into components and trying to evaluate and weigh these attributes through a reasoned comparison between options, whether real or imagined. This form of evaluation relies not on holistic judgements, but on information that is parsed down ... . Intuition is necessary to make evaluations and decisions that cannot be made rationally because the formal weighing of options does not contribute to the strength or intensity of the individual's emotions. (Illouz 2012: 93)

Denis de Rougemont argued that the love potion in *Tristan and Iseult* functioned as an 'alibi for passion', which freed sexual desire from the harsh judgement of the medieval Church by severing it 'from every kind of visible connection with human responsibility' (1983: 48). Other historians have stressed how the magical love potion was one of a number of devices used in the Tristan romances to protect love from being degraded to a profane, depersonalised and despiritualised force: 'There is no getting behind love to discover the cause of love. Love is the cause' (Schultz 2012: 78). When love is disenchanted and demystified, by contrast, resolute decision making and strong emotional commitments become harder to sustain, as indicated by Ann Swidler in her (admittedly more optimistic) reading of the interviews she conducted with eighty-eight middle-class Americans in the early 1980s. Like Illouz, she reports a widespread scepticism and disdain towards 'romantic love mythology', as she calls it, with the women and men she talked to preferring to describe their love lives with a 'prosaic-realism' that stressed – often in conventional formulas and equally time-worn motifs – the importance of hard work, compatibility, maturity, tolerance and sharing. Interestingly, however, Swidler also witnessed the intermittent re-emergence of the imagery of romantic love in the responses of many of her interviewees, with people 'suddenly slipping into a mythic vocabulary at variance with the ways they normally think' (Swidler 2001: 117). The recollection of a momentous, all-or-nothing choice; a belief in the 'rightness' and exclusiveness of that choice (the 'one true love'); the idea that love involves a heroic test of character in which precious things must be given up in order for something greater to be won; and the ideal of a love that lasts forever (alluded to in the common diagnosis that a relationship that failed could not have been 'real' love in the first place) all punctuated the otherwise dominant discourse of disenchanted realism. Swidler argues that mythic love retained its plausibility in the lives of her participants, most of whom were married or divorced, not because it was a 'realistic' description of their experience – in that respect prosaic love was clearly victorious – but rather because romantic love was a *mobiliser of action* in relation to the institution of marriage (or relationships 'modelled' on marriage). The popular culture of romantic love thus 'flourishes in this gap where action meets institution', helping cultivate 'that set of feelings, that reading of one's own psyche and the psyche of another, that internal propagation of firm decision and perpetual vigilance that can sustain a marriage' (2001: 131, 133).

> In order to marry, individuals must develop certain cultural, psychological, and even cognitive equipment. They must be prepared to feel, or at least convince others that they feel, that one other person is the uniquely right 'one'. They must be prepared to recognise the 'right person' when that person comes along … . Love, then, is the quality of 'rightness' that defines the particular, unique other that one does marry; it is the emotion that propels one across the gap that separates single from married life; and it is 'commitment', the psychological concomitant of the all-or-nothing, exclusive, enduring relationship constituted by marriage. The popular culture of love both prepares persons for and helps them to organise and carry through the aspects of marriage that depend on individual action. (Swidler 2001: 131)

Hierarchies of emotional competence

While Swidler found evidence that romantic love, although ostensibly subdued and repudiated, remained part of the middle-class habitus, Illouz's research emphasises how the dominant form of a cognitively literate, realistic and self-moderating love also favours the middle-class pursuit of intimacy. Pierre Bourdieu had argued in *Distinction* (1984) that both the 'aesthetic distancing' required for appreciation of the most prestigious forms of culture and indeed the 'role distancing' described in Goffman's dramaturgical account of social interaction presuppose a habitus shaped by those conditions of material affluence and freedom from necessity which make up 'the basis of the bourgeois experience of the world' (Bourdieu 1984: 54). Acknowledging Bourdieu's insight, Illouz suggests that the ability to distance oneself from, in order to scrutinise and rationally verbalise, one's emotions has a similar provenance, being 'the prerogative of those who have readily available a range of emotional options, who are not overwhelmed by emotional necessity and intensity, and who can therefore approach their own self and emotions with the same detached mode that comes from accumulated emotional competence' (1997: 56). This emotional competence also implies a habitus that makes one feel at ease addressing conflicts of feeling by means of controlled linguistic interaction. Such a 'view of language as an instrument to express the inner self constitutes a part of the cultural habitus of the new service class' whose 'professional competence depends on a successful presentation of self, of management of emotions and of linguistic performance'. It is the members of this class who are therefore 'more likely to practise the subtle form of reflexivity required to achieve the project of intimacy in the late modern era' (1997: 58).

To some extent these insights are not new. In *Natural Symbols* (1970) Mary Douglas drew on Durkheim to explore the shift from ritualised to individualised grammars of social organisation in affluent European and North American communities. She also made extensive use of the work of the socio-linguistic Basil Bernstein, who had already described how person-centred language codes are more typical of the offspring of the middle classes, with obvious implications for the educational progression of working-class children in a schooling system that devalues more communal modes of learning, knowing and communicating (Bernstein 1964, 1971). The novelty of Illouz's work, however, is that it shows how love and intimacy are now increasingly governed by the same person-centred speech code that Bernstein identified with the middle-class habitus, a construction of autonomous selfhood which Foucauldians like Nikolas Rose (1998) have definitively linked to the growth of the 'psy' disciplines. With hindsight, we can now see how the psychological revolution of the twentieth century produced a model of personal life that accommodated women's demands for greater emotional intimacy, but how in the very same process this normative model 'naturalised the emotional and verbal habitus of the romantic practices of members of the new service class, thus making intimacy another domain of cultural authority' (Illouz 1997: 52).

The sociological analysis of intimate life must therefore do more than simply expose the superficialisation of romantic bonds – a communitarian complaint that Illouz believes overlooks the social and historical construction of 'intimacy' and wrongly underestimates the extent to which the therapeutic ethos 'has still been a successful response to the current disarray of private life and selfhood' (1997: 61). It must also recognise how erotic love and intimacy in late modernity have been modelled on the emotional and verbal style of the professional middle classes, and how the habitus of the latter naturally makes them experts at the communicative forms of self-realisation and relatedness which make up what Giddens called the 'pure relationship'. The work and consumption practices of working-class women may to some extent bring them within the orbit of this therapeutic culture, Illouz notes, but working-class men are at a much clearer disadvantage. 'To put it bluntly: in the culture fashioned by late capitalism, the dominant definition of intimacy demands an *androgynous* emotional and verbal competence that has made "obsolete" whatever erotic, amorous or marital skills working-class men may have hitherto had at their disposal' (1997: 59).

As emotional intimacy has become a critical source of well-being for people in contemporary societies, we must therefore pay attention to the maldistribution of this resource and to 'new hierarchies of emotional well-being' (2007: 73). Class is one such hierarchy, but what about gender? Women's greater emotional literacy might lead one to assume that they too are more likely to be winners in this new environment of well-reasoned emotions. But we are talking here about relationships not solitary individuals, and heterosexual relationships require for their success some degree of mutual commitment and understanding between women and men. In *Why Love Hurts?* (2012), Illouz searches for a sociological explanation for why heterosexual women appear to suffer greatest from the marketisation of courtship in advanced capitalist societies. Although in this respect she shares the concern of Wendy Langford (1999) with the way women suffer, in Illouz's words, 'emotional domination' by 'commitment-phobic' men, Illouz is unwilling to dismiss romantic love as patriarchal ideology, noting how the cultural importance of love in Western societies has actually grown in tandem with the sexual emancipation of women.

An apparent paradox of sexual relations in late modernity is that at the same time as the body is relegated or displaced by the cognitive deliberations of online daters, it is also re-centred as *the* primary object of sexual desire. Beauty, to the nineteenth-century romantic imagination, was inseparable from moral character, which was in turn rooted in bodily practices as well as in social and economic signifiers of class. With the growth of the modern beauty industry, however, the female body in particular was increasingly thought of in terms of 'an aesthetic surface, detached from moral definitions of personhood' (Illouz 2012: 43). Beauty was replaced by 'sexiness', which is self-consciously manipulable and purchasable by means of fashion and beauty products, physical and dietary training, and mastery of the appropriate cosmetic codes. Two centuries of slow-growing affective individualism may have already undermined the traditional patterns of conjugal endogamy, where marriage choices were determined by the need to reproduce class membership, wealth and common values. But Illouz emphasises how the rise of sex appeal as a form of erotic capital subverts endogamy in a more decisive way, since visual attractiveness can now be freely traded for economic assets, thus allowing people previously excluded by age and class inferiority to participate in middle- and upper-class 'marriage markets'. This latter term, which is favoured by economists, in fact reflects a modern institutional construction that shows how the individualising process is tied up with the expansion of capitalism: 'The "great transformation" of romantic encounters is thus the process by which no formal social boundary regulates access to partners and an intense competition comes to prevail in the process of meeting others' (2012: 51).

Working-class women's use of erotic capital to secure upward mobility may be one reason why marriage and love are more important to some women than they are to men. But women's search for a mate is also more likely to be subsumed by awareness of their time-limited fertility, the window of which is for many women further narrowed by the need to gain an early foothold in the labour market. The negative impact of motherhood on women's earning power and career prospects also sharpens women's perceived need for a stable breadwinner as a partner. For women in their thirties and forties, in particular, there is likely to be an enhanced sense of urgency and a willingness to commit to a relationship earlier and faster. Affluent heterosexual men who enter the dating market can thus choose from a larger pool of potential mates, including younger, less affluent and less educated women. It is because they are faced with an excess of supply over demand, Illouz argues, that men find it easier to control the terms of the romantic exchange by devaluing the encounter and being more emotionally detached. This lack of emotional commitment also reflects the more contested nature of patriarchy in modern Western families, which no longer offer men a smooth route to masculine identity and power. Men today are, as Illouz puts it, 'far less normatively compelled to biological reproduction because the family is no longer a site of control and domination' (2012: 74). Instead they are more likely to seek status and identity through economic success and sexual conquest. Facing sexual discrimination in the labour market, and age discrimination in the heterosexual dating market, women, by contrast, tend to search instead for recognition and security through love.

The result of all this, Illouz argues, is that men are more likely to treat the dating market as a sexual market, and be less willing to leave it, 'whereas women tend to view the sexual market as a marriage market and would tend to stay in it for less time' (2012: 78). In these circumstances heterosexual women tend to suffer 'emotional domination' at the hands of men because men's greater sexual opportunities give them 'a greater capacity to control the emotional interaction through greater detachment, and greater capacity to exert choice and to constrain the choice of the other' (2012: 104). This is not because men are pathologically bent on dominating women, Illouz suggests, but rather because, once the rational logic of the marketplace takes hold in shaping people's attitudes to relationships, value can only be assigned to that which is measurably scarce. Stereotypical male avoidance behaviours, in other words, 'constitute a strategic attempt to *create scarcity*, and thus value, in a market where they cannot assign value, because women's sexual and emotional availability is in over-supply' (2012: 85). Relationship advice books for women that encourage cooler styles of romantic interaction are similarly interpreted by Illouz as a logical if misguided attempt to address the structural imbalance in the 'free market of sexual encounters' by getting women to better control the supply of their own emotional availability.

Illouz agrees with Beck and Beck-Gernsheim that sexual love has become more important to people's ontological security and sense of self-worth as traditional sources of identity and status have become more elusive and uncertain. The processes of individualisation, by dissolving objective criteria of moral worth, have made the search for validation through personal relationships both more intense and more challenging. Precisely because love addresses the totality of the person, attending to her imperfections as well as to her excellences, love is a vital counterweight to our everyday invisibility, becoming the prime authenticator of the self in an era that demands constant self-differentiation and uniqueness but yields very little in the way of lasting recognition. What is historically new, according to Illouz, is not so much the subjective profundity of love – this sentiment is, if anything, in retreat – but rather the social role that love plays today in providing a sense of identity and value that was previously calibrated by shared moral standards and clear status hierarchies.

Because love now plays such an important role in people's sense of worth, when relationships fail the result can be a catastrophic sense of humiliation. This is a risk borne in particular by women, Illouz argues, because fewer public channels to affirm their value are available to them and they are therefore more likely to rely on intimacy for personal recognition. Illouz also notes how her interviews with heterosexual women revealed the conspicuous absence of a normative language capable of criticising romantic betrayal or abandonment, with the contractual model of intimate relationships appearing to give male partners the perceived right to terminate relationships without moral censure. Even more puzzling was the tendency for women to blame themselves for male infidelity or the failure of a relationship, and to hold themselves responsible for 'loving too much'. In Illouz's view, this further demonstrates how hegemonic the anti-sociological paradigm of the 'psy-sciences' has become, which has transformed the issue of self-worth from a problem of social recognition – which of course cannot be self-generated – to one of emotional immaturity and a deficient personal capacity for autonomy, separateness and self-care (2012: 150–1). Sociology therefore has a vital role to play in exposing the societal determinants of our intimate lives; but sociology must also avoid colluding with the forces that damage those lives, and must defend a model of human flourishing that gives passion as well as reason its due.

Conclusion: Reclaiming
the romantic imaginary

Eva Illouz's work stands out from contemporary sociological treatments of love for the generosity with which it addresses something that social scientists more commonly regard with suspicion. Not only does she ask for a reappraisal of passionate love as an important source of human well-being, but she also shows how the frustrations and failures of intimate life reflect wider cultural and economic processes of rationalisation. Romantic fantasies of love have long been derided for their reactionary concealment of patriarchal interests, yet rational partner selection and egalitarian models of intimacy have brought with them new injuries and uncertainties, and Illouz's research suggests that women may not be clear beneficiaries of the growth of emotional capitalism.

The tension between thought and feeling, reason and passion, cognition and pleasure, is, we have seen, as old as Western civilisation itself. From Greek antiquity onwards, Western societies have sought to reconcile the rational pursuit of knowledge and understanding with the emotional longing for human connection, and the intellectual history of love bears testimony to this troubled endeavour, being a history of faith and fervour as well as of truth, tragedy and unhappiness. While the Greeks saw love as a miraculous force that could transfigure human consciousness, it would take more than a millennia of cultural and religious thinking before the idea took root that a particular human person could be the unique and unrepeatable object of the soul's creative pursuit of meaning and value. Centuries later, as social and economic relations were transformed by the impact of industrial capitalism, becoming more impersonal, more calculating and more impervious to acts of solidarity and kindness, the romantic ideals of a twelfth-century courtly culture were resurrected and redefined in order to imagine a place for emotional solidarity and tenderness amidst a functionally depersonalised world. Romantic love became an earthly comfort, a spiritual redoubt, a 'haven in a heartless world'. But in fleeing from an inhuman society, this romantic spirit, whose legacy we are still scrutinising and contesting today, also carried with it the contradictions and injuries of what it disdained. For although we may seek, through love, to establish a connection so uncompromising that the soul of another becomes inseparable from our own, to love the totality of another person must also be to grasp society's inexorable imprint on that person, in all its irrationality, inconstancy and injustice. Love is tragic because, while it longs for the sublime reconciliation of truth and happiness, of rational explanation and a beauty beyond words, this yearning is continually undone by knowledge of powerlessness, hurt and misery, or by the ignorance that is needed to safeguard our pleasures. 'Enjoyment and truth, happiness and the essential relations of individuals are disjunctions' (Marcuse 1968b: 166).

Love seeks a blissful harmony of selves, the construction of a new reality, the birth of a new standpoint which, as Alain Badiou (2012: 25–6) elegantly puts it, 'views the panorama of the world through the prism of our difference'. This 'paradox of identical difference', however, is always vulnerable to ideological abuse. The yearning for love may encourage withdrawal from and indifference to the alienations and injustices of the social world. Its heterosexual ideal, feminists have long argued, is often a spurious denial, and worse, a naively sentimentalised extension, of the male domination of women. Today's romantic imaginary needs to be agitated, revitalised and multiplied with the invention of new, diverse and more inclusive models of intimacy. Love must be subverted, queered and decolonised; we need to honour love in its diversity of contexts, show its earthly forms as well as its soaring ecstasies, reveal its entanglement in cultural values and material interests, observe its many different rhythms, premises, starting points and means of communication. If we fail to diversify the moral semantics of intimate life, not only do we devalue the multiplicities of human sociality and companionship, but we also invite the despotism of a universal love which leaves every singular lover doubting whether they are truly loving or loved.

Doubt in the domain of intimacy, nonetheless, cannot be fully eradicated – except by eradicating love as a longing and as an ideal, and with it the subversive power that comes from reckoning with the impossible. What is impossible must be imaginary, and what is imaginary is what reveals the defects and inadequacies of the real. The eighteenth- and nineteenth-century novel was so troubling to a male-dominated society because it changed women's social and emotional expectations of personal life, the idea of 'marriage for love' undermining the role of the family as a mechanism for the reproduction of male wealth and status. Western modernity had constructed woman as a natural, impulsive being, lacking in reason and unfit for rational public life, but in doing so it gave her a status that 'eluded utilitarian calculation', as Max Horkheimer put it. That same rational society inadvertently produced its subversive antithesis: women's passionate 'ability to love in contradiction to the world's norms' and to pursue fulfilment not through self-interest but through 'self-forgetfulness' (Horkheimer 1985: 16).

Today the more radical idea of 'love for love' has undermined marriage, but it has also played a role in shaking the domestic foundations of patriarchy, heteronormativity and other divisions, prejudices and constraints that have impeded the realisation of diverse and meaningful forms of intimate life. It would be naïve, however, to say that 'love is love is love' without recognising the social and economic conditions to which love must adapt if it is to speak in the prevailing language of logic, proof and justice. For just as images of love are susceptible to ideological rationalisation, so too are images of reason, in today's emotional capitalism, mobilised to legitimise and secure more manageable, but also more rational, kinds of love. This recalls the dangerous paradox of the 'dialectic of Enlightenment' described by Adorno and Horkheimer, in which the desire to subdue the irrational forces of the external world is won through an Odyssean cunning that disfigures the master as much as the enslaved. 'The subjective spirit which cancels the animation of nature can master a despiritualised nature only by imitating its rigidity and despiritualising itself in turn' (Adorno and Horkheimer 1997: 57). They continue:

> with the denial of nature in man not merely the *telos* of the outward control of nature but the *telos* of man's own life is distorted and befogged. As soon as man discards his awareness that he himself is nature, all the aims for which he keeps himself alive – social progress, the intensification of all his material and spiritual powers, even consciousness itself – are nullified, and the enthronement of the means as an end, which under late capitalism is tantamount to open insanity, is already perceptible in the prehistory of subjectivity. Man's domination over himself, which grounds his selfhood, is almost always the destruction of the subject in whose service it is undertaken. (Adorno and Horkheimer 1997: 54)

What makes love subversive is its imaginative appeal to that sensing, feeling, suffering subject whose censorship and renunciation, the Frankfurt School believed, is the price we have been forced to pay for our technological and economic advancement. But this appeal to love also conjures its own discord, for our routinised, rationalised and hyper-individualised lives rarely live up to our romantic ideals, while our romantic ideals continue to offer melancholic respite when conflict, alienation and the rule of self-interest prevail. For this reason love is not and cannot be mere escapism. We can no more escape an irrational society through the blessedness of love than we can escape our irrational selves by adapting to a rationalised world.

In escaping to love, moreover, we are led by moral and aesthetic ideals which, though structured and energised by shared cultural projects, narratives and imagery, always promise a meaning that is uniquely our own, and whose uniqueness we can trust and treasure only by a retreat from others, including those we love. One of the great paradoxes of the romantic imaginary is that its most profound visions of harmony and connectedness are formed in solitude, in private communion with literature, music or film, in a yearning that grows richer and deeper the longer its actual gratification is deferred and the more we are left alone with our fantasies and dreams. Only in solitude can we imagine a remedy for solitude; yet without that imagined remedy, how parlous, how profane, how docile would be our social isolation and estrangement? And how disenchanted and de-eroticised would be our love lives if there were no friction and withdrawal, no distance between the person we are and the person we want, and want to be?

This book has traced some of the key intellectual staging posts in the development of Western cultural understandings of erotic love, the aim being to enrich our romantic literacy and to complement the burgeoning field of sexualities studies with a more sophisticated appreciation of the history and meaning of love. Enchanting images of loving intimacy may of course beguile us with cheap and toxic fictions, but we have seen that the romantic imaginary can also be a gateway to the deepening of feelings, a licence for devotion, a catalyst for the suspension of disbelief, for the non-observance of competing alternatives and for the mobilisation of the total self in all its complexities and contradictions. It's no coincidence that when Max Weber wrote of the need for the scientist to 'put on blinkers' and give absolute personal dedication to the intellectual enterprise, he likened this commitment to a religious calling that to non-believers would always look absurd. It is ironic that intellectual inquiry is today increasingly recognised by social scientists to be an emotional project that must rely, at some level, on a blind leap of faith, yet in the rational analysis of our intimate lives the romantic vocation is commonly dismissed as an absurd and damaging delusion.

Love and science may not be the clear-cut adversaries they are made out to be, but what about love and politics? The exclusivity of erotic love means there can be no genuine republic of lovers. Politics and love belong in principle to different domains, not least because in the former we must deal sensibly with our enemies. The political mythologising of human bonds also has an ugly European history, romantic beliefs being entangled with fanatical nationalism, revolutionary violence and xenophobic hatred. For the individual political actor, romantic fantasies of the unlived life can easily become a way of colluding with a state of unhappiness, as yearning for the impossible conceals those painful changes, compromises and challenges that might yield genuine gains. Unlived dreams and ideals may defrost the icy hand of reason, but fantasies can, as the psychoanalysts have argued, deflect as well as condense the truth of our deeper feelings and needs.

Nonetheless, romantic ideals are never purely narcissistic delusions. When we love we may fantasise about our own happiness, but we also fantasise about the happiness of another person. In this process the imaginative history of romantic love gives us narrative resources that we can draw upon to combat the social conflicts and divisions that splinter our emotional selves, providing models of harmony and cohesion with which to contest the irrationality of what is real. And because this irrationality is our external as well as our internal worlds, romantic love and longing do not necessarily lead to political absenteeism. One may justly wonder how much suffering is caused or perpetuated not by our self-deceiving mental artistry but by our indifference to the unlived life, and how the lives we haven't lived – the lives of people different to and less fortunate than ourselves – stir no interest or compassion in us precisely because we have not made the effort to imagine them. Are we so shabby as to care for the plight of others only in so far as their situation is the same as our own? 'I saw people being abused, shouted at, spat at in the street', said former National Front and British white supremacist organiser Kevin Wilshaw who in 2017 renounced nearly 40 years of neo-Nazi activism after coming out as gay; 'it's not until it's directed at you that you suddenly realise that what you're doing is wrong'.[1] If this is the extent of our moral and political imagination then, as Fevre (2016) argues, we will remain in thrall to a jaundiced cognitive individualism which, elevating personal knowledge over the contestable authority of an ethical *belief*,

---

[1] In an interview broadcast on Channel 4 News on 17 October 2017. https://www.channel4.com/news/neo-nazi-national-front-organiser-quits-movement-comes-out-as-gay-kevin-wilshaw-jewish-heritage.

will never arouse the emotional convictions necessary for acts of solidarity and for the testing work of collective social change.

Love is not easy, it is often said, and you have to work at it if you want a relationship to last. This realist version of love is the after-image of a work-dominated society, the cultural echo of a productivist–consumerist paradigm which has become so dominant that its irrationalities become visible to us only in the form of our own personal defects and failures. But there is another image of love, the spectre of which survives in the interstices of logic, in fiction, reverie and the extravagance of aesthetics. This is love as a truthful, beautiful, ingenuous thing, which 'takes work' only because we have so little time for it, because we're unable to give it the effortlessness it deserves. A juvenile dream, perhaps, yet without the dream how glad, generous and humane are we really capable of being?

'A man cannot become a child again, or he becomes childish', Marx wrote in the *Grundrisse*, acknowledging that the epic poetry and arts of the ancient Greeks was the cultural product of a particular stage of social development which economic and technological advancements have long since surpassed. This materialist insight is, nonetheless, immediately qualified: 'But does he not find joy in the child's naiveté, and must he not strive to reproduce its truth at a higher stage?' (Marx 1973: 111). Today this higher truth not only opens the door to joyfulness but also answers our increasingly urgent need for the imagination to knit together people's separate actions and interests and to commit us to something – or to resist something – that lies beyond the sphere of our rational activity and its immediate results. Don't the social and environmental problems that face the world today require, from those who want to address them, a certain foolish faith? Must we not believe – blindly, madly, deeply – in our fellow humans, in our ability to set aside self-interest in favour of the greater good, and to imagine a good greater than the sum of individuals – greater, even, than our species itself? I am not preaching Tolstoyan mysticism here, but simply restating the human capacity to love, the artfulness of the romantic imagination, and the hopes and possibilities that they sustain.

Bibliography

Adorno, T., and Horkheimer, M. (1997 [1944]) *Dialectic of Enlightenment*. London: Verso.

Ahearn, L. (2001) *Invitations to Love: Literacy, Love Letters, and Social Change in Nepal*. Ann Arbor: University of Michigan Press.

Amato, P. R. (2010) 'Research on Divorce: Continuing Trends and New Developments', *Journal of Marriage and Family*, vol. 72, no. 3, 650–66.

Anderson, M. (1995) *Approaches to the History of the Western Family 1500–1914*. Cambridge: Cambridge University Press.

Andreas-Salomé, L. (2014 [1910]) *The Erotic*. Trans. J. Crisp. New Brunswick, NJ: Transaction Publishers.

Arendt, H. (1958) *The Human Condition*. Chicago, IL: Chicago University Press.

Arendt, H. (1977) 'The Crisis in Culture', in *Between Past and Future: Eight Exercises in Political Thought*. New York: Penguin, 194–222.

Ariès, P. (1962) *Centuries of Childhood*. Trans. R. Baldick. London: Jonathan Cape.

Aristotle (1976) *Nicomachean Ethics*. Trans. J. A. K. Thomson and H. Tredennick. Harmondsworth: Penguin.

Armstrong, N. (1987) *Desire and Domestic Fiction: Political History of the Novel*. Oxford: Oxford University Press.

Astell, M. (1986) *The Celebrated Mary Astell: An Early English Feminist*. Chicago, IL: University of Chicago Press.

Austen, J. (2003 [1813]) *Pride and Prejudice*. London: Penguin.

Badiou, A. (2012) *In Praise of Love*. London: Serpent's Tail.

Bakewell, G. W. (2013) *Aeschylus's Suppliant Women: The Tragedy of Immigration*. Madison: University of Wisconsin Press.

Barbalet, J. M. (2000) '*Beruf*, Rationality and Emotion in Max Weber's Sociology', *European Journal of Sociology*, vol.4, no. 2, 329–51.

Bauman, Z. (2000) *Liquid Modernity*. Cambridge: Polity.

Bauman, Z. (2003) *Liquid Love: On the Frailty of Human Bonds*. Cambridge: Polity.

Beard, M. (2017) *Women and Power: A Manifesto*. London: Profile Books.

Beauvoir, S. de (1972 [1949]) *The Second Sex*. Harmondsworth: Penguin.

Beck, U. (1999) *World Risk Society*. Cambridge: Polity.

Beck, U., and Beck-Gernsheim, E. (1995) *The Normal Chaos of Love*. Trans. M. Ritter and J. Wiebel. Cambridge: Polity.

Beck, U., Bonss, W., and Lau, C. (2003) 'The Theory of Reflexive Modernisation: Problematic, Hypotheses and Research Programme', *Theory, Culture and Society*, vol. 20, no. 2, 1–33.

Beck-Gernsheim, E. (1999) 'On the Way to a Post-Familial Family – From a Community of Need to Elective Affinities', in M. Featherstone (ed.), *Love and Eroticism*. London: Sage, 53–70.

Bell, D. (1976) 'The Cultural Contradictions of Capitalism', in *The Cultural Contradictions of Capitalism*. New York: Basic Books, 33–84.

Belsey, C. (1994) *Desire: Love Stories in Western Culture*. Oxford: Blackwell.

Benjamin, J. (2008) 'A Desire of One's Own: Psychoanalytic Feminism and Intersubjective Space', in A. Bailey and C. Cuomo (eds), *The Feminist Philosophy Reader*. New York: McGraw-Hill, 188–203.

Benton, J. F. (1961) 'The Court of Champagne as a Literary Center', *Speculum*, vol. 36, no. 4, 551–91.

Berger, P. L. (1963) *Invitation to Sociology: A Humanistic Perspective*. Harmondsworth: Penguin.

Berger, P., and Kellner, H. (1964) 'Marriage and the Construction of Reality: An Exercise in the Microsociology of Knowledge', *Diogenes*, vol. 12, no. 46, 1–24.

Berkner, L. K. (1972) 'The Stem Family and the Developmental Cycle of the Peasant Household: An Eighteenth-Century Austrian Example', *American Historical Review*, vol. 77, no. 2, 398–418.

Berkner, L. K. (1975) 'The Use and Misuse of Census Data for the Historical Analysis of Family Structure', *Journal of Interdisciplinary History*, vol. 5, no. 4, 721–38.

Bernstein, B. (1964) 'Social Class, Speech Systems and Psycho-therapy', *British Journal of Sociology*, vol. 15, no. 1, 54–64.

Bernstein, B. (1971) *Class, Codes and Control. Vol. 1. Theoretical Studies Towards a Sociology of Language*. London: Routledge and Kegan Paul.

Binion, R. (1994) 'Fiction as Social Fantasy: Europe's Domestic Crisis of 1879–1914', *Journal of Social History*, vol. 27, no. 4, 679–99.

Blanchard, R. (1929) 'Richard Steele and the Status of Women', *Studies in Philology*, vol. 26, no. 23, 325–55.

Bland, L. (2005) 'White Women and Men of Colour: Miscegenation Fears in Britain after the Great War', *Gender and History*, vol. 17, no. 1, 29–61.

Blassingame, J. W. (1979) *The Slave Community: Plantation Life in the Antebellum South*, 2nd edn. New York: Oxford University Press.

Bloch, R. H. (1991) *Medieval Misogyny and the Invention of Western Romantic Love*. Chicago, IL: University of Chicago Press.

Boase, R. (1977) *The Origin and Meaning of Courtly Love: A Critical Study of European Scholarship*. Manchester: Manchester University Press.

Bologh, R. W. (1990) *Love or Greatness: Max Weber and Masculine Thinking – A Feminist Inquiry*. London: Unwin Hyman.

Boone, J. A. (1987) *Tradition Counter Tradition: Love and the Form of Fiction*. Chicago, IL: Chicago University Press.

Boone, J. A. (1995) 'Vacation Cruises; or, The Homoerotics of Orientalism', *PMLA*, vol. 110, no. 1, 89–107.

Bourdieu, P. (1984) *Distinction: A Social Critique of the Judgement of Taste*. Trans. R. Nice. London: Routledge.

Brontë, C. (1993 [1853]) *Villette*. Ware: Wordsworth.

Brontë, C. (2006 [1847]) *Jane Eyre*. London: Penguin.

Brontë, E. (1992 [1847]) *Wuthering Heights*. Ware: Wordsworth.

Brown, W. W. (2004 [1853]) *Clotel: Or, the President's Daughter*. London: Penguin.

Brownmiller, S. (1976) *Against Our Will: Men, Women and Rape*. Harmondsworth: Penguin.

Bruckner, P. (2013) *Has Marriage for Love Failed?* Trans. S. Rendall and L. Neal. Cambridge: Polity.

Burgess, E. W. (1926) 'The Romantic Impulse and Family Disorganisation', *Survey*, no. 57, 290–4.

Butler, J. (2002) 'Is Kinship Always Already Heterosexual?', *Differences*, vol. 13, no. 1, 14–44.

Byrne, J. (1995) *A Genius for Living: A Biography of Frieda Lawrence*. London: Bloomsbury.

Campbell, C. (1987) *The Romantic Ethic and the Spirit of Modern Consumerism*. Oxford: Blackwell.

Chan, S. C. (2006) 'Love and Jewelry: Patriarchal Control, Conjugal Ties, and Changing Identities', in J. S. Hirsch and H. Wardlow (eds), *Modern Loves: The Anthropology of Romantic Courtship and Companionate Marriage*. Ann Arbor: University of Michigan Press, 35–50.

Chisholm, J. (1995) 'Love's Contingencies: The Developmental Socioecology of Romantic Passion', in W. Jankowiak (ed.), *Romantic Passion: A Universal Experience?* New York: Columbia University Press, 42–56.

Christian, B. (1980) *Black Women Novelists: The Development of a Tradition, 1892–1976*. Westport, CT: Greenwood.

Clark, A. (1919) *Working Life of Women in the Seventeenth Century*. London: G. Routledge.

Cole, J. (2009) 'Love, Money, and Economies of Intimacy in Tamatave, Madagascar', in J. Cole and L. M. Thomas (eds), *Love in Africa*. Chicago, IL: University of Chicago Press, 109–34.

Collins, J., and Gregor, T. (1995) 'Boundaries of Love', in W. Jankowiak (ed.), *Romantic Passion: A Universal Experience?* New York: Columbia University Press, 72–92.

Connor, W. R. (1984) *Thucydides*. Princeton, NJ: Princeton University Press.

Cristi, M. (2012) 'Durkheim on Moral Individualism, Social Justice, and Rights: A Gendered Construction of Rights', *Canadian Journal of Sociology*, vol. 37, no. 4, 409–38.

Davis, A. (2003) 'Racism, Birth Control and Reproductive Rights', in R. Lewis and S. Mills (eds), *Feminist Postcolonial Theory: A Reader*. Edinburgh: Edinburgh University Press, 353–67.

De Munck, V. C. (1996) 'Love and Marriage in a Sri Lankan Muslim Community: Toward a Reevaluation of Dravidian Marriage Practices', *American Ethnologist*, vol. 23, no. 4, 698–716.

D'Emilio, J., and Freedman, E. B. (1997) *Intimate Matters: A History of Sexuality in America*, 2nd edn. Chicago, IL: University of Chicago Press.

Demosthenes (1999) *Apollodoros 'Against Neaira' [D.59]*. Trans. K. A. Kapparis. Berlin: Walter de Gruyter.

Dickens, C. (1992 [1850]) *David Copperfield*. Ware: Wordsworth.

Dickens, C. (1992 [1861]) *Great Expectations*. Ware: Wordsworth.

Douglas, M. (1970) *Natural Symbols: Explorations in Cosmology*. Harmondsworth: Penguin.

Dover, K. J. (1974) *Greek Popular Morality in the Time of Plato and Aristotle*. Oxford: Basil Blackwell.

Dover, K. J. (1989) *Greek Homosexuality*. Cambridge, MA: Harvard University Press.

Downing, C. (1994) 'Lesbian Mythology', *Historical Reflections/Reflexions Historiques*, vol. 20, no. 2, 169–99.

Du, S. (2008) ' "With One Word and One Strength": Intimacy among the Lahu of Southwest China', in W. R. Jankowiak (ed.), *Intimacies: Love and Sex Across Cultures*. New York: Columbia University Press, 95–121.

DuCille, A. (1993) *The Coupling Convention: Sex, Text, and Tradition in Black Women's Fiction*. New York: Oxford University Press.

Duncombe, J. and Marsden, D. (1993) 'Love and Intimacy: The Gender Division of Emotion and "Emotion Work"', *Sociology*, vol. 27, no. 2, 221–41.

Duncombe, J. and Marsden, D. (1995) ' "Workaholics" and "Whingeing Women": Theorising Intimacy and Emotion Work – The Last Frontier of Gender Inequality?', *The Sociological Review*, vol. 43, no. 1, 150–69.

Duncombe, J. and Marsden, D. (1996) 'Whose Orgasm Is this Anyway? "Sex Work" in Long-term Heterosexual Couple Relationships', in J. Weeks and J. Holland (eds) *Sexual Cultures: Communities, Values and Intimacy*. Basingstoke: Macmillan, 220–38.

Durkheim, E. (1951 [1897]) *Suicide: A Study in Sociology*. Trans. J. A. Spaulding and G. Simpson. New York: Free Press.

Durkheim, E. (1961 [1925]) *Moral Education: A Study in the Theory and Application of the Sociology of Education*. Trans. E. K. Wilson and H. Schnurer. New York: Free Press.

Durkheim, E. (1964 [1893]) *The Division of Labour in Society*. Trans. G. Simpson. New York: Free Press.

Durkheim, E. (1978a) 'The Conjugal Family' [1892], in M. Traugott (ed. and trans.), *On Institutional Analysis*. Chicago, IL: University of Chicago Press, 229–39.

Durkheim, E. (1978b) 'Divorce by Mutual Consent' [1906], in M. Traugott (ed. and trans.), *On Institutional Analysis*. Chicago, IL: University of Chicago Press, 240–52.

Durkheim, E. (1978c) 'Review of Marianne Weber, *Ehefrau und Mutter in der Rechtsentwickelung*' [1906–9], in M. Traugott (ed. and trans.), *On Institutional Analysis*. Chicago, IL: University of Chicago Press, 139–44.

Durkheim, E. (1979) 'A Discussion on Sex Education' [1911], in W. S. F. Pickering (ed.) and H. L. Sutcliffe (trans.), *Durkheim: Essays on Morals and Education*. London: Routledge and Kegan Paul, 140–8.

Durkheim, E. (2001 [1912]) *The Elementary Forms of Religious Life.* Trans. C. Cosman. Oxford: Oxford University Press.

Eagleton, T. (1988) *Myths of Power: A Marxist Study of the Brontës,* 2nd edn. Basingstoke: Macmillan.

Elias, N. (1987) 'The Changing Balance of Power between the Sexes – A Process-Sociological Study: The Example of the Ancient Roman State', *Theory, Culture and Society,* vol. 4, nos. 2–3, 287–316.

Eliot, G. (1995 [1860]) *The Mill on the Floss.* Ware: Wordsworth.

Engels, F. (1942 [1884]) *The Origin of the Family, Private Property, and the State.* Trans. A. West. New York: International Publishers.

Engels, F. (1958 [1845]) *The Condition of the Working Class in England.* Trans. W. O. Henderson and W. H. Chaloner. Stanford, CA: Stanford University Press.

Evans, M. (1999) ' "Falling in Love with Love is Falling for Make Believe": Ideologies of Romance in Post-Enlightenment Culture', in M. Featherstone (ed.), *Love and Eroticism.* London: Sage, 265–76.

Evans, M. (2003) *Love: An Unromantic Discussion.* Cambridge: Polity.

Ferry, L. (2013) *On Love: A Philosophy for the 21st Century.* Trans. A. Brown. Cambridge: Polity.

Fevre, R. (2000) *The Demoralisation of Western Culture: Social Theory and the Dilemmas of Modern Living.* London: Continuum.

Fevre, R. (2016) *Individualism and Inequality: The Future of Work and Politics.* Cheltenham: Edward Elgar.

Finch, J., and Summerfield, P. (1991) 'Social Reconstruction and the Emergence of Companionate Marriage, 1945–59', in D. Clark (ed.), *Marriage, Domestic Life and Social Change: Writings for Jacqueline Burgoyne (1944–88).* London: Routledge, 6–27.

Firestone, S. (1979 [1971]) *The Dialectic of Sex: The Case for Feminist Revolution.* London: Woman's Press.

Fisher, H. (1995) 'The Nature and Evolution of Romantic Love', in W. Jankowiak (ed.) *Romantic Passion: A Universal Experience?* New York: Columbia University Press, 23–41.

Fitzgerald, F. S. (1990 [1926]) *The Great Gatsby.* London: Penguin.

Flandrin, J.-L. (1979) *Families in Former Times: Kinship, Household and Sexuality.* Trans. R. Southern. Cambridge: Cambridge University Press.

Flaubert, G. (2003 [1857]) *Madame Bovary.* Trans. G. Wall. London: Penguin.

Foreman, P. G. (1990) 'The Spoken and the Silenced in *Incidents in the Life of a Slave Girl* and *Our Nig*', *Callaloo,* vol. 13, no. 2, 313–24.

Foucault, M. (1980) 'Body/Power', in C. Gordon (ed.) *Power/Knowledge: Selected Interviews and Other Writings 1972-1977.* New York: Pantheon, 55–62.

Foucault, M. (1990 [1976]) *The History of Sexuality. Vol. 1: An Introduction.* Trans. R. Hurley. Harmondsworth: Penguin.

Foucault, M. (1992 [1984]) *The History of Sexuality. Vol. 2: The Use of Pleasure.* Trans. R. Hurley. London: Penguin.

Freud, S. (1955) 'Beyond the Pleasure Principle' [1920], in J. Strachey (trans. and ed.), *The Standard Edition of the Complete Psychological Works of Sigmund Freud. Vol. XVIII*. London: Hogarth, 7–64.

Freud, S. (1957) 'On Narcissism: An Introduction' [1915], in J. Strachey (trans. and ed.), *The Standard Edition of the Complete Psychological Works of Sigmund Freud. Vol. XIV*. London: Hogarth, 73–102.

Freud, S. (1991) 'Three Essays on the Theory of Sexuality' [1905], in *The Penguin Freud Library. Volume 7: On Sexuality*. Harmondsworth: Penguin, 31–169.

Freud, S. (2001) 'On the Universal Tendency to Debasement in the Sphere of Love' [1912], in J. Strachey (trans. and ed.), *The Standard Edition of the Complete Psychological Works of Sigmund Freud. Vol. XI*. London: Vintage, 177–90.

Fromm, E. (1956) *The Art of Loving*. New York: Harper and Row.

Gabriel, M. (2011) *Love and Capital: Karl and Jenny Marx and the Birth of a Revolution*. New York: Little, Brown.

Gane, M. (1993) *Harmless Lovers? Gender, Theory and Personal Relationships*. London: Routledge.

Gaunt, S. (1995) *Gender and Genre in Medieval French Literature*. Cambridge: Cambridge University Press.

Gay, P. (1986) *The Bourgeois Experience: Victoria to Freud. Volume 2: The Tender Passion*. Oxford: Oxford University Press.

Giddens, A. (1991) *Modernity and Self-Identity: Self and Society in the Late Modern Age*. Cambridge: Polity.

Giddens, A. (1992) *The Transformation of Intimacy: Sexuality, Love and Eroticism in Modern Societies*. Cambridge: Polity.

Giddens, A. (1998) *The Third Way: The Renewal of Social Democracy*. Cambridge: Polity.

Gilbert, S. M., and Gubar, S. (2000) *The Madwoman in the Attic: The Woman Writer and the Nineteenth-Century Literary Imagination*, 2nd edn. New Haven, CT: Yale University Press.

Goethe, J. W. von (1929 [1774]) *The Sorrows of Young Werther*. Trans. W. Rose. London: Scholartis.

Goodman, R. (2001) 'Beyond the Enforcement Principle: Sodomy Laws, Social Norms, and Social Panoptics', *California Law Review*, vol. 89, no. 3, 643–740.

Gouldner, A. W. (1967) *Enter Plato: Classical Greece and the Origins of Social Theory*. London: Routledge and Kegan Paul.

Gove, W. R. (1973) 'Sex, Marital Status, and Mortality', *American Journal of Sociology*, vol. 79, no. 1, 45–67.

Green, M. (1974) *The von Richthofen Sisters: The Triumphant and the Tragic Modes of Love*. New York: Basic Books.

Habermas, J. (1984) *The Theory of Communicative Action. Volume 1: Reason and the Rationalisation of Society*. Trans. T. McCarthy. Cambridge: Polity.

Habermas, J. (1987) *The Theory of Communicative Action. Volume 2: The Critique of Functionalist Reason*. Trans. T. McCarthy. Cambridge: Polity.

Halperin, D. M. (1986) 'Plato and Erotic Reciprocity', *Classical Antiquity*, vol. 5, no. 1, 60–80.

Hardy, T. (1993 [1874]) *Far from the Madding Crowd*. Ware: Wordsworth.

Hardy, T. (1995 [1878]) *The Return of the Native*. Ware: Wordsworth.

Hardy, T. (2004 [1878]) *The Woodlanders*. Ware: Wordsworth.

Hardy, T. (2012 [1882]) *Two on a Tower*. London: Penguin.

Hemmingway, E. (2004 [1941]) *For Whom the Bell Tolls*. London: Arrow Books.

Hennis, W. (1988) *Max Weber: Essays in Reconstruction*. Trans. K. Tribe. London: Allen and Unwin.

Hirsch, J. S., and Wardlow, H. (eds) (2006) *Modern Loves: The Anthropology of Romantic Courtship and Companionate Marriage*. Ann Arbor: University of Michigan Press.

Hirsch, J. S., Higgins, J., Bentley, M. E., and Nathanson, C. A. (2006) 'The Social Construction of Sexuality: Companionate Marriage and STD/HIV Risk in a Mexican Migrant Community', in J. S. Hirsch and H. Wardlow (eds), *Modern Loves: The Anthropology of Romantic Courtship and Companionate Marriage*. Ann Arbor: University of Michigan Press, 95–116.

Hochschild, A. R. (2003) 'The Commercial Spirit of Intimate Life and the Abduction of Feminism: Signs from Women's Advice Books', in *The Commercialisation of Intimate Life: Notes from Home and Work*. Berkeley: University of California Press, 14–29.

hooks, b. (2001) *Salvation: Black People and Love*. New York: William Morrow.

Horkheimer, M. (1985) 'The Concept of Man' [1957], in M. O'Connell (trans.), *Critique of Instrumental Reason: Lectures and Essays since the End of World War II*. New York: Continuum, 1–33.

Hornblower, S. (1991) *A Commentary on Thucydides, vol. 1*. Oxford: Clarendon.

Houlbrooke, R. A. (1984) *The English Family 1450–1700*. London: Longman.

Howard, V. (2003) 'A "Real Man's Ring": Gender and the Invention of Tradition', *Journal of Social History*, vol. 35, no. 4, 837–56.

Huxley, A. (1929) 'Fashions in Love', in *Do What You Will*. London: Chatto and Windus, 104–14.

Illouz, E. (1997) 'Who Will Care for the Caretaker's Daughter? Toward a Sociology of Happiness in the Era of Reflexive Modernity', *Theory, Culture and Society*, vol. 14, no. 4, 31–66.

Illouz, E. (1999) 'The Lost Innocence of Love: Romance as a Postmodern Condition', in M. Featherstone (ed.), *Love and Eroticism*. London: Sage, 161–86.

Illouz, E. (2007) *Cold Intimacies: The Making of Emotional Capitalism*. Cambridge: Polity.

Illouz, E. (2012) *Why Love Hurts: A Sociological Explanation*. Cambridge: Polity.

Jackson, W. T. H. (1985) 'The *De Amore* of Andreas Capellanus and the Practice of Love at Court', in J. M. Ferrante and R. W. Hanning (eds), *The Challenge of the Medieval Text: Studies in Genre and Interpretation*. New York: Columbia University Press, 3–13.

Jackson, S., and Scott, S. (1997) 'Gut Reactions to Matters of the Heart: Reflections on Rationality, Irrationality and Sexuality', *Sociological Review*, vol. 45, no. 4, 551–75.

Jacobs, H. (2001 [1861]) *Incidents in the Life of a Slave Girl*. Mineola, NY: Dover.

James, H. (1993 [1902]) *The Wings of the Dove*. Ware: Wordsworth.

James, H. (1993 [1904]) *The Golden Bowl*. Ware: Wordsworth.

James, H. (1999 [1881]) *The Portrait of a Lady*. Ware: Wordsworth.

Jamieson, L. (1998) *Intimacy: Personal Relationships in Modern Societies*. Cambridge: Polity.

Jamieson, L. (1999) 'Intimacy Transformed? A Critical Look at the "Pure Relationship"', *Sociology*, vol. 33, no. 3, 477–94.

Jamieson, L., and Simpson, R. (2013) *Living Alone: Globalisation, Identity and Belonging*. Basingstoke: Palgrave Macmillan.

Jankowiak, W. R., and Fischer, E. F. (1992) 'A Cross-Cultural Perspective on Romantic Love', *Ethnology*, vol. 31, no. 2, 149–55.

Jankowiak, W. R., and Paladino, T. (2008) 'Desiring Sex, Longing for Love: A Tripartite Conundrum', in W. R. Jankowiak (ed.), *Intimacies: Love and Sex Across Cultures*. New York: Columbia University Press, 1–36.

Johnson, P. (2005) *Love, Heterosexuality and Society*. London: Routledge.

Joyce, J. (1960 [1916]) *A Portrait of the Artist as a Young Man*. Harmondsworth: Penguin.

Kant, E. (1963 [1786]) 'Conjectural Beginning of Human History', in L. W. Beck (ed. and trans.), *Kant on History*. Indianapolis, IN: Bobbs-Merrill, 53–68.

Kaufmann, J.-C. (2011) *The Curious History of Love*. Trans. D. Macey. Cambridge: Polity.

Keller, E. F. (1985a) 'Gender and Science', in *Reflections on Gender and Science*. New Haven, CT: Yale University Press, 75–94.

Keller, E. F. (1985b) 'Love and Sex in Plato's Epistemology', in *Reflections on Gender and Science*. New Haven, CT: Yale University Press, 21–32.

Kelly, A. (1937) 'Eleanor of Aquitaine and Her Courts of Love', *Speculum*, vol. 12, no. 1, 3–9.

Langford, W. (1999) *Revolutions of the Heart: Gender, Power and the Delusions of Love*. London: Routledge.

Langhamer, C. (2013) *The English in Love: The Intimate Story of an Emotional Revolution*. Oxford: Oxford University Press.

Laslett, P. (1972a) 'Introduction: The History of the Family', in P. Laslett and R. Wall (eds), *Household and Family in Past Time*. Cambridge: Cambridge University Press, 1–90.

Laslett, P. (1972b) 'Mean Household Size in England since the Sixteenth Century', in P. Laslett and R. Wall (eds), *Household and Family in Past Time*. Cambridge: Cambridge University Press, 125–58.

Lawrence, D. H. (1917) *Look! We Have Come Through!* London: Chatto and Windus.

Lawrence, D. H. (1932) *The Letters of D. H. Lawrence*. New York: Viking.

Lawrence, D. H. (1961) 'À Propos of Lady's Chatterley's Lover' [1930], in *À Propos of Lady Chatterley's Lover and Other Essays*. Harmondsworth: Penguin, 85–126.

Lawrence, D. H. (1985) *Mr Noon*. London: Granada.

Lawrence, D. H. (1986) *Study of Thomas Hardy and Other Essays*. London: Grafton.

Lawrence, D. H. (1995 [1915]) *The Rainbow*. Ware: Wordsworth.

Lawrence, D. H. (1999 [1913]) *Sons and Lovers*. Ware: Wordsworth.

Lawrence, D. H. (2005) *Fantasia of the Unconscious* [1922] in *Psychoanalysis and the Unconscious and Fantasia of the Unconscious*. Mineola, NY: Dover, 53–225

Lawrence, D. H. (2007a) 'Twilight in Italy', in S. de Filippis, P. Eggert, and M. Kalnins (eds), *D. H. Lawrence and Italy*. London: Penguin, 1–136.

Lawrence, D. H. (2007b) 'New Eve and Old Adam' [1934], in *D. H. Lawrence: Selected Stories*. London: Penguin, 96–121.

Lawrence, D. H. (2013 [1928]) *Lady Chatterley's Lover*. London: Harper Collins.

Lawrence, F. (1959) 'Introduction: Frieda Lawrence Remembers…', in D. H. Lawrence, *Look! We Have Come Through!* Dulverton: The Ark Press, 9–16.

Leslie, C. R. (2000) 'Creating Criminals: The Injuries Inflicted by "Unenforced" Sodomy Laws', *Harvard Civil Rights-Civil Liberties Law Review*, vol. 35, no. 1, 102–81.

Levin, I. (2004) 'Living Apart Together: A New Family Form', *Current Sociology*, vol. 52, no. 2, 223–40.

Lewis, C. S. (1938) *The Allegory of Love*. London: Oxford University Press.

Lewis, C. S. (2012 [1960]) *The Four Loves*. London: Collins.

Lewis, J. (2001) *The End of Marriage? Individualism and Intimate Relations*. Cheltenham: Edward Elgar.

Lindholm, C. (1995) 'Love as an Experience of Transcendence', in W. Jankowiak (ed.), *Romantic Passion: A Universal Experience?* New York: Columbia University Press, 57–71.

Lindholm, C. (1999) 'Love and Structure', in M. Featherstone (ed.), *Love and Eroticism*. London: Sage, 243–64.

Lodziak, C. (1988) 'Dull Compulsion of the Economic: The Dominant Ideology and Social Reproduction', *Radical Philosophy*, no. 49, 10–17.

Ludwig, P. W. (2002) *Eros and Polis: Desire and Community in Greek Political Theory*. Cambridge: Cambridge University Press.

Luhmann, N. (2012) *Love as Passion: The Codification of Intimacy*. Trans. J. Gaines and D. L. Jones. Cambridge: Polity.

MacFarlane, A. (1986) *Marriage and Love in England: Modes of Reproduction 1300–1840*. Oxford: Blackwell.

MacIntyre, A. (1985) *After Virtue*, 2nd edn. London: Duckworth.

Mann, T. (1999 [1924]) *The Magic Mountain*. Trans. H. T. Lowe-Porter. London: Vintage.

Marcuse, H. (1968a) 'The Affirmative Character of Culture' [1937], in J. J. Shapiro (trans.), *Negations: Essays in Critical Theory*. Harmondsworth: Penguin, 88–133.

Marcuse, H. (1968b) 'On Hedonism' [1938], in J. J. Shapiro (trans.), *Negations: Essays in Critical Theory*. Harmondsworth: Penguin, 159–200.

Marcuse, H. (1972 [1955]) *Eros and Civilisation*. London: Abacus.

Marcuse, H. (1991 [1964]) *One-Dimensional Man: Studies in the Ideology of Advanced Industrial Society*, 2nd edn. London: Routledge.

Marx, K. (1973 [1858]) *Grundrisse*. Trans. M. Nicolaus. Harmondsworth: Penguin.

Marx, K. (1976 [1867]) *Capital vol. 1*. Trans. Ben Fowkes. Harmondsworth: Penguin.

Marx, K., and Engels, F. (1956 [1845]) *The Holy Family, or Critique of Critical Critique*. Trans. R. Dixon. Moscow: Foreign Languages Publishing House.

Marx, K., and Engels, F. (1967 [1848]) *The Communist Manifesto*. Trans. S. Moore. Harmondsworth: Penguin.

Masquelier, A. (2009) 'Lessons from *Rubí*: Love, Poverty, and the Educational Value of Televised Dramas in Niger', in J. Cole and L. M. Thomas (eds), *Love in Africa*. Chicago, IL: University of Chicago Press, 205–28.

May, S. (2011) *Love: A History*. New Haven, CT: Yale University Press.

McGlew, J. F. (1993) *Tyranny and Political Culture in Ancient Greece*. Ithaca, NY: Cornell University Press.

Meštrović, S. G. (1996) *Postemotional Society*. London: Routledge.

Meštrović, S. G. (1998) *Anthony Giddens: The Last Modernist*. London: Routledge.

Meyer, S. L. (1989) 'Colonialism and the Figurative Strategy of *Jane Eyre*', *Victorian Studies*, vol. 33, no. 2, 247–68.

Millett, K. (1970) *Sexual Politics*. London: Rupert Hart-Davis.

Milton, J. (2003 [1667]) *Paradise Lost*. London: Penguin.

Mitzman, A. (1970) *The Iron Cage: An Historical Interpretation of Max Weber*. New York: Alfred A. Knopf.

Moller, H. (1959) 'The Social Causation of the Courtly Love Complex', *Comparative Studies in Society and History*, vol. 1, no. 2, 137–63.

Monoson, S. S. (1994) 'Citizen as Erastes: Erotic Imagery and the Idea of Reciprocity in the Periclean Funeral Oration', *Political Theory*, vol. 22, no. 2, 253–76.

Moore, H. T. (1960) *The Intelligent Heart: The Story of D. H. Lawrence*. Harmondsworth: Penguin.

Morgan, D. (1991) 'Ideologies of Marriage and Family Life', in D. Clark (ed.), *Marriage, Domestic Life and Social Change: Writings for Jacqueline Burgoyne (1944–88)*. London: Routledge, 114–38.

Morris, C. (1972) *The Discovery of the Individual, 1050–1200*. Toronto: University of Toronto Press.

Mower, E. R. (1927) *Family Disorganisation: An Introduction to Sociological Analysis*. Chicago, IL: Chicago University Press.

Naylor, G. (1988) 'Love and Sex in the Afro-American Novel', *The Yale Review*, vol. 78, no. 1, 19–31.

Nietzsche, F. (1997 [1891]) *Thus Spake Zarathustra*. Trans. T. Common. Ware: Wordsworth.

Nietzsche, F. (2015) *Aphorisms on Love and Hate*. London: Penguin.

Nussbaum, M. C. (1990) 'Steerforth's Arm: Love and the Moral Point of View', in *Love's Knowledge: Essays on Philosophy and Literature*. Oxford: Oxford University Press.

Nussbaum, M. C. (2001) *The Fragility of Goodness: Luck and Ethics in Greek Tragedy*. Cambridge: Cambridge University Press.

Nussbaum, M. C. (2002) '*Eros* and Ethical Norms: Philosophers Respond to a Cultural Dilemma', in M. C. Nussbaum and J. Sihvola (eds), *The Sleep of Reason: Erotic Experience and Sexual Ethics in Ancient Greece and Rome*. Chicago, IL: University of Chicago Press, 55–94.

Nygren, A. (1953 [1936]) *Agape and Eros*. Trans. P. S. Watson. London: SPCK.

Ober, J. (1994) 'Civic Ideology and Counterhegemonic Discourse: Thucydides on the Sicilian Debate', in A. L. Boegehold and A. C. Scafuro (eds), *Athenian Identity and Civic Ideology*. Baltimore, MD: Johns Hopkins University Press, 102–26.

Office for National Statistics (2018) *Statistical Bulletin: Divorces in England and Wales: 2017*. https://www.ons.gov.uk/peoplepopulationandcommunity/birthsdeathsandmarriages/divorce/bulletins/divorcesinenglandandwales/2017.

Ortega y Gasset, J. (1933) 'The Nature of Love', *The Living Age*, February 1, 526–30.

Ortega y Gasset, J. (1957a) 'The Role of Choice in Love', in T. Talbot (trans.), *On Love: Aspects of a Single Theme*. New York: Meridian Books, 83–134.

Ortega y Gasset, J. (1957b) 'Love in Stendhal', in T. Talbot (trans.), *On Love: Aspect of a Single Theme*. New York: Meridian Books, 21–82.

Parsons, T. (1943) 'The Kinship System of the Contemporary United States', *American Anthropologist*, vol. 45, no. 1, 22–38.

Paz, O. (1995) *The Double Flame: Love and Eroticism*. Trans. H. Lane. New York: Harcourt Brace.

Perry, R. (1986) *The Celebrated Mary Astell: An Early English Feminist*. Chicago, IL: University of Chicago Press.

Perry, R. (2004) *Novel Relations: The Transformation of Kindship in English Literature and Culture 1748–1818*. Cambridge: Cambridge University Press.

Phelan, S. (2001) *Sexual Strangers: Gays, Lesbians, and Dilemmas of Citizenship*. Philadelphia, PA: Temple University Press.

Phillips, A. (2012) *Missing Out: In Praise of the Unlived Life*. London: Penguin.

Plato (1994) *Symposium*. Trans. R. Waterfield. Oxford: Oxford University Press.

Plato (1996) *Protagoras*. Trans. C. C. W. Taylor. Oxford: Oxford University Press.

Plato (1997) *Republic*. Trans. J. L. Davies and D. J. Vaughan. Ware: Wordsworth.

Plato (2002) *Phaedrus*. Trans. R. Waterfield. Oxford: Oxford University Press.

Plato (2004) *The Laws*. Trans. T. J. Saunders. London: Penguin.

Polhemus, R. M. (1990) *Erotic Faith: Being in Love from Jane Austin to D. H. Lawrence*. Chicago, IL: University of Chicago Press.

Poster, M. (1978) *Critical Theory of the Family*. London: Pluto.

Price, A. W. (1997) *Love and Friendship in Plato and Aristotle*. Oxford: Clarendon Press.

Rebhun, L. A. (2007) 'The Strange Marriage of Love and Interest: Economic Change and Emotional Intimacy in Northeast Brazil, Private and Public', in M. B. Padilla, J. S. Hirsch, M. Munoz-Laboy, R. Sember and R. G. Parker (eds), *Love and Globalisation: Transformations of Intimacy in the Contemporary World*. Nashville, TN: Vanderbilt University Press, 107–19.

Reddy, W. M. (2012) *The Making of Romantic Love: Longing and Sexuality in Europe, South Asia, and Japan, 900–1200 CE*. Chicago, IL: University of Chicago Press.

Rilke, R. M. (1912) 'Requiem für eine Freundin' [1908], in *Requiem*. Leipzig: Insel Verlag, 7–21.

Rose, N. (1998) *Inventing Ourselves: Psychology, Power and Personhood*. Cambridge: Cambridge University Press.

Rougemont, D. de (1983 [1940]) *Love in the Western World*. Princeton, NJ: Princeton University Press.

Ruskola, T. (2005) 'Gay Rights versus Queer Theory: What Is Left of Sodomy After *Lawrence v Texas?*', *Social Text*, vol. 23, nos. 3–4, 235–49.

Russell, B. (1967[1932]) 'In Praise of Idleness', in E. Fromm (ed.), *Socialist Humanism*. London: Allen Lane, 225–37.

Said, E. W. (1979) *Orientalism*. New York: Vintage.

Sartre, J.-P. (1956) *Being and Nothingness*. New York: Philosophical Library.

Sawyer, S. M., Azzopardi, P. S., Wickremarathne, D., and Patton, G. C. (2018) 'The Age of Adolescence', *The Lancet: Child and Adolescent Health*, vol. 2, no. 3, 223–8.

Scaff, L. A. (1987) 'Fleeing the Iron Cage: Politics and Culture in the Thought of Max Weber', *American Political Science Review*, vol. 81, no. 3, 737–56.

Schultz, J. A. (2012) 'Why Do Tristan and Isolde Make Love? The Love Potion as a Milestone in the History of Sexuality', in J. Eming, A. M. Rasmussen and K. Starkey (eds), *Visuality and Materiality in the Story of Tristan and Isolde*. Notre Dame, IN: University of Notre Dame Press, 65–82.

Schwarz, B. (1996) 'Black Metropolis, White England', in M. Nava and A. O'Shea (eds), *Modern Times: Reflections on a Century of English Modernity*. London: Routledge, 176–207.

Scott, W. (1991 [1819]) *The Bride of Lammermoor*. Oxford: Oxford University Press.

Seccombe, W. (1992) *A Millennium of Family Change: Feudalism to Capitalism in Northwestern Europe*. London: Verso.

Seidman, S. (1991) *Romantic Longings: Love in America, 1830–1980*. New York: Routledge.

Sensabaugh, G. F. (1940) 'Platonic Love and the Puritan Rebellion', *Studies in Philology*, vol. 37, no. 3, 457–81.

Shakespeare, W. (2000 [1597]) *Romeo and Juliet*. Ware: Wordsworth.

Sharpe, K. (1987) *Criticism and Compliment: The Politics of Literature in the England of Charles I*. Cambridge: Cambridge University Press.

Shorter, E. (1977) *The Making of the Modern Family*. Glasgow: Fontana.

Shumway, D. R. (2003) *Modern Love: Romance, Intimacy, and the Marriage Crisis*. New York: New York University Press.

Simmel, G. (1950a) 'Types of Social Relationships by Degrees of Reciprocal Knowledge of Their Participants' [1906], in K. H. Wolff (ed. and trans.), *The Sociology of Georg Simmel*. New York: Free Press, 317–29.

Simmel, G. (1950b) 'The Metropolis and Mental Life' [1903], in K. H. Wolff (ed. and trans.), *The Sociology of Georg Simmel*. New York: Free Press, 409–24.

Simmel, G. (1968) 'The Conflict in Modern Culture' [1918], in K. P. Etzkorn (ed. and trans.), *The Conflict in Modern Culture and Other Essays*. New York: Teachers College Press, 11–26.

Simmel, G. (1971) 'Eros, Platonic and Modern' [1921], in D. N. Levine (ed.), *George Simmel: On Individuality and Social Forms*. Chicago, IL: University of Chicago Press, 235–48.

Simmel, G. (1984) 'On Love', in Guy Oakes (ed. and trans.), *George Simmel: On Women, Sexuality, and Love*. New Haven, CT: Yale University Press, 153–92.

Simmel, G. (1991 [1907]) *Schopenhauer and Nietzsche*. Trans. H. Loiskandl, D. Weinstein and M. Weinstein. Urbana and Chicago: University of Illinois Press.

Simmel, G. (2004 [1900]) *The Philosophy of Money*, 3rd edn. Trans. T. Bottomore and D. Frisby. London: Routledge.

Singer, I. (1984) *The Nature of Love. Vol. 1: Plato to Luther*, 2nd edn. Chicago, IL: University of Chicago Press.

Singer, I. (2009) *The Nature of Love. Vol. 2: Courtly and Romantic*. Cambridge, MA: MIT Press.

Sloterdijk, P. (1988) *Critique of Cynical Reason*. Trans. M. Eldred. London: Verso.

Smith, A. (1982 [1759]) *The Theory of Moral Sentiments*. Indianapolis, IN: Liberty Fund.

Smith, D. J. (2006) 'Love and the Risk of HIV: Courtship, Marriage, and Infidelity in Southeastern Nigeria', in J. S. Hirsch and H. Wardlow (eds), *Modern Loves: The Anthropology of Romantic Courtship and Companionate Marriage*. Ann Arbor: University of Michigan Press, 135–56.

Smith-Rosenberg, C. (1975) 'The Female World of Love and Ritual: Relations Between Women in Nineteenth-Century America', *Signs*, vol. 1, no. 1, 1–29.

Sølbeck, D. E. (2010) ' "Love of the Heart": Romantic Love Among Young Mothers in Mali', *Culture, Health and Sexuality*, vol. 12, no. 4, 415–27.

Sorokin, P. A. (1950) *Altruistic Love: A Study of American 'Good Neighbours' and Christian Saints*. Boston, MA: Beacon Press.

Spivak, G. C. (1985) 'Three Women's Texts and a Critique of Imperialism', *Critical Inquiry*, vol. 12, no. 1, 243–61.

Spronk, R. (2009) 'Media and the Therapeutic Ethos of Romantic Love in Middle-Class Nairobi', in J. Cole and L. M. Thomas (eds), *Love in Africa*. Chicago, IL: University of Chicago Press, 181–203.

Stendhal (1975 [1822]) *Love*. Trans. G. Sale and S. Sale. London: Penguin.

Stigers, E. S. (1981) 'Sappho's Private World', *Women's Studies*, vol. 8, nos. 1–2, 47–63.

Stone, L. (1990) *The Family, Sex and Marriage in England 1500–1800*. Abridged and revised edn. London: Penguin.

Swidler, A. (2001) *Talk of Love: How Culture Matters*. Chicago, IL: University of Chicago Press.

Tadmor, N. (1995) 'The Concept of the Household-Family in Eighteenth-Century England', *Past and Present*, vol. 151, no. 1, 111–40.

Tanner, T. (1979) *Adultery in the Novel: Contract and Transgression*. Baltimore, MD: Johns Hopkins University Press.

Thomas, K. (1959) 'The Double Standard', *Journal of the History of Ideas*, vol. 20, no. 2, 195–216.

Thompson, S. (1995) *Going All the Way: Teenage Girls' Tales of Sex, Romance, and Pregnancy*. New York: Hill and Wang.

Thucydides (2013) *The War of the Pelopennesians and the Athenians*. Trans. J. Mynott. Cambridge: Cambridge University Press.

Tilly, L. A., Scott, J. W., and Cohen, M. (1976) 'Women's Work and European Fertility Patterns', *Journal of Interdisciplinary History*, vol. 6, no. 3, 447–76.

Tolstoy, L. (1987) 'A Confession'[1882], in J. Kentish (trans.), *A Confession and Other Religious Writings*. London: Penguin, 19–80.

Tolstoy, L. (2004a) 'Afterword to "The Kreutzer Sonata"' [1890], in *The Death of Ivan Ilyich and Other Stories*. Ware: Wordsworth, 200–205.

Tolstoy, L. (2004b) 'The Death of Ivan Ilyich' [1886], in *The Death of Ivan Ilyich and Other Stories*. Ware: Wordsworth, 77–130.

Tolstoy, L. (2004c) 'The Kreutzer Sonata' [1889], in *The Death of Ivan Ilyich and Other Stories*. Ware: Wordsworth, 131–200.

Tribe, K. (1988) 'Translator's Introduction', in K. Tribe (trans.), *Max Weber: Essays in Reconstruction*. London: Allen and Unwin.

Troyes, C. de (1975) *Arthurian Romances*. London: Dent.

Turner, J. (1990) 'The Otto Gross-Frieda Weekley Correspondence: Transcribed, Translated, and Annotated', *The D. H. Lawrence Review*, vol. 22, no. 2, 137–227.

Vlastos, G. (1981) 'The Individual as Object of Love in Plato', in *Platonic Studies*, 2nd edn. Princeton, NJ: Princeton University Press, 3–34.

Wandhoff, H. (2012) 'How to Find Love in Literature: Reading Gottfried von Strassburg's *Tristan* and His Cave of Lovers', in J. Eming, A. M. Rasmussen and K. Starkey (eds), *Visuality and Materiality in the Story of Tristan and Isolde*. Notre Dame, IN: University of Notre Dame Press, 41–64.

Wardlow, H. (2006) 'All's Fair When Love Is War: Romantic Passion and Companionate Marriage among the Huli of Papua New Guinea', in J. S. Hirsch and H. Wardlow (eds), *Modern Loves: The Anthropology of Romantic Courtship and Companionate Marriage*. Ann Arbor: University of Michigan Press, 51–77.

Warner, M. (1999) *The Trouble with Normal: Sex, Politics, and the Ethics of Queer Life*. New York: Free Press.

Waterfield, R. (1990) 'The Dinner-Party: Introduction', in H. Tredennick and
R. Waterfield (trans.), Xenophon, *Conversations of Socrates*. London: Penguin.

Weber, M. (1949) '"Objectivity" in Social Science and Social Policy' [1904], in E.
A. Shils and H. A. Finch (eds and trans.), *The Methodology of the Social Sciences*.
New York: Free Press, 49–112.

Weber, M. (1965 [1922]) *The Sociology of Religion*. Trans. E. Fischoff.
London: Methuen.

Weber, M. (1970a) 'Science as a Vocation' [1917], in H. H. Gerth and C. W. Mills (eds
and trans.), *From Max Weber: Essays in Sociology*. London: Routledge and Kegan
Paul, 129–156.

Weber, M. (1970b) 'Politics as a Vocation' [1919], in H. H. Gerth and C. W. Mills (eds
and trans.), *From Max Weber: Essays in Sociology*. London: Routledge and Kegan
Paul, 77–128.

Weber, M. (1970c) 'Religious Rejections of the World and Their Directions', in H.
H. Gerth and C. W. Mills (eds and trans.), *From Max Weber: Essays in Sociology*.
London: Routledge and Kegan Paul, 323–59.

Weber, M. (1978 [1922]) *Economy and Society: Volumes 1 and 2*. Trans. and eds G. Roth
and C. Wittich. Berkeley: University of California Press.

Weber, M. (1994) *Max Weber Gesamtausgabe: Briefe 1909–1910*. Tübingen: Mohr.

Weber, M. (1999) 'Letters from Ascona', in S. Whimster (ed.), *Max Weber and the
Culture of Anarchy*. London: Macmillan, 41–71.

Weber, M. (2002 [1905]) *The Protestant Ethic and the Spirit of Capitalism*, 3rd edn.
Trans. S. Kalberg. Los Angeles, CA: Roxbury.

Weber, Marianne (1975 [1926]) *Max Weber: A Biography*. Trans. H. Zohn.
New York: John Wiley.

Weeks, J. (1999) 'The Sexual Citizen', in M. Featherstone (ed.), *Love and Eroticism*.
London: Sage, 35–52.

Weeks, J. (2007) *The World We Have Won: The Remaking of Erotic and Intimate Life*.
London: Routledge.

Weitman, S. (1999) 'On the Elementary Forms of the Socioerotic Life', in M.
Featherstone (ed.), *Love and Eroticism*. London: Sage, 71–110.

Whimster, S. (1995) 'Max Weber on the Erotic and Some Comparisons with the Work
of Foucault', *International Sociology*, vol. 10, no. 4, 447–62.

White, F. C. (1990) 'Love and the Individual in Plato's *Phaedrus*', *The Classical Quarterly*,
vol. 40, no. 2, 396–406.

Whitman, W. (2009 [1891]) *Leaves of Grass*. Oxford: Oxford University Press.

Wilcox, J. (1930) 'Defining Courtly Love', *Michigan Academy of Science, Arts and Letters*,
vol. 12, 313–25.

Williams, R. (1977) *Marxism and Literature*. Oxford: Oxford University Press.

Wilson, H. E. (2005 [1859]) *Our Nig. Or, Sketches from the Life of a Free Black*.
London: Penguin.

Winterson, J. (2017) 'We need to be more imaginative about modern marriage',
     The Guardian, 8 April. https://www.theguardian.com/books/2017/apr/08/
     jeanette-winterson-marriage-monogamy-wedding.
Woolf, V. (1966a [1931]) 'Professions for Women', in *Collected Essays: vol. 2*.
     London: Chatto and Windus, 284–9.
Woolf, V. (1966b [1929]) 'Women and Fiction', in *Collected Essays: vol. 2*.
     London: Chatto and Windus, 141–8.
Woolf, V. (1968) 'The Novels of Thomas Hardy' [1928], in *Collected Essays: vol. 1*.
     London: Hogarth Press, 256–66.
Worthen, J. (2005) *D. H. Lawrence: The Life of an Outsider*. New York: Counterpoint.
Xenophon (1990) 'The Dinner-Party' [*Symposium*], in H. Tredennick (trans.) and R.
     Waterfield (trans. and ed.), *Conversations of Socrates*. London: Penguin.
Zelizer, V. (2005) *The Purchase of Intimacy*. Princeton, NJ: Princeton University Press.
Žižek, S. (1999) 'Courtly Love, or Woman as Thing', in E. Wright and E. Wright (eds),
     The Žižek Reader. Oxford: Blackwell, 148–73.
Žižek, S. (2008) *The Sublime Object of Ideology*. London: Verso.
Zonana, J. (1993) 'The Sultan and the Slave: Feminist Orientalism and the Structure of
     Jane Eyre', *Signs*, vol. 18, no. 3, 592–617.

Index